New Dynamics
in National Strategy

New Dynamics in National Strategy

The Paradox of Power

Foreword by
General Maxwell D. Taylor

with contributions by faculty members
of the United States Army War College

Thomas Y. Crowell Company
New York   Established 1834

Manufactured in the United States of America

Library of Congress Cataloging in Publication Data
Main entry under title:

New dynamics in national strategy.

Bibliography: p.
1. United States—National security. 2. United States—Foreign relations. 3. World politics—1965- 4. Strategy. I. United States.
Army War College.

UA23.N38   1975   355.03'3073   74-34250
ISBN 0-690-00685-3
        0-8152-0377-2 (Apollo paperback)

1 2 3 4 5 6 7 8 9 10

Contents

Foreword

General Maxwell D. Taylor

This compilation of essays represents a notable departure for the US Army War College as I have observed it. Since its establishment in 1903 as the capstone of the Army school system, the College has exerted an important influence on the intellectual formation of generations of senior Army officers. However, its work has usually been carried out internally with little activity perceptible from beyond its walls. This compilation, in open publication, demonstrates serious academic work not evident heretofore, which I applaud, and is continuing evidence of the College's claim as a center of innovative thought in the field of national security policy and strategy.

Despite the institutional orientation of the Army War College toward the Army and military matters, the scope of these essays gives evidence of a broad interest in national policy rather than a narrow concentration on its military component. Of the fifteen papers herein only one, dealing with the possible uses of precision weaponry in the defense of Western Europe, could be considered essentially military. The largest number examine various aspects of great power relationships, particularly as they come together in Europe, the Middle East, and Northeast Asia. Several testify to a growing sense of importance of economic and ecological factors in security policy. Frequent references are made to domestic factors and to the importance of enlisting public support and understanding for security programs. In the aggregate, the articles present a mosaic of the problems of the external and domestic environment in which our leaders will pursue national goals in the coming decade and of the forces which will oppose or facilitate their efforts.

The mosaic, as I perceive it, is a turbulent scene dominated by unstable governments and strained economies among the great powers and by diminishing resources and disappointed hopes among the weak. The troubles of both great and small will often stem from the consequences of population growth—increases in consumer demand, scarcities, prices, inflation, and government burdens; decreases in income, food, raw materials, production, and confidence in government. The latter will cause frequent changes in political regimes, a trend already visible among the democracies of the West. In industrial countries, inflation will be a prime cause of this discontent, one for which no world leader has yet found an acceptable remedy. In the developing countries with pressing population problems, the prospect is for recurrent disasters arising from famine, flood, drought, revolution or local wars.

Despite the military background of most of the authors, there is surprisingly little mention of the role of strategic or major conventional war in adjudicating the issues anticipated in the environment portrayed. There seems to be a general assumption that a continued strategic equilibrium will deter nuclear war and decrease the likelihood of major conventional wars. The industrial powers, which alone are capable of waging major wars, are likely to be restrained by reciprocal economic dependence, by scarcities in war sustaining resources such as oil, and by the uncertainties of popular support for prolonged war in any form. However, rivalry over markets, competition for the riches of the seabed, and the universal political turbulence anticipated are cogent grounds to fear a high incidence of minor conflicts leading in some cases to military involvement.

One speculates as to the role of the oil rich nations in this setting, a role which is sure to be important but difficult to predict. Will these nations use their great wealth for political leverage to influence the foreign policy of their customers and possibly as a disruptive factor for world trade and money markets if the leverage fails? Or will they use it responsibly to improve the lot of their own people and to help other emerging countries which are without valuable exports to pave the way to prosperity? Their affluence opens to them the possibility of great achievements or great follies.

Against this environmental background, the authors of several essays appraise the nature of the balance of power which we should seek with the other four power centers—Western Europe, the USSR, Japan, and the Peoples Republic of China (PRC). They seem in general agreement that our relations with Western Europe should remain the cornerstone of our foreign policy while recognizing the many divergencies of policy which developed between ourselves and our allies during the Yom Kippur War. The *sauve qui peut* among our European friends at the outset of the Arab oil embargo did little to establish the worth of the alliance in a serious pinch affecting national economic interests. As depicted by one writer, Europe is torn between conflicting forces of integration and disintegration and wracked by apprehensions over the reliability of the United States as an ally, the cohesion of the Common Market, and occasional indications of eastward drift on the part of West Germany. However, these fears do not augment the willingness of Europeans to expend resources to improve North Atlantic Treaty Organization (NATO) defenses against possible aggression by the Warsaw Pact. But despite perceiving their primary dangers as nonmilitary and essentially economic, most Europeans still want the American troop presence as an earnest indication of continued involvement in their interests.

With respect to the defense of NATO, one author contributes a very interesting discussion of the possible use of precision conventional weaponry as an additional defensive option for the alliance. However, even if one accepts the most favorable assumption as to the availability and accuracy of such weapons, the tactical and logistical dispositions of the defensive forces would require space for dispersion and maneuver which does not exist today behind the NATO front. When President de Gaulle withdrew France from military NATO in 1966 and obliged the United States to roll up the American line of communication extending from Bordeau to southern Germany, he took the capablity of conducting a defense based on maneuver in depth from NATO.

Several contributors undertake to evaluate the future behavior of the USSR, particularly in the Middle East/Indian Ocean region and in Northeast Asia. One expresses considerable doubt regarding the meaning of detente as viewed by Moscow and the sincerity of the Soviet purpose in current negotiations, especially in those dealing with strategic armaments and the reciprocal reduction of forces in Western and Central Europe. The point is well made that the Soviet negotiators have never been willing to release official information on their military establishment without which our side could never be sure of the size of the force remaining after a negotiated reduction in strength. However, it seems clear that, for the moment, the Soviets wish to adhere to those aspects of detente which offer the possibility of US assistance in the development of their natural resources.

As to Soviet policy in the Middle East, there is a tendency to attribute Soviet intervention largely to a traditional interest in the area, coupled with a compulsive inclination to fish in troubled waters wherever found. It does not appear that the Soviets have a "vital" interest in the area for which they would risk anything like a military confrontation with the United States. Their naval activities in the Mediterranean are viewed as being more for political than for military purposes and their emergence into the Indian Ocean as little more than a flag-flying exercise to indicate an interest in the Persian Gulf and the intention to look after Soviet interests thereabouts.

Essayists discussing the opening of the Suez Canal regard it as a desirable development which should be of advantage politically to the United States, commercially to Western Europe and South Asia, and militarily to the USSR. However, the military advantage to the Soviet Navy is not viewed as too important since their ships east of Suez will still have a long and exposed line of communication leading through defiles to the Black Sea or to more distant bases. The US Navy will also be far from home in these waters and, even in small numbers, it will certainly need the facility presently planned on Diego Garcia.

Japan is properly regarded as the key to American policy in Asia, a part of the world in which the United States must prevent the formation of any hostile coalition capable of marshalling the vast resources of the region against it. Because of an urgent need for access to raw materials, Japan might be seduced one day from its present political orbit by the offer of a reliable supply base. The USSR would be the most likely to make such an offer—in fact, it is bargaining now with Tokyo for assistance in developing its eastern oil and gas fields. It will be in the US interest, one would think, to oppose any Soviet attempt to develop a commonality of economic interest with Japan and to help the Japanese to find alternative sources to the desired raw materials. One way might be to form a Pacific economic partnership consisting of Japan, the United States, Canada, Australia, and Indonesia—countries with the means to satisfy many of the

Japanese needs. This quandary could serve as a reminder of the timeliness of overall review of our present alliances and commitments in the light of the new economic factors which are appearing on the international scene.

In treating Japan's problems, I cannot give a high probability to military dangers arising for Japan by way of Korea or Taiwan. An American military presence should certainly remain in Northeast Asia but I see nothing sacrosanct about the present troop dispositions. Our nuclear umbrella is still of value as a psychological reassurance and tends to dampen any enthusiasism on the part of the Japanese for seeking nuclear power status. However, the credibility of that umbrella encounters the same questions as in Europe.

I have serious doubts regarding the viability of the treaty arrangement whereby Japan is largely dependent upon the United States for its military security. It is a situation humiliating to many Japanese who resent its suggestion of a client status and it certainly causes unhappiness to many American taxpayers who object to footing Japanese defense bills indefinitely. Personally, I view the treaty as an unwholesome long-term relationship for both sides which, if we are not careful, will eventually break up in a mutual exchange of recriminations. At some appropriate time, we should consider replacing the security treaty by an unwritten understanding of "special relationship" after the model of our relationship with the United Kingdom.

In these essays the attention accorded the PRC arises largely from the importance of its relationship to the USSR and Japan. Obviously the United States should do everything possible to prevent any revival of the old Sino-Soviet relationship as its existed before the rupture or the development of serious Chinese economic dependence upon the USSR. On the other hand, an outbreak of military hostilities between the two is a horrendous prospect with consequences too unpredictable to warrant a present judgment as to the proper American course of action in such a contingency.

Several essayists identify factors on the domestic scene which will affect national security and popular attitudes toward its claims for support. They point to the proliferation of militant minorities dedicated to group interests and stress the public skepticism as to the needs of the Armed Forces and the importance of their mission. This antimilitary bias raises doubt as to the feasibility of maintaining large forces over long periods of peace when they will appear to many Americans as "chimneys in summer"—to use an English phrase.

Under such circumstances it will require able and articulate spokesmen to justify military forces and budgets. The task is made particularly difficult by the drum fire of criticism from the media continually directed at all symbols of authority ranging from the President to the corner policeman. The Armed Forces and the military industrial complex will continue to be favorite targets as long as the media feel honor-bound to assume an adversary position vis-a-vis their government and all of its works. As one paper points out, governmental leaders, in presenting their case, must find better ways to communicate the facts about national security to the electorate in an era when, as the current cliche puts it, "the people have a right to know" practically everything. One sensible suggestion made is that our officials improve their own practices, put an end to excessive security classification of documents, and refrain from trying to manage the news for partisan political advantage. Apart from other reasons for candor, high officials should be reminded that they usually get caught when they try to beguile the public for long.

In the heat of the public relations difficulties of the Johnson administration over Vietnam, I tried in vain to stir up interest in a way to permit recurrent TV interpellation of government officials on matters related to the war. It did not seem unreasonable to propose to the three principal TV networks that they reserve one hour of prime time each week for the interrogation of some senior official involved in Vietnam policy by a panel chosen by the network. The central theme of the question period could be announced in advance—for example, the bombing campaign against North Vietnam—and the public would be invited to send in questions to the host network for selected use by the panelists. The overall program could be given a title such as "Your Government Reports on Vietnam."

Since the idea never found a sponsor in the Johnson entourage, it must have had something seriously wrong with it. However, it does indicate my sympathy with the essayist who feels that the executive branch, without getting directly into the media business, should find ways to establish a regular two-way channel of communication between the governing and the governed. Boiler-plate government handouts will not accomplish the purpose.

In discussing our domestic problems, no writer in this compilation has mentioned the low estate of the Presidency and its likely effect upon national security. The disrepute of this high office is to some degree an aspect of the general derogation of authority and institutions which characterizes the national attitude, but it also reflects a mood of self-disparagement whereby individual citizens exhibit their personal loss of confidence and morale. These negative attributes in combination create an image of national weakness which nullifies much of the deterrent effectiveness of the Armed Forces and weakens the ability of our leaders to influence international events in accordance with national interest. Thus at a time that we talk of the importance of the "perceived strength" of our strategic weapons, we are displaying perceptible weakness in many forms to the detriment of national security.

Often in these articles there is a question raised or implied as to the role of the Armed Forces in the future which we are contemplating. A few specific missions are mentioned as falling to the military under the new dispensation. With our increasing concern over resource shortages, the military must assure communications with overseas sources not only for ourselves but for our principal allies as well. The exploitation of the seabed, and activity fraught with many possibilities of international controversy, will require military protection of the development sites, and eventually of the pipelines and shipping linking sites and the homeland. We must be ready to assert our right of innocent passage through straits and coastal waters brought under national jurisdictions by extensions of territorial limits.

A nonmilitary role for the Armed Forces might be employment on civil tasks related to nation-building such as flood prevention, pollution control, and reforestation. As an alumnus of the Civilian Conservation Corps (CCC) in 1933, I can testify that such programs, if desirable, are feasible. However, the workers on CCC projects were not soldiers but jobless youths working for little pay at a time of national economic depression. Army personnel merely provided them with living accommodations and administrative assistance. Today, at current military pay scales, Army troops would no longer be cheap labor.

My excuse for this lengthy foreword is the variety and scope of the essays comprising the book. Without pretense of doing full justice to the articles, I have tried to give at least some of their flavor as I savored it in my reading. Inevitably, my selections for comment are influenced by personal interest and predilection which, I fear, may have caused me to overlook much that deserves particular mention. I hope, however, that the ultimate result of my contribution will be to encourage the thorough reading which the papers deserve. They provide, by their range and style, indisputable evidence that the Army War College is not an institution preparing to refight the last war.

MAXWELL D. TAYLOR

Washington, D. C.

Introduction

The chapters within this book are products of individual research and analysis conducted by officers and professional civilians of the US Army War College. They represent solely the author's views, but exemplify the College's commitment to serious academic study and writing in the field of national security. This compilation does not encompass all areas of national security; rather focuses on selected subjects to act as a catalyst for further research and thought on the issues addressed. Only through such study will challenges confronting the nation in today's changing international arena be clarified and an informed public be enabled to participate in national dialogue.

During the time these papers were developed, Major General Franklin M. Davis Jr. served as Commandant of the College, a position which Major General DeWitt C. Smith Jr. now holds. Brigadier General Robert G. Yerks serves as Deputy Commandant.

The Strategic Studies Institute, a department of the College with primary responsibility for research on national military strategic affairs, is directed by Colonel Joseph E. Pizzi. A majority of the book's contributors work within the Institute. Mr. John R. Cameron, Assistant to the Director, and Mrs. Marianne P. Cowling, the Institute's editor, were especially helpful in preparation of this compilation; Lieutenant Colonel Llyle J. Barker assisted before his assignment to the student body of the Class of 1975. The College's Department of Military Planning and Strategy also is represented among the contributors. In addition, many other individuals provided comments, advice, and secretarial support.

Perceived errors in thought or content are attributable only to the individual author; none of the material should be considered as representing the official view of the US Army War College, the US Army, the US Marine Corps, or the Department of Defense.

ONE

Establishing the Framework

1

The Evolving Domestic Forum for National Security Debates

Anthony L. Wermuth

We live in interesting, challenging times. Every day, we are provoked by new challenges to reexamine and justify to ourselves what we are doing. In 1973, at the 30th reunion of his Harvard class, Adam Yarmolinsky became exasperated by the flood of familiar questionnaires with their oft-repeated questions—"What political party do your support?" "What is your income bracket?" "What foreign countries have you visited?" and so forth.

He startled his classmates with what he called a counter-questionnaire, containing these among a number of provocations:

What are you really curious about?

How often are you astonished these days?

Whom are you currently trying to impress?

What's most wrong with this world? Is it anybody's fault? Can it be fixed?

Does God love you? Do you care?

Where are you likely to spend eternity?

Which of these questions was hardest to answer?

One would have been highly astonished at such questions themselves a generation ago, but today we seem to be more willing to take them in stride.

THE AQUARIAN LANDSCAPE

Not too many decades ago, decisionmaking on matters of national security could be accomplished, so to speak, in a forum not much larger than a breadbox. Today, the elements and actors influencing any nation's security policy are seen to be legion. Having recourse to the rule of parsimony, I speak here mainly of policymaking in the domestic context, in both abstract and concrete terms. The primary dynamic pervading this paper is consideration of change, making the environment for national security planners more difficult, complex, and circumscribed. That this is an evolving context is, of course, no secret to the planners themselves; indeed, few institutions have been so energetic as the military institutions in adjusting many procedures to the so-called Age of Aquarius.

Obviously, a host of factors are relevant, even crucial, to this environment. Changing factors in the international context will exercise tremendous influence; after all, the primary thrust of national security policy is external, outward, intended to protect this society against harm from foreign sources. Some developments in the international context contain what are clearly seeds of potential future conflict, such as competition over the dwindling fossil fuels in the earth's crust; the looming conflicts over exploitation of resources in the oceans and seabeds; the anomalous role of multinational corporations; the potential tensions between the have and have-not nations; the pressures building up from expanding populations; the uncertainties contingent upon monetary and fiscal interchange; not to mention the realities of nuclear arsenals, space satellites, intercontinental missiles—all are factors which becloud the future relations among nations. To raise a single specific question, for example—what effects on America's world status will emerge from relinquishment of American control over the Panama Canal? It is probably too early even to conjecture.

As previously mentioned, however, I should like to concentrate more on the domestic forum than the foreign or international. Even the domestic context is too much to handle in a brief span. The context of domestic political change alone is a formidable challenge. For example, the War Powers Resolution, the 60-day limit now in effect on the President's authority to commit US forces overseas without Congressional endorsement, may have a currently-imponderable but profound future effect on a number of domestic military affairs, such as on the Reserve and National Guard system. The domestic economic context, too, is certainly formidable, as we wrestle with the largest-ever peacetime military budget. In the remainder of this paper, however, I should like to emphasize the probable impacts of change in American social and cultural contexts, which necessarily overlap the areas of politics, economics, and foreign relations.

At the outset, I shall propound a few questions that are deliberately provocative. Their relevance should emerge during the course of our discussion—such questions as these:

• In an age of mass media and mass opinion, are we more, or less, vulnerable to prevailing "wisdom" that is sometimes inaccurate and misleading?

• Can a community preserve its integrity if individual conscience is accorded priority overriding all other considerations?

• Which value, achievement or equality, will contribute most to the realization of social cohesion in future society?

• If America must eventually fight a particular war, is it more desirable to fight it, if possible, on foreign soil, or to wait and fight it on American soil?

• Is the prevailing attitude of Americans really biased against the military, or is that a recurrent myth which certain writers keep telling us is so?

• Or Samuel Huntington's question: "How can a liberal society provide for its military security when this requires the maintenance of professional military forces and institutions fundamentally at odds with liberalism?"[1] These and many other questions suggest themselves as being invested with increased significance in the modern context of military affairs. Answers to these questions are, as usual in dynamic times, not clear.

MORE OR LESS FAMILIAR THEMES

Underlying my comments is one firm assumption: that the military function remains important to American society—not only that it be performed, but also that, when it is needed, it be performed well. It is essential that military expertise be fostered, developed, and maintained in advance of need; over a long training period, despite indifference, misunderstanding, and alienation. As one of the Marine Corps slogans has it: "Nobody wants to fight, but somebody has to know how."

Cyclical approval and alienation is one problem the military has wrestled with through the ages in all societies, bespoken by the poets from Homer to Housman. Kipling's lines have become perhaps overfamiliar (but to the rising generation?):

> Oh, it's Tommy this and Tommy that
> And "Chuck 'im out, the brute."
> But it's "saviour of 'is country"
> When the guns begin to shoot.

In fact, a peculiar strain runs through the history of American national defense which intermittently tends to extol the role of the part-time citizen soldier over that of the military professional. In his biography of Franklin Pierce, Nathaniel Hawthorne wrote, through a haze of misperception:

The valor that wins our battles is not the trained hardihood of veterans, but a native and spontaneous fire; and there is surely a chivalrous beauty in the devotion of the citizen soldier to his country's cause, which the man who makes arms his profession and is but doing his duty cannot pretend to rival.

In the wider context of international power dynamics, there has also in the past recurred a certain American naivete, sometimes refreshing, sometimes exasperating, even dangerous. One recalls the incident of Henry L. Stimson, as Secretary of State, breaking up the decoding section of the State Department on the grounds that "gentlemen do not read each other's mail."[2] Or one recalls the incident of Woodrow Wilson in the White House in 1915, holding up a copy of that day's *Baltimore Sun*, livid with rage at an item which revealed that the Army General Staff was developing contingency plans for use in case of a possible war with Germany. Wilson furiously directed the Acting Secretary of War to investigate and, if he found the story to be true, to relieve every officer on the General Staff and ship them out of Washington.[3] A difficult forum for military planners; for, of course, only two years later we *were* at war with Germany. To what extent has that context of naivete changed?

ONE TYPOLOGY OF CHANGE

In contemplating change, we may discern three types: fads, cycles, and long-term changes. All of them must be coped with, and they all affect the processes of developing national security policy.

Fads may be of relatively short duration but also be highly intense and almost irresistible while they last. The youth element of the ferment of the 1960's furnishes an example, although many an aspect was something more than a fad. It is still difficult to realize what hit us in the 1960's. Norman Ryder and Daniel Moynihan have contributed one valuable insight, regarding the 14-24 age group, the locus of most social ferment. Between 1890 and 1960, that age group increased during each decade by an overall net gain of something over one million. During the whole 70 years till 1960, the cumulative net gain in the 14-24 age group amounted to 12 ½ million persons. But during the single decade of the 1960's, that age group exploded by adding 13.8 million persons, more than the previous 70 years altogether, far beyond anything in our previous national experience.[4]

We expanded schools and colleges madly, but we were not sufficiently aware of many other aspects—such as the connections between this explosion and teenage unemployment, crime, drug abuse, and subcultures encapsulated from the rest of society. The tidal wave of youngsters in the 1960's provided the physical underpinnings for the youth movement and the emphasis on personal "liberation" as a transcendent value, and certainly played a role in opposition to the Vietnam War.

It is interesting to note, in passing, that during the 1970's, the 14-24 age group will gain numbers of less than one million, and during the 1980's, that age group will suffer a net loss in numbers—thus making surplus a sizeable proportion of our schools, teachers, and professors.[5]

A second type of change is cyclical, producing recurrences of pressures which we have felt before, though perhaps in different forms or degrees. For example, the end of every war witnesses an ebbing tide of interest in military affairs and a rise in hedonistic, individualistic pursuits. The lines from Kipling suggest analogous situations to those in which American military establishments have found themselves before.

This cyclic recurrence, coupled with the emergence of fads, is related to the evocation of "prevailing wisdom," the pervasive domination within a society of one among several contending explanations of major events. It is usually difficult to resist or to counter; although when reconsideration later sets in, we sometimes wonder how on earth we could have been swept along at the time.

American society does not ordinarily sustain passion very long. Harvard sociologist S. M. Lipset calculates that in America those movements that attain the level of obsessions, from Know-Nothingism to McCarthyism, generally have a life cycle of four to five years, and then rather quickly fade. This phenomenon is related to General George Marshall's assertion at the end of World War II that a democracy will not fight a long war.[6]

In analyzing the internal divisiveness of the late 60's and early 70's historian Eric Goldman predicts that an American consensus will gradually reemerge in the 1970's, in which "the young will not be so critical of the old and ... the old will not be so rigidly protective of their values."

The third type of change sometimes is, but mostly is not, as dramatic or intense as fads and cycles. Some protracted revolutions are subtle and imponderable, but relentless nevertheless. This enduring type of secular change is like a series of peaks on a continuous wave of human progress, an extended movement whose destination lies far beyond any horizon that we can see. None of the most important themes in this wave were invented today—in the youth movement, or in any other cultural area. They have been universally cited as common aspirations in all cultures and all societies, such as justice, freedom from want, from fear, and from servitude. They bear continuous witness to the myths, the rationalizations, and the shortfalls in social performance; and they advance the human condition by some degree. Their effects are more or less permanent.

Examples spring readily to the mind of anyone with a sense of history. I shall cite only one: the disappearance of the concept of the divine right of kings, and the triumph of the concept of the sovereignty of the people. DeTocqueville observed that since the 11th Century, the whole course of Western civilization has steadily moved in the direction of egalitarianism. Some residue of fads and cycles remains from their ups and downs, the ebbs and flows, the backing and filling, to reinforce the course of permanent change. All major institutions of society are affected, and the course of the military function is not exempted.

I have identified three types of change; whereas, of course, there are really dozens of types of change occurring simultaneously, at different paces and in different directions. Nor should we neglect to observe that some aspects of society are changing very little, or not at all—for one example, the persistent tendency in all of us to see, or hear, not what is to be seen or heard, but what we want to perceive.

It is perhaps helpful to employ some such typology of change, in order to manage the data, to cope with the complex phenomena occurring at any one time. Such a classification system is relatively easy to set up, but it is much more difficult to recognize which category is appropriate for labeling any particular change and to assess the intensity and probable duration of a particular change. Is it a fad that will eventually blow away, never to return? Or is it like something we have seen before, that left behind lessons we ought to recall? Or are we dealing here with some tenacious deviance from familiar processes—perhaps a new perspective or value shift that is not going to go away, however much we might wish that it would? It may contribute to further illumination to turn the spotlight on some more or less specific changes, the effects of which we perceive with varying degrees of uncertainty.

MORE EXPENSIVE KNOWLEDGE, COORDINATION, AND TIME

Daniel Bell is one who steers a careful course between the utopians and the doomsayers.[7] Some look at the future with concern in terms of scarcity, in terms of *how much,* meaning the *amount* of goods and services that will be available. Bell says, however, that, economically speaking, the possibility of abundance is real, and that we have passed beyond the problem of survival. He says, "The question before the human race is not subsistence but standard of living, not biology but sociology." Bell insists that the critical question is not *amount,* but relative *costs.* Here, I take it, he means not accretion, but redistribution—the monetary, social, and psychic costs of redistribution. How much will various actors—governments, organizations, groups, and individuals—be willing to pay? In the post-industrial society, three hitherto inexpensive factors will escalate sharply in costs: information, coordination, and time. Each of these factors will compound the policymaking process.

Information becomes more costly simply because of the escalating scale of information we need in every field. Knowledge is proliferating (doubling about every 15 years); but the more knowledge we develop, the more we need, in many ways. For example, there are now 150 independent nations in the world and thousands of transnational agencies and organizations to keep track of. Moreover, the information we need becomes increasingly technical, specialized, and complex; consequently, we need more intermediaries for explanation, translation, and synthesis. At the same time, we become more conscious of the finite limitations on the amount of information that any one person, however brilliant, can absorb. More and more closely, we are approaching the condition in which no one person, not even the specialist, can provide all the knowledge needed to cope with single problems or issues. For the security analyst and the strategist, as well as every other specialist, this means increasing dependence upon teams whose members pool their knowledge—interdisciplinary teams, interagency teams, teams aware of the vital necessity for incorporating multiple perspectives. The major security dilemmas are no longer susceptible of resolution primarily by the State Department, or a military department, or the Defense Department, or even the State-Defense team.

I am speaking here primarily of formally organized knowledge. We need also to be aware of the more diverse sources of knowledge available outside formal structures today, especially to the young. The director of a French prep school recently observed that in the previous generation, 75 percent of what students knew they had learned in school, whereas today 75 percent of an adolescent's knowledge comes from outside the school. It is food for reflection that the average high school graduating senior today has already spent some 15,000 hours watching television, compared to 12,000 hours attending school.[8] What stereotypes of the military, for example, have coalesced in his mind out of that experience?

In any event, in an increasingly technological society, the costs of information, of acquiring, analyzing, and disseminating data, increase; even more, it becomes increasingly expensive to research, study, and ponder the *significance* of the interrelated mosaics of data.

What Bell calls the costs of coordination are also rising sharply—not only monetary costs, but also costs in time and in social cohesion. Along with technology, perhaps the principal engine of change is education. As education permeates a society, more and more participants enter the political process. Educated people tend to be more discerning and less gullible about the political process, and more determined to exercise a role in governing themselves. One aspect is that interest groups splinter and multiply, representing fragments of political parties, consumer interests, ethnic minorities, industrial associations, organized labor, professional socities, religious denominations, even domestic and foreign policy issues. In sum, they raise more issues, assessing issues more deeply, generating more mediation and bargaining, requiring more contacts, more transportation, more communication. Some become essentially veto groups.

In a broad sense, greater education and abundance bring greater personal freedom, mobility, and diversity. At the same time, they inevitably also generate greater complexity and conflict, which in turn demand more organization, more planning, and eventually more social control and regulation—else the society bogs down in chaos.

The principal proponents in the development of national security policy will be increasingly constrained by the necessity to coordinate, directly or indirectly, with proliferating interest groups which develop political sophistication and political clout—not to neglect mention of their potentially valuable insights. Other aspects of coordination warrant mentioning; some will be taken up later.

Bell's third area of rising costs is that of time. As society becomes more complex, individuals and agencies confront intensifying dilemmas over how to apportion their own time, how to establish priorities among various claimants on their time, how to apportion more money out of rising incomes to hire more costly services in order to save their time. When only a few persons in a society are affluent, the services of others to save one's own time are relatively cheap; but when affluence is widespread, services become scarce and hence expensive.

Bell uses the simple illustration of doing one's laundry. When laundresses are cheap, one sends it out, paying modest amounts of money to save one's time. When laundresses can make more money doing something else, the fewer available laundresses become expensive. Should one spend one's time then doing one's own laundry? Is a laundromat a reasonable trade-off device between one's time and one's money?

A more complex illustration might involve essential research by security agencies. Which is least expensive in time and money: the establishment of an in-house research and study group that includes all the essential disciplines, perspectives, and specialists, or contracting the problems to external agencies which are competently staffed? This is one specific problem, incidentally, that will nag future security-policy agencies indefinitely, as the costs of time, including the costs of in-house manpower time, continue to climb.

CORE PHILOSOPHY AND ITS CONTENDERS

The Vietnam War and the military have been to some extent catalyst-scapegoats for the unrest and discontents that have been running deep since long before shooting conflict erupted in Indo-China, as the traditional sources of value have been drying up and consequent decay has occurred in uniform beliefs. Max Weber and Emile Durkheim felt that modern man would find solace only in allegiance to larger solidarities; they felt that the way to individual security lies in collective normalcy, in the maintenance of norms and binding customs. Social health, they felt, derived from emphasis on conformity with the group.

That belief, while still receiving substantial support, is strongly opposed by the rising emphasis on individuality, on personal autonomy, on the transcendance of individual conscience over group or collective interests. Joseph Fletcher, in *Situation Ethics,* endorses this premise: "Every man must decide for himself according to his own estimate of conditions and consequences; and no one can decide for him or impugn the decision to which he comes."[9] A few years ago, in Massachusetts, the Rabbinical Court of Justice of the Associated Synagogues rendered a verdict questioned by other Jews: "The foremost Jewish law," it said, "is that nothing is greater or more important than the single individual, not the society, its institutions, or one's country."[10] This is heady wine for many, young and old.

Amitai Etzioni notes that in periods of transition, several social philosophies contend for preeminence. The old core philosophy may be displaced by one of the contenders; the old one will not then disappear, but will remain, somewhat changed, influential as a subculture. Meanwhile, one of the contenders will move into the core status, but also be changed in the process. Etzioni describes today's waning central pattern as legitimating current economic patterns and institutions, such as ever-increasing productivity, and emphasizing concern for this world, and for austerity, rationality, discipline, and achievement.

Etzioni identifies four competing subcultures as contenders:[11]

• *literati* subculture, a lifestyle of nonpurposive learning, with focus on self and avoidance of socially useful labor. Offering no justification for efforts on behalf of justice or any other social cause, it might provide a basis or a society with less competition, conflict, and tension.

• an *empathetic* subculture, stressing the quality of positive relationships with others, on personal and small group levels, over interests of the large society.

• a *political-activist* subculture, emphasizing the primary of public life, and such public goals as justice, and education as the primary criteria for meaningful lifestyle.

● a *hedonistic* subculture, endorsing natural inclinations with few prohibitions, aiming to free mankind from norms, based on belief in the natural goodness of man.

Which subculture is likely to become the dominant one? Etzioni suggests that an amalgam of the *political-activist* and *empathetic* subcultures will emerge as the central core of the future. All contenders contain implications for national planning, for security as for other essential purposes.

INDIVIDUALISTIC vs COLLECTIVE VALUES

Of course, there is nothing new in the existence of tension among contradictory values accepted within the same society. DeTocqueville pointed out a century and a half ago—and such diverse thinkers as Warner, Parrington, and Lipset have echoed the idea since—that the two supreme values in American culture are essentially antithetical: liberty (achievement) and equality. Still, we continue to endorse both values and to live with the inconsistencies.

Which will emerge in the dominant position—individual values or collective values? It is probably that we shall evolve some kind of compromise and continue to support both values but in some altered relationship. Hasan Ozbekhan speaks of our "commitment to detailed molecular disorder."[12] David Riesman's term, "antagonistic cooperation," may become even more accurate.[13]

Nevertheless, some predict the inevitable dominance of collective values in an increasingly complex society. Professor Jack Douglas insists that without society, man cannot exist or possibly fulfill himself.[14] Garrett Hardin offers an interesting aphorism suggesting a new definition of freedom: "Freedom is the recognition of necessity, and all must accept mutual coercion mutually agreed upon."[15] Others suggest that collective values will necessarily become so dominant that the individual will be considered abnormal if he fails to conform to group norms. If such a value structure is on the way, it appears to be yet a long way off.

Meanwhile, national planners must cope with today and tomorrow amidst a context that intensifies internal dissidence. Obviously, highly organized societies are highly vulnerable. I mentioned veto groups earlier. One is repeatedly impressed by the capability of some small group to immobilize large polities, such as the crippling of New York City by successive work stoppages by garbage collectors, elevator

11

operators, taxi drivers, engravers, or bridge tenders. Even, in Montreal, by the police. Political, legal, economic, social, ethnic, professional, and work groups have less and less hesitancy in adopting militancy as a technique to further their interests. This is one manifestation of the diffusion of power that is taking place.

One should note the evolving role of professional organizations and societies. More and more professional associations are being established, formulating standards for professions, and to some extent eroding the loyalty of their member professionals to work organizations. For example, medical societies, not only the Military Medical Services, establish many performance standards and procedures for military medical professionals. Similar movements are taking place among lawyers, chaplains, engineers, journalists, and other professional specialties. Thus greater interchange between specialist members of policymaking bureaucracies and their professional associations is bound to occur.

All professional associations have suffered attempts over recent years by "Young Turk" movements to take over associations for purposes of political activism. One such group within the American Political Science Association (APSA), for example, in the summer of 1973, (unsuccessfully) demanded that the APSA condemn Henry Kissinger on the grounds that Kissinger, as a political scientist, was accountable to his professional peers as well as to his formal public superordinates.[16]

Speaking of bureaucracies, one should also note some positive aspects of the role that organizations play in bureaucracies. Aaron Wildavsky has pointed to the Watergate affair and the relative success of representatives of well-established organizations—the CIA, the military services, the FBI—to resist corrupting overtures toward involvement in questionable activities. Along another line, Max Lerner points to the inconsistency of Watergate with the myth that locates the danger to American freedom in the "military-industrial complex." The American military clearly continues its traditional neutrality in partisan domestic politics.[17]

The makers of security policy will probably find it more difficult to develop national compromise or consensus that supports one course of action or another. A number of trends in the general society compound this difficulty. One is the decline in acceptance of the Great Man syndrome; a citizenry that is better educated and more politically sophisticated is more aware of the warts and flaws of leaders, and is unwilling to accept the old assurances that "Papa knows best." John

Stuart Mill once asked: "Was there ever any domination that did not appear natural to those who possessed it?";[18] but the familiar elites will be permitted less autonomy in running future societies or communities. More and more citizens are intolerant of societies or communities. More and more citizens are intolerant of social domination, and are increasingly successful in resisting, for example, manipulated information or edicts handed down without explanation from on high.

There is less compunction in raising various moral dilemmas surrounding authority and its exercise. Lord Acton is widely quoted these days:

> The person who authorizes the act shares the guilt of the person who commits it . . . If the thing be criminal, then the authority permitting it bears the guilt . . . I cannot accept [the] canon that we are to judge Pope and King, unlike other men, with a favoured presumption that they did no wrong. If there is any presumption, it is the other way, against holders of power, increasing as the power increases . . . Power tends to corrupt and absolute power corrupts absolutely. Great men are almost always bad men, even when they exercise influence and not authority . . .[19]

In repeated samplings of public opinion, there is reported widespread lack of confidence in government.[20] It is, of course, not always clear whether this reflects declining confidence in the government or administration of the moment, or declining confidence in government in general. Moreover, the widening suspicion of, and resistance to, the use of "national security" to justify withholding of information and explanations appears to be spreading within the government itself, as well as in general American society. In November 1973, the Watergate Special Prosecutor Leon Jaworski said: "In the recent past, national security has been invoked by officials at widely disparate levels of government service to justify a wide range of apparently illegal activities."[21] Even setting aside illegal actions, pressure mounts for fuller, more candid, and more cogent actions, undertaken under the rubric of "national security." For, of course, if one cannot learn anything about them, one cannot arrive at a judgment as to whether they are legal or not, let alone whether they are necessary or wise. The outcome will probably be that greater public accountability and more extensive explanation will be exacted of national planners.

There are fewer existing restraints to publication of private or public sensitive material. For example, no federal libel law exists (and there has been none since the controversial Alien and Sedition Acts of 1798). Current Supreme Court decisions have set very demanding requirements for public officials and public figures to meet in order to defend themselves against libel. President Nixon termed the situation "virtually a license to lie about political leaders, inviting slanderous attacks on them or their families."[22]

The point here is that the public climate in which government policy is developed grants considerable latitude for misrepresentation and misstatement via exploiters of the media, often without needed correctives. This situation will be a fact of life for some time. Even classified documents and discussions are no longer as untouchable as they used to be. The Pentagon Papers are stolen, reproduced, and published, with the protection of the courts. Former trusted government specialists, having sworn never to reveal specific matters, publish books or testify in open hearings about intelligence procedures, the CIA, and sensitive inter-nation discussions. These are new and formidable encumbrances in the formulation of security policy. Two related developments are instant "kiss-and-tell" revelations by departees from sensitive positions, and "whistle-blowing," the revelation by a member of any agency, public or private, of institutional practices which he personally questions. Greater access to public forums is now available for dissenting subordinates——through Congress, the media, and activist groups; and increasing numbers of subordinates have no inhibitions about exploiting such access for any of a variety of motives.

PREVAILING WISDOM

A particularly difficult trend to cope with is that of developments in the media, the press, and mass communications in general. The technical equipment has become so advanced and so ubiquitous that we are becoming inundated with the spoken and printed word. Techniques of presenting public information resemble those of dramatic presentation, including selection, omission, slanting, and suspense. Competition becomes so intense at times that the most passionate adversary with the loudest bullhorn and the most offensive invective is the one who gets to tell the story. Access to the media, and skill in exploitation of them, become effective in building up pervasive climates of opinion. Regarding Vietnam, for example, C. L. Sulzberger wrote a short time ago: "Vietnam has been for so long a code word for disaster that most people lose all semblance of intellectual reasoning once they hear it."[23]

Gradually, certain myths arise and take hold; and from then on, those who subscribe to the other side must contest, not reality, but the myth. This is one of the most ambiguous challenges to future policymakers in the field of national security. For example, since the middle of the Vietnam War we have been assured in a steadily rising crescendo from revisionists that the United States acts in the fashion of imperialism, and actually started the Cold War.

The revisionist school is not exactly a monolithic group, including as it does a gamut from serious, frequently healthy skeptics, to a handful of superficial and intolerant denouncers in several disciplines. A reviewer of a recent work in this genre describes the typical revisionist script on the Cold and Vietnam Wars as picturing:

> Truman and a number of industrialists, generals, and self-righteous crusaders from Foggy Bottom conspiring to double-cross the goodhearted Stalin . . . setting in motion an imperialistic adventure in Indo-China, impelled by the imperatives of American capitalism, [leading] to a genocidal campaign by the United States against Oriental peasants, in which, fortunately, the United States was militarily defeated.[24]

This radical collection of cliches became the prevailing wisdom, the preferred rationale, for many, especially on the campuses and in the adversary press in the late 1960's. It was skillfully exploited by the orchestrators of the Communist propaganda apparatus worldwide. How much truth was in it? Any? A little? A lot? Actually, as those who lived through the tense, frustrating early years of the Cold War should know, this version is preponderantly a myth, congenial to the double-standard perception of democracies and totalitarian regimes of the Right as corrupt and repressive, while totalitarian regimes of the Left are to be indulged as benign tyrannies.

This is not the place to debate the Cold War; but it is useful to point out the power of modern media to saturate, with rhetoric and partisan premises, our limited absorbing capacity. Even the 1971 White House Conference on Youth expressed one. resolution in this way, the implications of which for national planning are self-evident:

> We are concerned about the incredible strength of the media in all phases of our lives. We recognize the potential for danger that lies in this widespread penetration.[25]

One asks again, is it really possible that there can be created in modern times a prevailing climate of opinion that is largely myth? The evidence is ambivalent but suggestive. S. L. A. Marshall said a while ago that for five years of the Vietnam period it was not possible to publish a pro-war or pro-military article in a number of eminent American journals.[26] A young academician recalled recently that, over the same period, in the faculty club of a prestigious Ivy League university, to espouse the American cause in Vietnam was to invite instant and complete ostracism. The Vietnam War, incidentally, as reported by Art Hadley, was perhaps the first one in our history in which Ivy League participation was conspicuously minimal.[27]

Our failure to make sufficient early efforts to explain fully the issues and the options of the war in Vietnam to the American people seems, in retrospect, almost self-defeating. We assumed too much about the state of American opinion at the time, neglecting, for example, the advice of W. E. H. Lecky, who wrote a century ago that the success of any opinion depends "less upon the force of its arguments, or upon the ability of its advocates, than upon the predisposition of society to receive it."[28] In our day, Carl Becker makes the same point: "Whether arguments command assent or not depends less upon the logic that conveys them than upon the climate of opinion in which they are sustained."[29] Of course, Plato suggested many centuries ago that the pursuit of the good and the true has nothing to do with the state of prevailing mass opinion.

Some of the major arguments advanced in opposition to the Vietnam War were inaccurate and incredible; but the weight of general opinion, not without help, gradually coalesced around opposition. In a number of respects, it did not really matter what the real issues were, or the pros and cons about each; when the climate of national opinion hardened around opposition to the war, no supporting argument, however sound, was welcomed. It seems clear that far greater efforts will be required in the future to inform and explain the facts and the arguments which have persuaded national leaders toward a major course of action—certainly concerning such a course as entering a war.

GETTING TO THE RISING GENERATION

How pervasive was opposition to the Vietnam War? How successful were antiwar, opinion-molding elites in disseminating their views? One population area of particular significance for the future is that of children; both Lenin and the Jesuits have emphasized in the past the importance of indoctrinating children. In an interesting exercise, a political scientist at Wilberforce reported results of his 1971 interviews of 2,700 pupils in grades 3 through 8 (ages 8-14) in New York, New Jersey, and Maryland on their attitudes toward the war. Only one-third of the children felt that the United States was "right" in Vietnam. Half thought the United States should withdraw its forces "even if they lose." Fewer than one-third thought President Nixon was "doing the right thing" in Vietnam. Only 22 percent believed the President always told the truth about the war. The older the child, the more skeptical he or she was about confidence in government.[30]

I am not suggesting that this one survey necessarily reflects nationwide opinion accurately, nor am I suggesting that the opinions of 8- to 14-year-olds on the war are persuasive in themselves. These findings are cited in order to identify some efforts to cultivate attitudes of skepticism, even hostility, toward government among the rising generation. One asks, "Where did these children get these ideas?" The investigator concluded that the children's *knowledge* about the war depended more on the media than on parents or schools. On the other hand, he concluded that the children's *attitudes* were influenced more by parents and schools than by the media.

One wonders about "the other side." What prevailing wisdom exists in the rising Soviet generation, whose indoctrinated perceptions of America we will have to cope with for a long time ahead? Hans Morgenthau has expressed his skepticism about the euphoria which affects some Americans when they contemplate the term "detente." He singles out the recent book by Andrei Gromyko's son, who is head of the foreign-policy section of the Soviet Academy of Science's Institute of the USA, the main source of Soviet information about the United States. Morgenthau's opinion is that the book is a frightening experience, a compendium of every nonsense ever uttered by Soviet propagandists about the United States, which is portrayed as the incarnation of evil. Morgenthau remains suspicious of "any government that cuts itself and its people off from objective contact with the outside world, that becomes the prisoner of its own propaganda." He considers that detente can be no more than a breathing spell in an ongoing struggle for world stakes—a breathing spell that primarily "serves the interests of the Soviet Union, whom we are providing with economic and technical potential without any assurance of its ultimate uses." Morgenthau says, "the Soviet Union is bound to be an unreliable

17

partner." We must retain some skepticism about the probable effects on future cooperation of indoctrination of several generations of Soviet youth.[31]

THE OPTION OF GRADUALISM

Earlier, General Marshall's conclusion was cited that a democracy will simply not fight a long war. This is probably a reliable conclusion, which leaders in America have had to learn over and over again. It may be recalled that, in the Civil War, Grant was described as "a butcher" for his heavy losses in aiming to destroy Lee's army. In reality, Grant was anything but reckless with the lives of his men; he insisted, however, that it was better to endure losses and achieve the primary object of the war than to *continue* to endure losses for the stalemate in which the eastern armies had already floundered for three years.[32]

Grant, incidentally, would not criticize Joseph E. Johnston's delaying tactics. He thought them the correct tactics for the South, the only rational ones, based on a hope that stretch out of the Civil War for still another year might result in foreign recognition for the South and might strain Union resolve and support of the war to the breaking point.[33]

The lesson for future military planners, accentuated by the Vietnam experience, is that a strategy of creeping gradualism in a future war will probably not be a viable choice.[34] If it is true that the American public will not support a long war, one of the essential constraints on American strategic decisionmakers will be to see to it, so far as it is within their power to do so, that it will not be a long war.

DUBIOUS SOLACE

While considering dynamic developments and uncertainties in the United States, we may extract some solace from the fact that we are by no means alone. Uncertainty, internal tension, and instability are widespread around the world. Peculiarly, the discord seems most evident, despite high standards of living, in free democratic countries. Few, if any, national leaders are accorded worldwide approval and prestige—such as was granted to Churchill, DeGaulle, Eisenhower, even Nasser. There are few world heroes left. Government upheavals have taken place in France and Britain. Recent Italian governments have had to serve with slim parliamentary margins. Sweden operates under a minority government. The Dutch and the Danes have strong opposition party combinations. Belgium went on for months without a government. Germany walks something of a tightrope, with less than expected results from its *Ostpolitik.*[35]

A recent Japanese incident may illustrate how universal is the malaise of transition, as military ethos from the past attempts to make its compromises with a changing society: the return of Lieutenant Onoda after 30 years of hiding and fighting in the Philippines.[36] His return deeply stirred mixed emotions in each person in Japan; for those 30 years occurred *after* the war ended. This is an example, with a vengeance, of the principle that "there's always someone who doesn't get the word."

The lieutenant's return evoked the Japanese spirit of "gimu," a broad sense of obligation of the individual Japanese to his family, associates, institution, and society. While the Japanese repudiate the spirit of militarism that sent Lieutenant Onoda into the Philippines long ago, they felt great satisfaction with his faithfulness, his sense of duty, his fidelity to the soldier's code. They marveled that, even after 30 years in the jungle, his gun was clean.

We have mixed feelings about that incident, too, in which exasperation is no doubt prominent. We have difficulty in understanding that degree of sustained, totally unquestioning, obedience to orders. American units have, on occasion, fought to the last man (one recalls immediately the Battle of the Bulge, and the Chinese and North Korean whirlwind invasion of South Korea, during which a number of American units complied with orders to fight to the last man). But those stands each had a clear battle purpose—the protection of the main forces. The steadfastness of the few saved the many. But individualistic Americans have difficulty in understanding the passive acceptance of Lieutenant Onoda. Could he not have initiated some effort over 30 years to learn whether the war was over?

Something bothers us. Is there some echo here of Eichmann and the fanatical SS units, and the Nuremberg defense that "I was only carrying out orders"? American values do not include a comparable high place for "gimu." We may marvel at such blind obedience; but while it stirs us, it also mystifies us. The point here is that it also alienates some of the Japanese, especially the young. Many young politicians are rising in Japan, who arrived at maturity after the war and have somewhat differing perspectives, respecting many of the traditional Japanese qualities but also exasperated by some of those qualities.[37] The younger ones tend to seek to add idealism to the hardheaded pragmatism of the older leaders. The Onoda incident is peculiarly Japanese, but it also suggests the ambivalence of some profound changes in the military ethos in democratic societies.

THE ELUSIVE ETIOLOGY OF WAR

Highly articulate groups invariably arise in postwar democracies, with the conviction that war can be, or even soon will be, eliminated from human experience. Yet, we recall that in *Ecclesiastes,* it is said:

> For everything there is a season and
> a time to every purpose under heaven—
> A time to be born and a time to die,
> A time to plant and a time to reap.
> . . . a time for war and a time for peace.

Few passages are as eloquent on the relentless repetition of the cycles of life.

Thomas Jefferson, no less, once wrote:

Wars then must sometimes be our lot; and all the wise can do, will be to avoid that half of them which would be produced by our own follies, and our own acts of injustice; and to make for the other half the best preparations we can.[38]

We need not pause here to explore the roots of war—whether war stems inexorably from aggressive instincts in man's psyche, from one or more of the seven deadly sins, from the contradictions inherent in capitalism or communism, from ideologies, from ignorance or miscalculation, from strength, or from weakness. Most of all the familiar theories are at least partially unsatisfactory. If I may mention one that always seemed to me to be particularly unpersuasive, even in this age of advanced communications, it is the theory that, if people knew each other better and communicated more, wars would be avoided. This ignores the fact that most wars have been fought among neighbors, and the evidence on the personal level that most murders occur between people well known to each other, frequently members of the same families. We shall continue to explore its roots with the purpose of eliminating war from the human condition, but we cannot know whether another war will bedevil us until it arrives.

What does appear to be changing in the context of war, however, is the nature of whatever war may come, and the organization of the conduct of war. We appear to have learned from experience—or have we? Despite long acquaintance with the insights of Machiavelli and Clauzewitz, we did not successfully mesh military and political objectives in World War II. At the outset of World War II, a crusty sundowner, Admiral Ernest J. King, moved into the position of Chief of Naval Operations, observing wryly, "When things get tough, they send for the sons of bitches." At the end of the war, when he, among others, was asked what should be told to the people during a war, he answered (in something of a pose, I'm sure): "Tell them nothing. When it's over, tell them who won." Nevertheless, we learned very much during World War II about the necessity for maintaining psychological cohesion on the home front; but when the Vietnam War approached, we neglected to explain the war persuasively enough, and *early* enough, to our own people.

When Lincoln installed Grant in command of the eastern armies, he told Grant that he enjoyed Lincoln's confidence and should proceed, and that he, Lincoln, did not want to know Grant's plans.[39] Through World War I (and to some lesser extent, through World War II) we adhered to the principle that when war comes, its direction is largely turned over to the military. In the past two decades, this situation has been reversed. By the time of the Vietnam War, technological advances in communications, as well as political and other factors, had made it feasible, and in the Administration's view desirable, to apply a host of limitations and restraints on military operations—even for the White House to pass on the suitability of the next day's specific targets. It is not likely that this trend will be reversed. The communication facilities now exist, and they are sure to be used by any wartime political leadership. Thus, while some aspects of power are being diffused, others are being centralized.

Louis Halle, pondering the future of war, suggests that, in the past 30 years, the very few wars in which the fighting has extended for years—the Greek Civil War, Korea, Vietnam—were all aftermaths of residual issues unresolved at the end of World War II. Otherwise, fighting periods have been brief. Halle suggests that the time has gone forever of great formal wars, duly declared and openly contested, and especially of great wars involving great powers on both sides.[40] However, he foresees the continuous eruption of violence on lesser scales—interventions, clandestine conflicts, guerrilla wars—which appear to be more difficult for democracies to cope with.

21

A host of important developments in progress are related to the domestic context of military affairs—too many to be cited here, including many affecting the search for the proper postwar roles for the military establishment. Alfred de Vigny provides a passage that may be somewhat overstated:

> When a modern army ceases to be at war, it becomes a kind of constabulary. It . . . knows neither what it is nor what it is supposed to do, . . . It is a body searching high and low for its soul and unable to find it.[41]

There is unquestionably a military role to be found; but its ethos, its terms, its rationales, its civil-military equations, are particularly difficult to identify in the seething peacetime context of current postwar American society. It is particularly difficult to evolve appropriate modern conditions of service that make sense to young entrants pre-indoctrinated by an ambivalent general society, to utilize its manpower most efficiently, to receive its share of qualified people and yet avoid the connotations of stockpiling large numbers of talented men and women who may never be used in the military's primary function over a long period, to avoid what Morris Janowitz calls the "chronic underemployment" of peacetime military service.[42] And the strongest pressures concerning this aspect will come, not only from changing social and cultural perspectives, but from the hard realities of competition for talented manpower in an increasingly complex and specialized society.

SMOKE IN THE POWERHOUSE

The erstwhile naivete of Stimson and Wilson, symptomatic of earlier, isolationist times, have been overtaken by more realistic approaches to the international context of power. But are we still constrained by the emergence of other myths, such as, perhaps, misunderstanding of American internationalism as "imperialism"? How accurate are our current perceptions of other nations—and of ourselves?

Within our own borders, the elusive nature of national interest even in domestic terms; the erosion of consensus; the conflict among special interests and militant veto groups; the limited tolerance of Americans for sustained emergencies; the proliferation and splintering of knowledge; the complexity of coordination within government; the fundamental tension between increased autonomy for the individual and imperatives for emphasis on group values; the generalist-specialist tug-of-war; declining confidence in government and rising suspicion of the rationale of "national security"; ambiguous expansion in the role and power of the media; the perennial unpredictability of the nature of future war—all these facets of change compound the challenge to national security planners.

Thus, to summarize what's happening to this process, we might employ several upgraded cliches to the effect that for national security planners, the heat in the kitchen will become more intense, the goldfish bowl will become less opaque, and there are sure to be more lions in the arena.

We have raced through here a bewildering array of changes in the domestic context, some only dimly seen, and yet we have merely scratched the surface. Perhaps one reacts as to those instant flashes of scenes they use on TV and the movies these days; in many instances, they seem more disconcerting than informative.

Some of these changes will prove to be fads and wither away. Some will prove to be cyclic, and wax and wane from time to time. But some will prove to be inexorable and irresistible. The crucial question is, which are which?

In April 1972, the University of Texas sponsored an international symposium, assembling the most eminent thinkers on the theme: "Problems of the 21st Century." At the end of three days of the most lively and provocative discussion, the distinguished British anthropologist, H. Max Gluckman, was asked to sum up. He tried, then threw up his hands and said, "I can't do it—it's really impossible!" He proposed a toast to the Queen instead.[43]

In lieu of summing up the foregoing discussion, I propose a toast to those men and women of the future who, whatever the challenges, will succeed in developing appropriate security policies for the United States, as well as to those who will risk their lives, as have so many in the past, in whatever dangerous enterprises American society calls upon them to endure.

2

Public Opinion
in a Time of Troubles

Richard O. Gillick

The consent of the governed, from which all American governmental power is derived, is bound to be elusive. Based partly upon the bedrock of national heritage—on the rights, rationality, and perfectability of man—it is also sensitive to the realities of today—on the drives for individual advantage and survival, the needs of the family, the community, the state. Thus consent, though essential, cannot be ordered up simply or quickly, and much political misery is attached to relearning that lesson.

Consent, or its lack, flows largely from the opinions of the governed. Hence, the conduct of a nation's affairs within and beyond its borders, if it is to be based on the consent of the people, must make reference to the opinion of the people. Public opinion, which can sustain or frustrate national strategy, should be a factor in the development of that strategy. The process by which variable elements are weighed in national security decisionmaking is now called "net assessment." Should not public opinion be an element of that process?

Robert E. Osgood, in his ground-breaking study of limited war, described well the cloudy yet dynamic nature of public opinion.

(It) is not a monolithic entity with concise and immutable views on foreign policy. It is a heterogeneous mass of fluctuating opinions and

24

predispositions, partial information and misinformation, together with a large measure of ignorance and apathy, filtered through a vast variety of institutions, pressure groups, and other media of expression. If it is possible at all to determine what constitutes public approval or rejection of foreign policy, one cannot assume that approval or rejection is a predestined or unalterable verdict; for opinion is a mutable and malleable thing, arranged into an endless succession of kaleidoscopic patterns under the impact of events and the weight of political leadership, acting upon each other.[1]

Osgood's description of public opinion will be useful as we consider the net assessment environment in which it must play a role.

A TIME OF LIMITS AND BALANCE

Net assessment is just good, solid, scientific problem-solving—a systematic analysis of key variables in relation to each other and to options. One is tempted to ask, "What's new?" What is new is the acknowledgement by our national strategy decisionmakers that the restraints implicit in the net assessment method are appropriate limitations to place upon matters involving national survival. Net assessment, as a strategy-building model, grew from the realization that the nation could no longer do everything; our plans should be based on realities. "Realistic" is itself a qualification, implying an accommodation with the facts of life.

In 1972, Melvin Laird, then Secretary of Defense, discussed "Net Assessment and the Threat" in a statement before the Senate Armed Services Committee. "It is important to re-emphasize," he said, "that any realistic assessments and resulting plans for military forces and new weapons systems must include political, economic, and social considerations."

> ... In these assessments we weigh the capabilities of potential enemies against our capabilities and those of our allies. At the same time, we must give careful consideration not only to the strengths of potential adversaries, but also to the deficiencies in their capabilities and the various constraints with which they must cope.[2]

To this point a cynic might view the net assessment process as merely a quasi-scientific method of reducing the threat to fit a preconceived response. But Secretary Laird partially dispels that interpretation when he speaks of the Four Realities upon which net assessment must be based. They are: the Strategic Reality, the Political Reality, the Fiscal Reality, and the Manpower Reality.[3] That these titles could come directly from the thoughts of Chairman Mao or from Thomas E. Lawrence's *Seven Pillars of Wisdom* is not coincidental. They are realities which must be faced by any leader who would maximize great but limited resources against vague and limitless threats. In the nuclear age they are realities to be faced by all.

A part of Secretary Laird's comments on the Political Reality are particularly germane to the subject at hand.

> ... As Secretary of Defense I also must take explicit account of both international and domestic political realities. From my perspective as a defense planner, these include: ... The difficulty of maintaining broad domestic public support for those programs necessary to assure national security.[4]

Our interest in the role of public opinion in the development and implementation of national policy—specifically national security policy—is heightened by the awesome imperatives which brought "net assessment" into our lexicon. The magnitude of the responsibilities: to have adequate defenses without being buried economically in the process, and to respond to domestic demands as well—these make it politically as well as morally essential that public opinion be gauged. But the same factors which make public support so essential also make it less certain, as the diversity of threats and the ultimate irrationality of nuclear war have caused an old idea to return as a new imperative: The concept of limited war.

This then is the test of public opinion in the nuclear age:

> One must wonder if a proud and aggressively idealistic nation can find within the somber prospect of indefinite containment sufficient incentives for enduring the frustrations and sacrifices of a protracted period of cold-and-limited war. In the trying process of harnessing a natural exuberance and moral enthusiasm to prosaic purposes, in the unending tedium of adjusting national power and will to the shifting demands of a strategy of limited objectives, might the nation not lose the vitality that has made America great and creative? And one must wonder if any democratic people today can be expected to sacrifice life and happiness, without ever exerting the full military strength of which it is capable, in order to preserve a balance of power in remote portions of the globe. A small professional army, a colonial garrison, could be expected to perform this chore; but when a whole nation is materially and emotionally involved in foreign affairs, will it permit its sons to die for the sake of holding some secondary position on the rimlands of Asia?[5]

Osgood raised those prescient questions in 1957. His answer then was, "perhaps"—if the political leadership explained the alternatives with candor and without embellishment, openly acknowledging that fundamental changes had settled upon the world and that victory was no longer an absolute.

A modern task for government, then, is to ease the public's accommodation to a condition in which danger is more real than apparent. Surely some part of this function will involve the government communicating with the people; not talking, announcing, proclaiming to, but *communicating with* the public about complex and subtle things. From such communication may come support.

Support for national programs has always been the outcome of lively debate, and pockets of resistance have inevitably defied the national will. But as the United States came upon the world scene in this century, and developed quickly a sense of power and of destiny, a President (or Commander-in-Chief of the Armed Forces) could rely on his sense of the national mood. The people were not simple, but the institutions and problems were, by current standards.

And though the refusal of Americans to acknowledge the acceptability of war as an element of foreign policy has found us ill-prepared for first battles, a dormant national spirit became martial and ferocious once the battle began. The people only required that the war be a crusade.

What will be the source of national consensus in the ambiguous, noncrusade, trials ahead? Now that traditional appeals seem inappropriate, how will subtle signs become rallying points? The institutions which once were leaven for the national will—church, school, home perhaps—have changing and less dominant roles.

What can and should government do to fill the gap, to build consensus out of pluralism, to affect the public opinion? The question is not whether government can affect it—surely its every action and inaction does that. The question is over the capability of the executive branch to take positive, preplanned, and substantial action directed at informing the public.

THE IDEA MARKET

Jack Anderson, preeminent investigative reporter, set the stage for controversy when he wrote,

It is the mission of the press to give the people an alternative to the official version of things, a rival account of reality, a measure by which to judge the efficacy of rulers and whether the truth is in them, an unauthorized stimulus to action or resistance.[6]

A question is inspired by Mr. Anderson's description: "How do the people get the official version of things, to which the press offers alternatives?" or, "How does the public know?"

Even before television revolutionized communications, Zechariah Chafee, Jr., foresaw the issue:

> The principle of freedom of the press was laid down when the press was a means of *individual* expression, comment, and criticism. Now it is an industry for profit, using techniques of mass suggestion and possessing great power. . . . Is the old principle of *Areopagitica* applicable to this new situation?[7]

Chafee referred of course to John Milton's eloquent description, in 1644, of the inevitable victory of "truth" in a fight with "falsehood." "Give her but room," said Milton.[8] The idea of the "free trade in ideas," "that the best test of truth is the power of thought to get itself accepted in the competition of the market," these strong appeals from Justice Oliver Wendell Holmes[9] have their origin in that same faith in the ultimate triumph of "right." But where is the market place, and how complete is access to it?

The problem of government access to the marketplace does not evoke much sympathy outside of government. James Reston sees scientific and political trends "enhancing the power of the President more than they are increasing the power of Congress or the press."[10] He sees a major danger in the excessive use of that power. But this too confuses the issue—for the presidential power perceived by Reston can at best, or worst, only limit further the public's access to information. It cannot, as presently exercised, increase the availability of other views.

Chafee, while noting the tendency of some elements of the press to exaggerate or distort, or even to lie, condemns the government's only response as a cure worse than the illness.

> Lying in the press is bad, but (outside such traditional and well-marked areas as libel and false advertising) the state cannot do anything against lies without inevitably supplying to the public its own brand of truth. There is nothing more deceptive than a state truth.[11]

The President's ability to influence public opinion, to tell the official view persuasively, is frustrated from many directions: by public suspicion, which, with Chafee, equates official statements with propaganda; by media awareness of the "preferred freedom" which protects it; by government's proclivity to secrecy. The task is further complicated when the executive and legislative branches are controlled by different parties. Then, Congress' role as communications link between the Federal Government and the people may be subordinated to the natural desire to take political advantage of opposition weakness.

Other factors cut across the roles of players in this drama of consent. The technological revolution makes transmission of information more certain than communication of ideas. Television delivers reality surrogates—requiring the viewer to place them in some context, to take them out of the artificially linear layout in limited time which characterizes television, and to gain meaning and insights from the bits.

Max Lerner described Americans as "spottily informed and basically bewildered." Writing before television became a predominant influence, Lerner attributed the chaotic state to the reliance on news media which present news as separate and unrelated items, offering the American few "patterns of meaning." As a result, wrote Lerner, "the process of history becomes for the newspaper reader a series of raging yet meaningless and impenetrable battles."[12] Television has surely not added warp and woof. It may, in fact, because of its illusion of reality, compound the trouble.

Economic imperatives have also had their effect. The cost of survival in the communications industry has caused a significant drop in the number of newspapers and, thus, in the number of communities which enjoy competition between news sources. A separate but related manifestation of cost is the common ownership of radio and television stations and newspapers within geographic areas.

Looking at the phenomena of centralization and consolidation, one need not conclude that the quality of information reaching the public has deteriorated. But the variety of views, including perchance the official one, has clearly been restricted.

As a source, the government is understandably chary in the dissemination of information. Thus the office which performs the security control over the release of public statements in the Army is titled the Freedom of Information Office. This euphemism gets the Department of the Army nowhere, of course, so long as the public perception of the information program is of a group of tax-supported officers setting out to "Sell the Pentagon." CBS won journalistic awards for exposing that malfeasance,[13] and within the profession received plaudits for criticizing one of its own, Walter Cronkite, who, in an earlier and simpler time, had said kind things about the Navy while riding aboard an aircraft carrier.

The question returns: How does one get the official view of reality? Specious, obsolete, inadequate it may be, but how will the people know until they see and hear it at its best, in the contest with other views of reality?

The inability of the press and the government—more specifically the executive branch—to acknowledge any common interest, and in that sense to cooperate, is largely due to growing acceptance of the theory of inevitable feud. This concept, institutionalized now in the term "adversary relationship," assigns a dog-cat relationship to the press and government. The idea has developed a life of its own and, to the extent that it receives acceptance from both sides, assures the existence of the dysfunction it describes.

The adversary theory, pro and con, could remain an academic argument—good debate material—except for the fact that a debate requires an adversary relationship, as does a jury trial, a basketball game, or a war. The essence of each contest is competition between sides, each using his resources to his best advantage—within some minimal set of rules—with the objective of winning. Winning requires a loser. Who wins when the government loses? Is this a part of what John Adams meant when he said, "There never was a democracy that did not commit suicide"?[14]

Professor Ithiel de Sola Pool gives a compelling minority opinion on the issue of the "adversary relationship," and in so doing replies to Adams. "If the government were the public's enemy," he said, "then (the adversary theory) would be a valid thesis, as to some extent it is."

> But to some extent a democratic government is also the expression of the people. And if that is so, then it is equally true, though equally partial, that the media are not the government's adversary but rather its ally in the struggle for national goals.[15]

And later:

> If the press is the government's enemy, it is the free press that will end up being destroyed.[16]

The pernicious nature of the adversary theory lies in its easy

30

acceptability by both "sides." In a time of rising acceptance of advocacy journalism—by definition subjective and biased—and of government's tendency toward defensiveness and secrecy, the adversary theory cannot possibly contribute to enlightenment.

PERCEPTIONS OF PROBLEMS AND POWER

Within the executive branch muted signals acknowledge the increased importance of public support. Mr. Laird's reference to the Political Reality is such. But though he spoke of the Political Reality as a major part of the assessment process, it has yet to achieve that status in practice. The structure for net assessment within the Department of Defense is in a formative state, but its present appearance—in personnel and charter—is impressively oriented toward the comparative analysis of systems and things rather than toward the consideration of psychological factors (at least in the domestic sense).[17] I suspect that this apparent void has resulted from the inability to square domestic psychological operations with the American heritage.

Psychological programs have been suggested before and, in the less sophisticated days of crusade, have been conducted. In the current environment, Hadley Cantril wrote in 1966 of the need for systematic consideration of psychological factors in the development of foreign policy.[18] His emphasis was upon the prompt and routine measuring of opinions, foreign and domestic, and upon considering those opinions in making and implementing policy. Cantril, a social scientist with extensive experience in public opinion research, would have a group appointed as advisers to the President, probably within the National Security Council system, specifically tasked to work in the psychological field, to understand the "psychological and political dynamics of the peoples involved. Careful consideration should also be given to the kind of information to be distributed to the American people, in order that they may understand the relevance of foreign policies to their personal welfare."[19]

The Cantril proposal could easily be applied to the narrower domain of military security, but while such a suggestion might fill a void in current assessment techniques, it has ominous overtones of the "manipulated information" to which, as Dr. Wermuth has noted, the public has become increasingly resistant. Whatever short-range benefits might flow from a committee on psychological factors, I am sure that the dangers of its misuse would make such a venture politically unthinkable through the foreseeable future. It was probably the assessment of *that* reality which caused the gap between the Secretary's broad concept and the relatively narrow and hardware-oriented implementation which followed.

There also are weak signs that our private institutions sense danger in the current trends. Stephen S. Rosenfeld, editorial writer and columnist for *The Washington Post,* has written of the new importance of domestic support for foreign policy and of the difficulties of achieving it in an era of pluralism. He is sensitive to the problems of a president, any president, who may, in the temper of these times, find "negotiating with his foreign adversaries . . . the easier part of his job."[20]

But Rosenfeld, after acknowledging that there is official anxiety over the depth of public support for an adequate defense budget, goes on to describe that anxiety as not warranted.

> The power of the President to alert the nation to security needs and to rally support for defense spending remains, after all, huge. It is not a misfortune but the defining strength—and risk—of a democracy that the national security managers must convince the country of what the national security requires.[21]

The concept of presidential power has unfortunate uses. It permits the executive branch to delude itself into confusing passage of a defense budget with popular support for the implications of that budget. Thus it permits the national security managers to think of "maintaining broad domestic public support" rather than of acquiring it. On the other hand, the exaggeration of presidential power encourages the press to consider itself the inferior contestant in the adversary relationship and to act accordingly.

While our population fragments and our news sources consolidate, national security has become a nonissue with most of the people. A Harris Poll, conducted for a congressional subcommittee in September 1973, asked approximately 1600 adults to cite "2 or 3 biggest problems facing the country . . ." The only national security issue cited by the respondents was the war in Indochina and it received minimal attention (less than 10%).[22]

Are we helpless then to improve the flow of information between the national security manager and the people, and to thus enhance awareness and support? Could "freedom of the press" become the self-inflicted wound of which John Adams wrote?

As Dumas Malone reminds us, Thomas Jefferson tells us "why" not "how."[23] Times do change, and it is the American ability to accommodate change which has enabled her to survive. A free press makes sense only in the context of a free and flourishing society. The First Amendment protects not the press as an institution but the people and their right to know. Governmental attempts to expand that vista, by encouraging competition, by expanding the sources of information, even by entering the communication enterprise itself, are possible ways by which the official views might be transmitted.

Such options might not be palatable. A Chief Executive operating from a position of reduced domestic support might not advance the implementing programs. In his assessment, he might opt for more conventional means or for none at all.

At the same time, the media might make an assessment of their own, and conclude that they *do* have a role in the grand experiment, that there are ways, open to the press, by which the public's ability to know can be enhanced without the watchdog lowering his vigilance. With that understanding, the press might voluntarily make some changes in policy. Specifically, newspapers, radio and television networks could occasionally offer prime time or prominent space for the Federal Government to state its view on specific or general topics. Such statements could be prominently identified as such, obviating any hint of endorsement. But at the same time, the media might feel less obligation to attack the view, instantaneously and with force.

Wire services might perform a similar service by placing the government view on the wire—thus encouraging small stations and papers, so dependent upon that service, to use the material. Adequate labelling would again be used.

The suggested proliferation of government information offers a risk as well as an aid, and the practice should be overseen. Though the bureaucracy and Congress are sure to take interest in that function, I would hope that press councils would take the lead in monitoring the "public information" program. In the expanded marketplace, under professional scrutiny, gross distortions would probably be rare and short-lived.

The role of press council suggests new awareness of objectives which transcend the news industry—a modest bow to national interest. The same spirit which permitted the formation of a national press council,[24] albeit with significant protest from within the news media, might also work toward the sublimation of the adversary relationship. The press can be watchdog without the government being cat.

Though there are limits to proper governmental action in influencing public opinion, national security managers can probably do more than merely note its existence. Deep public sentiment and transitory public moods can be gauged and should be considered. To the extent that information influences opinion, the flow of information becomes a legitimate concern of government, and actions which increase that flow should be considered.

The restoration of public confidence in government is not solely, or even primarily, the function of the press. This confidence grows from the congruity between official statements and perceived truth. Thus openness and candor will enhance the official view and will help to close the credibility gap. Patience, too, will help, as will acknowledgement of the obvious but oft-obscured truth that the official view is by necessity an institutional one, not shared by all members of the institution.

Finally, by manifesting a respect for public opinion, by making "right to know" a test superior to "need to know," the defense managers will encourage a recognition of the common interest which should bind us together.

A free press may be, to many, folly, but as Judge Learned Hand so eloquently put it, "... we have staked upon it our all."[25] The willingness of all parties to see that commitment as part of the larger one: to the survival of the democratic idea in the democratic state in a time of obscure but very real troubles, may determine our destiny.

3

Ecostrategy: The Ecological Crisis and National Security

Erwin R. Brigham

Pollution is an old problem—past civilizations were bothered by it, but important differences exist today. The scale is global, with new and dangerous aspects of the problem, which has reached crisis proportions— an ecological crisis.[1] The true nature of this crisis is only beginning to emerge and there is disagreement among writers concerning both the extent of the problem and possible solutions.[2]

The ecological crisis affects national security in many ways. Some which will be discussed are how the economic, political, military, and social aspects of the crisis affect the security of the United States; criticism of the military on ecological grounds; and how the ecological crisis might affect military roles, missions, organizations, and budgets in the future.

GLOBAL ECOLOGICAL PROBLEMS

Before discussing the relationship of the ecological crisis in national security, it is necessary to briefly review certain aspects of three global environmental problems: explosive population growth and the directly related phenomena of air and water pollution. The currently enormously expanding global population growth rate impacts in many ways on the earth's environment. More people, with rising living standards, mean an increase in consumption and production, giant growth of cities, expansion of industry and agriculture, and in turn, generation of wastes. If the world's population were growing slowly, as it did prior to the 18th century, the consequences for the earth's atmosphere and oceans would be easier to handle. However, in less than four centuries, population has grown from an estimated half billion people to seven times that number, 3.5 billion, and is expected to reach 11 billion by 2050.

What are the national security implications of the population explosion? One leading authority, Philip M. Hauser, writes that as a consequence of population problems:

> ... it may be expected that at least during the remainder of this century there will be increased, not decreased social unrest; more, not less, political instability; greater, not lesser threats to world peace; and intensified, not diminished cold war between capitalist and communist blocs or between have and have-not nations. Given the world population, economic and political outlook, it is reasonable to expect increased rather than decreased military and security expenditures...[3]

Whether or not the emerging detente between the East and West continues, US commercial and financial interests; access to resources and markets; use of overseas military bases; and the security of American citizens abroad may be detrimentally affected by world population growth, and its associated problems, particularly in underdeveloped areas.

Another aspect of the ecological crisis, directly related to population growth, is air pollution—excessive amounts of carbon dioxide and other matter in the atmosphere. Carbon dioxide alone has increased by 10 percent during the last century and could, with increasing production, rise by 25 percent by the year 2000.[4] The effect on climate and weather is uncertain but could be extremely serious. Experts disagree concerning the extent and nature of the problem.

Some authorities believe that continued air pollution will raise the temperature of the earth's atmosphere, indeed that it already has, but sufficient data are not available to substantiate this hypothesis. This warming of the earth's atmosphere, or "greenhouse" effect, may explain the fact that today the seas are warming and polar ice caps are thinning and shrinking. On land the snow line is retreating and glaciers are melting. If these trends continue long enough, many of the world's largest cities would be inundated.

On the other hand, world temperatures may decrease as a result of growing global murkiness caused by air pollution which shades the earth and decreases the amount of sunlight reaching it. Such a process might, if it continues, lead to a new ice age.[5] If air pollution were to cause either form of "invasion" by floods or glaciers, its long-term effects would be calamitous.

Another aspect of the ecological crisis is the pollution of inland and coastal waters and the oceans. The capability of the oceans and seas to absorb waste materials has been questioned for many years. Now there is little doubt that, at least in some areas, the capacity for the oceans to absorb pollution is shrinking rapidly. US National Science and Atmospheric Administration authorities reported "vast areas of the Atlantic Ocean, from Cape Cod to the Caribbean, were befouled by floating oil, tar, and plastics. In the summer of 1972, 665,000 square miles of ocean were covered by chemicals, sometimes in heavy concentration of fist-size debris."[6]

The significance of water pollution is seen in an agreement reached in November 1971 by 91 countries, including all major maritime nations, which signed a convention to end the dumping of poisonous waste matter at sea.[7]

OTHER ENVIRONMENTAL FACTORS

The global ecological problems considered here are limited primarily to explosive population growth and resultant pollution of the earth's air and water. However, the depletion of the earth's raw materials is equally important. In this regard, one writer concludes that if the world's population were to try to rebuild the existing industrial-urban civilization, as it would have to after a thermonuclear war:

> We could not possibly develop our industrial civilization in the way that we have . . . Copper, tin, zinc, lead, gold, silver, and, increasingly iron are all in short supply, increasingly subject to ever more sophisticated methods of extraction, methods which are increasingly costly per unit per production.[8]

Energy resources, especially petroleum, would be included in any current list of nonrenewable resources. Before the October 1973 Middle East War, supplies of various fuels had become critical in certain areas of the United States, beginning with natural gas in 1970, fuel oil in the winter of 1972, and gasoline in the summer of 1973.[9]

Some other aspects of the environmental crisis in its broadest sense can only be mentioned here, including contamination or waste of the earth's surface through strip mining, inefficient farming, pesticides, improper solid waste disposal, deforestation, and other man-induced erosion. Additionally, the whole human environment, economic, social, and political, is profoundly degraded by the following: the contamination of humans by drugs and alcohol;[10] deaths and damage from motor vehicle accidents—in the United States alone, 54,700 were killed and 2,000,000 injured at an estimated cost of $10.8 billion in 1970;[11] the rot in mass transportation; the decay of political corruption and crime; the deterioration of human resources through malnourishment, illiteracy, poor education, unemployment, and inadequately treated but curable diseases; and the debasement of society through prejudice and discrimination. All of these human environmental deficiencies are detrimental to American society. In their totality, these factors influence, directly or indirectly, the nation's security in various, unquantified, yet undeniable ways.

CONFERENCE ON THE HUMAN ENVIRONMENT

Widespread concern about the ecological crisis led to the First United Nations Planetary Conference on the Human Environment in June 1972, held in Stockholm, in which 130 nations participated. Its major results were: (1) approving action programs for approximately 200 recommendations ranging from promoting birth control and preserving vanishing plant and animal species to monitoring climate change and oceanic pollution; (2) establishing an environment fund for programs not financed by specialized agencies and national governments; (3) recommending methods to coordinate worldwide environmental programs to eliminate duplication and fill existing gaps; and (4) achieving a consensus on a declaration of agreed principles.

The conference was an important demonstration of the growing significance of the ecological crisis. In this regard, the noted anthropologist, Margaret Mead, said:

This is a revolution in thought fully comparable to the Copernican revolution by which, four centuries ago, men were compelled to revise their whole sense of the earth's place in the cosmos. Today we are challenged to recognize as great a change in our concept of man's place in the biosphere. Our survival in a world that continues to be worth inhabiting depends upon translating this new perception into relevant principles and concrete actions.[12]

AN INTERNATIONAL ENVIRONMENTAL ORGANIZATION?

In spite of the successes of the Conference, prominent persons, including George F. Kennan, believe that global ecological problems can be best solved outside the apparatus of existing international organizations, including the United Nations.[13] Kennan maintains that because the more advanced industrial states, primarily those in Europe, Japan, and North America, are responsible for most of the world's pollution, those nations will have to take effective collective action to combat the problem. One approach would be for these countries to form a new international organization. To be effective, advocates of such an organization maintain that each member must be assured participatory rights proportional to its political, economic, and military importance. There would be no one nation-one vote representation as in the United Nations.

How such a world authority would insure compliance by national governments regarding ecological standards and population growth programs cannot be clearly foreseen. Economic sanctions might be invoked and if these failed, more stringent procedures, including military action, might be necessary.

Assuming for the moment that this organization could significantly reduce world pollution, are there any other benefits which might possibly result from the efforts of such a body? To achieve its primary ecological goal would require an unprecedented level of effective and continuous cooperation among these advanced industrial states. Once such a pattern had been developed, it might lead to other forms of cooperation in economic, scientific, political, and even military areas; even the ultimate ecological disaster, thermonuclear war, might be prevented.

Such a success seems remote. However, remembering the bitterness, belligerence, and bloodshed among Western European countries for centuries, who would have predicted the degree of cooperation and progress that has been realized in the North Atlantic Treaty Organization[14] and the European Economic Community? Whether or not such an international organization is established, the ecological crisis already has unalterably affected many aspects of national sovereignty and related military and economic aspects of international relations.

ECONOMIC, POLITICAL, AND MILITARY FACTORS

The United States, currently responsible for approximately one half of the world's pollution, consumes about one half of the world's raw materials, and will be progressively more involved in complex and relatively inflexible international affairs arising in part from environmental problems.[15] In the future some of its relations with selected nations may become as binding for ecological reasons as they have been in the past for traditional political, economic, and military reasons.

The ecological crisis has raised novel and perplexing problems concerning a nation's obligations to protect its people and its territory from external encroachment of an entirely new kind. For ecological reasons, nations are being forced to reevaluate traditional matters of sovereignty. Subjects which only a short time ago were considered by nations as wholly internal and domestic affairs are now open to examination and question by foreign states. Nations already have acted to revise traditional relationships with their neighbors, both friend and foe. Environmental sanctions against a current ally and proposals for joint clean-up programs conducted with a strategic foe are conceivable.

Regardless of a given state's power, ecological problems alter traditional objectives and the means of obtaining them to an appreciable extent. While states must continue promoting the security and economic interests of their populations, they will do so increasingly at the risk of generating protest, making unwanted concessions and experiencing retaliation or interference because of ecologically related events.

How nations attempt to insure their territorial integrity in the new ecological sense remains to be seen. All states will have to protect their land, air and waters from "invasion" by pollution as well as by conventional threats from land, air, and sea weapons systems. Some states, including Canada and Iran, have already begun to do so; others will begin in the near future. Conceivably, military power may be required to prevent territorial damage from pollution on the same priority basis as it has been used in the past to control territory.

The growing requirement for resources including clean water and air obliges industrial nations to expand operations into areas of less developed countries. Other reasons for such expansion include lower production costs, more favorable tax policies, direct access to raw materials such as petroleum, and easier entry into foreign markets in developed and developing countries. This trend is achieved mostly by multinational corporations, controlled by the industrial nations, which establish operations that frequently increase ecological problems in developing countries. Consequently, policies must be evolved for foreign expansion with minimal friction and competition, particularly between major powers.

Compared to Western European states and Japan, the United States has not appreciably expanded operations in the less developed areas yet, because its needs have not been as great as those countries. The requirement for significantly increased importation of resources by the United States may arrive much sooner than formerly realized however. One study, released in May 1973, indicates that "the ravenous American appetite for minerals will lead to severe shortages in the next few decades unless the nation stops wasting resources and starts employing better ways of finding and exploiting low grade ores . . ."16 However, if the United States postpones such a move until the ecological problems are severe or a growing number of natural resources are scarce, it may find that such development is impossible. The Western Hemisphere is the most likely area for such expansion by the United States.

Greater dependence on oceanic resources is certain, and the United States probably will have to reverse its historic opposition to the extension of territorial limits. The United States should be prepared to consider extending its suboceanic rights initially to the edge of the continental shelf and eventually to any distance warranted by developing technology. Under such a policy, nations would stake out multiple claims to areas ranging from a few hundred square yards to many square miles in size throughout the oceans of the world, regardless of the distance from their own shores. Just as in the past, in the United States, when oil wells spouted on land without regard to political boundaries, so will extraction of raw materials, aquatic "farming," and other commercial ventures spread over and under the ocean surface. The oceans will break out in economic-political rashes, or "pin points" of sovereignty. Such "pin point sovereignty" will create numerous problems in international law, ecology, and conceivably have military repercussions. A divergent approach to the oceans' effect on national security is found in the chapter by Pappageorge and O'Shei.

The United States has begun to acknowledge, as have many of its allies and major opponents, that ecology is a major international issue with political, economic, and military effects. In the future, ecological factors will reduce the likelihood that relations between any two nations will be wholly cooperative, or wholly antagonistic. Under such conditions, US military alliances could deteriorate appreciably in areas where our allies might strongly oppose us for ecological reasons.

41

Host nations may increasingly use ecological factors as an argument to raise the price to the United States for in-country bases. Threats to the biosphere may be used to justify demands for increased rental fees, higher wages for native personnel, and occasional unprogramed lump sum payments for damages.

Ecological considerations will require that the United States remain strong militarily, especially in conventional, general purpose forces to protect its interests and achieve its objectives while it simultaneously encounters increased pollution and growing competition for resources from abroad.

For these reasons conventional threat analysis techniques and force planning procedures must be altered to include adequate sensitivity to ecological issues. The Federal Government requirement for environmental impact analyses and statements before any major construction programs in the United States can be approved illustrates the significance of this factor. Traditional elements of national power should be reexamined, and the conventional factors, such as technological superiority, economic strength, and military power, should be augmented by ecological considerations.

COSTS OF ECOLOGICAL PROGRAMS

Factors which increase the cost of military materiel and operations or, conversely, reduce funds available for military purposes impact on national security both directly and indirectly. Expenditures for ecological programs affect defense programs in both ways.

All of the long-term aspects of ecological programs are not known, but the total cost of proposed programs could increase the price of products and services of those industries which are the primary polluters by as much as 20 percent.[17] Total costs of about $10 billion a year in 1970 are expected to increase to more than $33 billion annually by 1980. The total cost to protect the American ecology in the 1970's has been estimated by the US Council on Environment Quality at $287 billion.[18] Some experts, such as Barry Commoner, estimate that the cost for "environmental measures would approach $40 billion annually for the next 25 years."[19] The Chase Manhattan Bank has predicted "... that an increase in annual expenditures in the dimension of ... 1½ to 2 percent of the gross national product can be expected by 1975 ..."[20] The impact of such developments on the military may be both unclear and distant; however, there are other pragmatic ramifications, including cost, which bear directly on the military now and in the future.

US MILITARY ECOLOGICAL PROBLEMS

The military services of the United States cannot be considered independent of the ecological problems that confront the world today. Military aircraft, ships, other equipment, and bases contaminate the air, water, and land. Certain types of pollution are unique to the military, including pollution from chemical and nuclear weapons, and until recently, biological weapons.

In the past 11 years, the following events have occurred: In 1963, the Nuclear Test Ban Treaty was ratified; in 1969, the United States reaffirmed its earlier renunciation of first use of chemical warfare weapons, and unilaterally stated that it would never engage in biological warfare; in April 1972, the USSR, the United States, and 68 other nations signed a convention outlawing biological weapons and requiring states to destroy their stocks of such weapons;[21] the full impact of the SALT I agreements remain to be seen, and the results of SALT II are even further away. Add to these events such developments as the cancellation of the American supersonic transport plane project by the US Congress in 1971,[22] the US ban on overflights of its territory by foreign supersonic aircraft, the delays in building the Alaskan pipeline, and a trend is clear. Additionally, one of the most important and expensive developments has been the evolution of tactical nuclear weapons.

A multimillion dollar program by the United States to develop, produce, and deploy an entirely new inventory of tactical nuclear weapons began in the 1950s. The availability of these weapons considerably broadens the options of this country and reduces our reliance on high yield strategic nuclear weapons, particularly in the initial stages of a conflict. At the same time, these "clean," or very low yield, weapons appreciably reduce the extent of possible future nuclear pollution.

Indications are that subsequent environmental developments will continue to affect operations and planning. In the recent past the following have aroused concern about military pollution, particularly chemical and nuclear pollution:

... the use of herbicides in Vietnam; the death of thousands of sheep as a result of a nerve gas accident in Utah in March 1968; and accidental release of nerve gas stored in Okinawa in July 1969; and a series of controversies over transportation of chemicals including the dumping of two train loads of nerve gas off the Florida coast in August 1970.[23]

Actions taken by the United States to eliminate the hazards of biological weapons and reduce the dangers from chemical and nuclear weapons have been mentioned. However, there are ongoing sources of militarily linked nuclear radiation which are significant. Other than atmospheric tests by nonsignatories of the 1963 Nuclear Nonproliferation Treaty, ways in which nuclear weapons can add to pollution are: (1) the manufacture and testing of nuclear weapons; (2) operation of nuclear powered ships; and (3) transportation and storage of radioactive byproducts. Although several of these problems also result from civilian activities, it is their military aspect that concerns us here.

The 1963 partial test ban treaty did not end nuclear weapon testing, and the Atomic Energy Commission (AEC) has detonated more than 250 underground explosions since then. Several of these have "vented," resulting in unintended radioactive contamination of the atmosphere. Most of the venting has been minor in nature, but on at least three occasions radioactivity from the leaks has been detectable from outside of the United States.[24]

In addition to nuclear testing dangers, the production and use of nuclear materials creates other problems. Large quantities of nuclear waste are accumulated and waste byproducts have in turn generated concern about the leakage of storage containers caused by earthquakes or other national disasters. Consequently, the AEC began solidifying atomic waste at Hanford, Washington, but " ... the amount being solidified was no more than just keeping up with the requirements for new storage, rather than reducing the quantity of hazardous liquid storage."[25]

Most nuclear powered ships are military, and although they have an excellent safety record, it is unlikely that there is any certain way of preventing serious nuclear contamination in the event of collision or other major accidents.

Reviewing the ecological role of the military in the biological, chemical, and nuclear areas, James A. Barber states:

... the military services have proved themselves capable of carrying out some pretty dubious and ecologically hazardous undertakings when such

44

projects have been either ignored by the public or hidden behind a screen of secrecy. [However] ... publicity and public controversy have been extraordinarily effective in obtaining modification of military policies ... to include greatly increased care in the transportation, storage, and disposition of chemical warfare materials, limitation on the testing of such material, plans for complete destruction of all biological warfare materials, withdrawal of nerve gas stored in Okinawa, a pledge from the Secretary of Defense that the United States would never dump nerve gas in the sea again, and a sharp cutback in the use of herbicides in Vietnam. [Additionally] ... an extensive program has been initiated by each of the military services to bring other kinds of environmental pollution resulting from their activities under control.[26]

CORPS OF ENGINEERS AND POLLUTION

No one need be reminded of the tremendous impact the media has on national security. An example of critical writing which directs attention to the military's relationship to ecology is Elizabeth B. Drew's article, "Dam Outrage: The Story of the Army Engineers."[27] After stating that "there is no question that the civil works program of the Army Corps of Engineers, viewed over its long history, has benefited the country," Drew adds that:

... now, however, it is a prime example of a bureaucracy that is outliving its rationale, and that is what is getting it into trouble ... It has brought down upon itself the wrath of more and more people disturbed about the effects on the environment. A secret poll taken by the White House last year showed environmental concerns to be second only to Vietnam in the public mind. This rather sudden general awareness of the science of ecology ... has brought projects which disturb the environment and the ecology, as the Corps projects do, under unprecedented attacks.[28]

In conclusion, she states:

If there are to be a Corps and a Corps Public Works Program, then proposals to expand the Corps' functions make sense. Making the Corps responsible for sewage treatment, for example, would give it a task that needs to be done, local governments a benefit which they really need ...[29]

Approximately two years after Drew's article, one of the important aspects of the Army's "new look" at the environment is the reorientation by the Corps of Engineers Civil Works Program to become more responsive to a revised set of national priorities, to include urban studies programs of regional waste treatment management systems throughout the United States.[30]

COST OF MILITARY ECOLOGICAL PROGRAMS

When discussing the overall impact of the ecological crisis on national security, specific ecological expenditures by the military services must be considered. The total cost of ecological measures by the military has not been calculated precisely, but the expense is rising. In the Department of Defense budget for Fiscal Year (FY) 71 and 72, the expenditures clearly identified for environmental control equaled almost $366 million. The FY 73 budget included another $314 million and the amount will increase significantly in the next few years. The Navy expects to spend as much as one billion dollars in the next five years on environmental quality programs.[31] The cost to the Army for research on pollution abatement alone was $12 million in FY 74.[32]

If these forecasts are reasonably accurate, the impact of such an added expense on military budgets is apparent, particularly when competiton for the budget dollar is increasing and especially if inflation continues.[33] The cost of ecological programs will continue to affect the price of buying, using, and maintaining military equipment and supplies. Estimates for equipping a civilian vehicle with emission controls have run from $225 to $860,[34] and the cost for controls on military vehicles presumably would be more expensive. Not only do emission controls use more fuel, but the US armed forces, with the largest automotive inventory in the country, expected a 35-40 percent increase in petroleum costs in FY 74 alone.[35] Expense is but one indicator of the ecology's importance. Another indicator is the significance it has to military personnel.

MILITARY AWARENESS

Military personnel, including some of the highest ranking officials, are becoming increasingly aware of environmental problems. Expenditures to reduce pollution demonstrate the conviction of some top defense officials in this matter. Recently the Deputy Under Secretary of the Army, Henry L. T. Koren, cited a US Army War College survey of 4,000 officers which demonstrated that Army personnel with up to five years of service consider pollution to be the "single greatest danger to the United States." Additionally, all other military personnel polled included the environment among the perceived dangers.[36]

To the extent that weapons systems, their cost, capabilities, quantities, and political-psychological implications, affect the formulation and execution of strategy, the events summarized here have already impacted on national security. Quite probably other events, which cannot be accurately forecast, will affect military programs and policies in the future. Environmentally generated political, economic, and social pressures will continue to require the military to adapt its policies accordingly.

CRITICISM OF THE MILITARY

Ecological programs undertaken by the services have not eliminated criticism of the military on ecological grounds. Some criticism of the military, particularly regarding its ecological role, is all encompassing. An example is Barbara Ward and Rene Dubos' recent book, *Only One Earth.* While their views may seem extreme to some, especially to the military, the authors are well known and their publications widely read. They state that the:

> ... developed economies have a "slack" to take in of at least $150 billion devoted every year to the most senseless, wasteful, and inflationary activity, the production of armaments. All governments of genuinely "advanced" countries know that war between them will be nuclear and hence the ultimate and irreparable pollution. Most of them might now reflect on such lessons as Algeria or Vietnam and ask whether limited wars, involving great powers in less developed areas, can be anything but profoundly wasteful and counterproductive. The largest environmental benefaction any government could bestow on its own people is first to keep the peace and then reduce the cost of preserving it to the levels of an international police force.37

The authors' point of view should not be dismissed as another tirade in the long series of statements opposing war. Nor should their position be shrugged off as an updating of a recurring theme in history to disarm either partially or completely. The authors' position on armed conflict reflects the desires of much of humanity through the ages. The "nuclear element" in modern warfare adds a factor of extreme urgency and raises warfare to a level of gravity unique in human history. For these reasons, such points of view on the futility of war and the need for disarmament will be more influential than at any time in the past. In any case, such opinions are among the many ecologically related factors that will have both short and long-term impact on national defense policymakers.

FUTURE US MILITARY ROLE

As ecological problems become more critical, remedial actions by the government, private organizations, and individuals have multiplied. An increasing amount of our resources have been used to cope with the situation and more effort may be needed, including possible involvement by Defense Department personnel in defensive roles. In an era of expanding East-West detente and reduced US military presence overseas, it is conceivable that the US armed forces might be used in large-scale, nationwide ecological reaction programs. Such missions could change US military force structure and operational priorities for some units, at least in the short run.

If the magnitude and severity of the ecological crisis warrants, sufficient historical precedence for use of the military in such a role exists. In addition to "winning the West," the US military has built roads, canals, railroads, and dams across the nation and overseas, and it had operational responsibility for the Civilian Conservation Corps in the 1930's. The military was responsible for managing the programs that developed the atomic bomb. Armed services personnel have played an important role in polar expeditions and pioneered development of naval and aerospace technology. Also, military personnel have been used to assist in domestic crises, ranging from national disaster relief to riot control.

As distasteful as it may be to some in the military, a large number of troops might be diverted to ecological duty, to nation rebuilding. Use of US military units in major ecological programs would be within the broad interpretation of the military's obligation to support and defend the Constitution of the United States against all enemies, foreign and domestic.

Military ecological involvement could operate under a wide spectrum of conditions. Least involvement would be in a role similar to the present, in which ecological considerations are secondary, for the most part, and primarily financial. Special attention would continue regarding the ecological impact of nuclear and chemical weapons. Other aspects would include local pollution abatement programs at forts, bases, and other installations, and attempts to reduce equipment emission pollution.

The other extreme would be maximum commitment of military forces under one or both of the following conditions. First, in the event of a thermonuclear exchange, the military, along with all other surviving elements of the US society, would be deeply involved in emergency civil support operations and longer term rebuilding programs. Second, severe ecological conditions requiring large-scale military involvement would arise in the remote event that either the ocean levels should rise appreciably or an "ice age" returns.[38]

A third possibility lies somewhere between, closer to the first one. In such a situation, military units might perform many tasks, including patrolling and monitoring for pollution—both domestically and offshore; operating a nationwide ecological communications warning network; transporting and disposing waste on an unprecedented scale; and participating in continental flood control and reforestation projects.

Commitment of US armed forces on a national scale in a coordinated program with other governmental agencies, private organizations, and individuals, would require the development of a comprehensive "ecostrategy."[39] The future ecological role of the military depends in large part on two, directly related, factors: first, the magnitude of the ecological crisis, and second, the capabilities of the nation to cope with the situation without major assistance from the armed forces.

ENVIRONMENTAL WARFARE

In this discussion of possible roles of the military regarding the ecological crisis, the armed services have been considered in a passive or defensive posture. They might react to ecological situations arising over the long term, through negligence, ignorance, or carelessness on the part of individuals, industries, or governments. The armed forces also might be used in the development and employment of offensive environmental weapon systems.

The former Department of Defense Director of Research and Development, Dr. John S. Foster, has stated that the military will study the "formation, growth, and dissipation of clouds, fog, and rain . . ." during the coming years. These measures probably would be primarily passive or reactive; however, advances made in these areas could eventually be adapted to offensive use. If the military can dissipate clouds and fog, it probably could generate these conditions at times and places desired. The "fog of war" would be literal as well as figurative.

Activity in these and related areas has caused the US Senate to overwhelmingly resolve that the United States should take the lead in seeking an international agreement to prohibit "environmental warfare," such as past rainmaking practices in Southeast Asia.[40] A "sense of the Senate" resolution to this effect was adopted by a vote of 82 to 10 on July 11, 1973. Senator Claiborne Pell, who sponsored the resolution, noted that the "potential military use of environmental modification ranged from simple rainmaking to possible earthquake stimulation, steering of ocean currents or tidal wave stimulation," as well as "the danger of unforeseeable repercussions from such tampering with natural forces." He added that he "would be very much surprised if some of the other superpowers have not taken steps to develop their own offensive military weather—modification capabilities.[41]

Dr. Gordon J. J. MacDonald, a geophysicist, has stated that other possible methods of altering natural forces for military purposes include changing the earth's temperature and creating a "hole" in the shielding layer of ozone that absorbs much of the sun's ultraviolet radiation. Other experts have testified concerning experiments by the military during the past five years regarding prevention of lightning and increasing snowpacks on mountains.[42] Senator Pell's committee, in considering the resolution, "was in general agreement that the use of rainmaking as a weapon of war can only lead to the development of vastly more dangerous environmental techniques whose consequences may be unknown and may cause irreparable damage to our global environment."[43]

Such a development has occurred, at least regarding rainmaking. In May 1974 the Department of Defense acknowledged that US military forces had participated in multimillion dollar top secret rainmaking operations in North Vietnam from 1967-72. The effectiveness of this weather modification is disputed; however, the intent of the program is clear—to slow the movement of North Vietnamese troops and supplies along the Ho Chi Minh Trail.[44] Remembering the accomplishments of the United States in nuclear warfare and in space, it is quite possible that other offensive and defensive ecological weapon systems could be initiated.

CONCLUSIONS

In any area as uncertain as ecostrategy, only the most tenuous, preliminary deductions can be made. Among these conclusions are the following.

Certain ecological problems have reached or are approaching the global crisis level, and have become strategically significant within the past five to ten years, with the result that the ecological factor now must be included in any analysis of traditional elements of power.

US armed forces generate some ecological problems that are unique, and criticism of the armed forces' role vis-a-vis ecology was a factor in the abandonment of biological weapons, brought on major restrictions of chemical weapons, and made nuclear weapons the most severely controlled and closely guarded ever.

It is conceivable that the US military could be used in large-scale, nationwide ecological programs, and, if so, such missions would change US military priorities, force structure, and type of operations. Additionally, US military forces might be committed to monitor and perhaps assist with international environmental program enforcement. The US economy, technology, and population have grown and developed to the extent, however, that the nation does not have to rely on its military forces today to resolve current ecological problems in a way that it did to assist in the nation's expansion and growth in the past two centuries.

Even without direct, large-scale involvement by the US military to alleviate environmental problems, aspects of the ecological crisis will affect national security in numerous ways. Many of these are highly important today and others will become critical in the future. Expenditures for ecological programs will both increase the cost of military materiel and operations and reduce funds available for defense purposes. Other elements of the ecological crisis, which cannot be precisely evaluated, bear on the nation's general well-being and upon its national security. For these reasons, the ecological crisis has obliged many nations to begin reexamining conventional concepts of sovereignty, and it has raised novel and complex issues concerning their obligation to defend their population and territory from encroachment of an entirely new kind.

In addition to possible reactive or defensive ecological roles by the military, the United States may develop and employ offensive environmental weapon systems. Military activity in this area has caused the US Senate to overwhelmingly resolve that the United States should take the lead in seeking an international agreement to prohibit environmental warfare. The potential possibilities of such conflict range from rainmaking to setting off earthquakes and tidal waves, steering ocean currents, changing the earth's temperature, and burning holes in the earth's ozone.

Depletion of the earth's raw materials has made it impossible to rebuild the present urban industrial nations of the world, a fact especially significant for the United States, which consumes about one half of the world's raw materials and causes approximately one half of the world's pollution. Consequently, the United States will be increasingly affected by international affairs related to environmental problems. Thus, it must remain strong militarily, especially in conventional, general purpose forces, to protect its interests and achieve its objectives while experiencing growing competition for resources from abroad.

4

Economic Interdependence and Strategy

John F. Scott

Two kinds of interdependence compete for our attention in the literature of international affairs. One, the popularized view, goes by other names—"One World," "The Global Community"—and is as legitimate as the elite, eclectic view which seems to concern academic writers. The latter is, however, the view that is the substance of this essay. A word on the distinction is appropriate.

The popular view of world interdependence seems to stem from the idea that exposure to information leads to beliefs that our fate and the fate of distant peoples and nations are connected. What happens to one affects the other and what one does affects the other. We are interdependent because we *think* we are. Fifty years ago a West African drought could have led to the starvation of people whose existence was unknown to us. Today, their plight is likely to make the front page of *The New York Times,* and the reedy bones and bloated abdomens of dying children will likely be shown on the evening news. We can choose to be indifferent, but not unaffected. Then, too, there are connections, sometimes mysterious, between Asiatic poppy growers and some of our children's ideas of psychic experiment. England exports a style of music (and a style of musician) and we retaliate with hamburger stands in Picadilly. The Bolshoi passes the Cleveland

Symphony in mid-Atlantic. All of this in addition to the somber, rational, trading and calculating of economic and political relations marks the popularized view.

The eclectic view might have gained its momentum not in spite of the popular view, but because of it, partly as a reaction to its tendency to oversimplify. We in the United States enter security alliances with other countries but we are not always as dependent on them for our security as they are on us for theirs. Perhaps in some phychological sense we are, but without distinctions everything is important and nothing is important. Dependent relationships are not necessarily measured by the volume of intercourse alone. The test seems to be that change must bring about like or greater change. A dependent relationship is one that is very costly to break. In the popular view, there is effect, impact, awareness, consciousness, but not necessarily *interdependence* in the sense of actions and reactions or of action and resultant atrophy. The witnesses to drama are not a part of it, no matter how many tears fall in after-theater wine. Let us call the popular concept "awareness" and the eclectic concept "interdependence." The popular conception is not less important to us than the eclectic, but there are differences, and the future security and prosperity of the world might not be served by confusing the two.

INTERNATIONAL ECONOMIC INTERDEPENDENCIES

Capital, commodities and services, labor, technology, and management skills move across national borders with greater ease and on a greater scale than at any time in the history of modern economic relations. But does this mean a rising level of economic interdependence? Economic interdependence "normally" refers to the dollar value of economic transactions[1] either in absolute terms or relative to the total transactions of a nation—that is, relative to its total annual production or gross national product (GNP). Absolute dollar values reveal little about interdependence. The amount could rise each year in noninflated dollars only to tell us that foreign trade is becoming *less* important if the trading economies are growing at faster rates at home.

When the dollar value of an economy's international trade is high relative to other nations and relative to its own total product, a dependent, if not interdependent, economic relation with its correspondent economies seems self-evident. Among eighteen

Organization for Economic Cooperation and Development (OECD) members for the period 1968-70, foreign trade of goods and services ranged from 49.2 percent for the Netherlands to 5.9 percent for the United States.[2] Still, these are gross figures and though the Netherlands is clearly more dependent on the international economy for its own economic welfare than is the United States, our ideas about what these figures mean in terms of influence on and from other economies might change if the same percentages were for Singapore and Chad. Perhaps the most that should be said for percentage figures for any one nation is that they represent an economy's relative potential susceptibility to external economic events, in terms of that nation's year to year internal growth and stability. To have political meaning the concept of interdependence requires criteria not necessarily inherent to the theory of international trade.

International trade and finance has potential political and social costs for a nation's sovereignty and autonomy, on the safe assumption that these two attributes of nationhood are highly valued by all states. A trade-off point presumably exists between economic welfare and sovereignty/autonomy when the former is damned if it means giving up any more of the latter. One need only think of the national security rationale for avoiding too much dependence on imported materials when domestic supplies or substitutes are available, even if at a higher dollar cost and therefore at greater economic opportunity costs.

Sovereignty in the present context is the relative freedom of a state to act in its relations with other states, recognizing possible constraints on the range of choice stemming from international economic relations. The choices of the oil importing states of West Europe—their sovereignty—were rather narrow in regard to their political stand toward the warring sides and the warfare issues during and after the 1973 Mideast crisis.

Autonomy refers to a state's freedom to choose its domestic economic policies for growth, development, and stability—although autonomy includes as well other social institutions and cultural values that might be changed by processes initiated by economic events. There would be little argument that US short-run choices for encouraging full employment of its labor force are circumscribed by its international economic obligations.

These broad political values then—sovereignty and autonomy—are the political criteria for assessing economic dependence and interdependence. When economic relations between nations are such that sovereignty and autonomy can be circumscribed, the relations are politically significant. When relations are such that conscious political decisions can and might be made to use economic developments purposefully to influence another's sovereignty and autonomy, the situation is strategically significant.

Richard Cooper uses the concept of sensitivity to economic transactions between two or more nations to economic developments within these nations as the context and concept of interdependence.[3] The concept goes beyond dollar volume and relative-to-GNP volume; both could be high without sensitivity. Also, volume might be low and sensitivity high. This concept for interdependence is not simple because the word often evokes an image of economic influences quite different from a technical meaning of "sensitivity." By sensitivity we mean the Princess and the Pea, not a bull in a china shop. Sensitivity is greatest when measurably small changes in economic developments in one national economy give rise to change in another. The stimulating changes might be in incomes, costs, prices, or exchange rates, for example. A slight increase in the price of commodity X, brought about by an increase in the price of labor to produce it, could greatly decrease that commodity's sales in a sensitive importing country. The importer would make more of its own commodity X, shifting resources from the foreign to the domestic sector.

The reason for this kind of sensitivity is the "convergence of production cost structures, among industrial countries, which is likely to continue as capital accumulates and as technical knowledge flows even more easily across national boundaries. . ."[4] If the costs to produce most commodities are roughly the same in two countries, the gains from specialization and subsequent international trade are relatively small. There is little if any economic advantage remaining in such trade relations. International trade then becomes less valuable for increasing the economic welfare of the nations involved in such a subsystem.

A sensitivity relationship is not politically benign. It might seem so because it implies small and even natural adjustments in relatively free domestic economies—production need not stop while a frantic search for other sources of supply goes on. But change there is, and the affected people might not like the consequences in their own economy from these small changes in another economy. Foreign changes are influencing decisions and processes the affected people should like to have complete control over themselves—their own economic systems and organization. Surely, the world will have gone to hell if a Zurich gnome can determine the price of a Texas rancher's beef. Some autonomy will have been lost.

With low national barriers to the movement of economic factors between most developed nations, "countries desiring to pursue tax and regulatory policies that deviate widely [from others] will find themselves stimulating large inflows or outflows of funds, firms, or persons; these induced movements will in turn weaken the intended effects of the policies . . . Economic policies that have hitherto been regarded as exclusively domestic will come under increasing influence from the international environment."[5]

Cooper contends that "economic issues are becoming . . . more problematic in relations among advanced non-Communist countries . . . Indeed, the trend toward greater economic interdependence among countries will require substantial changes in their approach to foreign policy in the next decade or so."[6]

This is probably true. Nevertheless, caveats are in order that might make the required changes seem less dramatic. First, Cooper's focus is on the economic relations between the most industrialized countries, the Atlantic community and Japan. The generalizations about interdependence, if true, are true for the larger world system to the extent that sensitivity applies, and it probably does not apply when the developing nations are brought into the picture. Second, the generalizations about increased sensitivity must be qualified by respect for product differentiation, economies of scale, and increased national protection of agriculture, each of which, in a word, limit price and cost sensitivity.[7] Finally, the United States is more of an exception to the rule than others. Because of its size and the use of the dollar in international trade, it "retains much more autonomy in the use of monetary policy for domestic purposes than do other countries, for its own actions strongly influence world monetary conditions."[8]

Another kind of sensitivity to external economic developments concerns an economy's dependence on material imports that it cannot find domestically or cannot easily substitute for at home. This kind, which we can simply label dependency, should not, but is, confused with the first kind of sensitivity, and appears to have more dramatic political and strategic implications. But the appearance is not reality.

The GNPs of industrial nations have grown faster than their demand for primary products, partly because of larger service sectors and partly because raw materials represent a lesser proportion of the cost of final products. We have noted the mobility of capital across national borders; its accumulation

> greatly reduces the *natural* differences among nations on which traditional trade was based. Some resources are highly specific to the production of certain goods and can be used in the production of other goods only with greatly increased cost. A rise in the capital stock relative to other factors reduces this specificity of production.[9]

Moreover, as Kenneth N. Waltz contends, reliance on imports per se does not represent dependence. One must consider the nearness to the source of imports (this can be deceiving as materials far away might be easier to get than the same materials just across a border); the numbers of suppliers of a commodity; stockpiles and the nature of war (is it likely that the United States would be in the kind of war where sufficient essential imports would be denied?); and, technology as a way to substitute for the questionable materials, and for the recovery of materials already used in production (e.g., scrap metals).[10]

Both in trade and investments, the United States has "plenty to lose," but for it to happen all at once would require a catastrophe on the order of war. "The question becomes one of who needs whom more."[11] The net influence of power, if you will, is the important ratio between economically interdependent countries. Exporters of raw materials do need to sell their products to expand their own economies. The supply cannot be turned off and on like a spigot for political advantage when the net effect on the whimsical exporter is to reduce his own economic welfare. The oil sheiks are the exception—the short-run exception at that—and not the rule. Perhaps the raw materials exporting countries should worry more about industrial countries finding cheaper substitutes than the industrial countries should worry about an assured supply of the raw materials.

Nevertheless, an interdependent relationship exists between importers and exporters of raw materials and some potential for strategic manipulation also exists. This power probably is not systematically symmetrical however, and in the case of the United States, not necessarily strategically important in terms of vulnerability, compared to other countries.

Barring dramatic national policy decisions, economic interdependence will probably not decrease in the next decade for the total world system. How does one know this, especially when quantitative criteria seem absent? Accepting national autonomy and sovereignty as the qualitative criteria, and with a fair idea of how and why these can be influenced by economic events in other countries, interdependence can be seen as a function of the continuation of the conditions which determine and allow this influence on autonomy and sovereignty. That is to say, increasing interdependence is a function essentially of low national barriers to the in and out flow of production factors, and, in the case of industrialized countries, the greater convergence of the price of these factors. There is more to be said about the determinants of economic interdependence, of course. Stipulated here is a reasonably high degree of total system interdependence—stemming from good economic reasons: motivated by the desire to increase economic welfare. We must be aware, however, that economic interdependence is a generalization covering subsystem relations which are more properly seen as dependence-dominance situations, and that economic interdependence does not mean dependence and attendant political vulnerability as a knee jerk deduction.

ASYMMETRIES AND THEIR EFFECTS

If foreign economic relations had little or no influence on the autonomy of states, they would have no strategic significance because affected states would have no reasons on these bases to take political actions to protect or retaliate in ways that harm others and harm their own societies. For case studies of foreign economic influence on autonomy, the multinational corporations tend to be the villains of the piece. When mutual state-private firm back-patting is the alleged source of influence, the United States, the home base to the majority of influential firms, tends to be the villain. US based enterprises account for 10 or 12 percent of the national production of countries outside these borders.[12] This potential for subtle influence creates unease.

Whenever the United States government seeks to extend its influence by means of its enterprises, as it has been known to do in the case of trading-with-the-enemy controls and antitrust policies, the affected countries are reminded of the great potential power and reach that the United States government represents. Occasional reminders of that power are sufficient to keep the uneasiness alive.[13]

Examples of US influence with and within other countries range from forbidding IBM-France to sell certain types of computers to the

French government[14] to a continuing near monopoly on nuclear reactor systems and the fuel they use, an asset with proven and latent political power.[15] But it is one thing to recognize these instances of combined US government-private corporation influence and quite another to infer an institutionalized conspiracy with political purpose. The US government frequently is at odds with its own multinationals[16]—with antitrust suits against oil companies, capital export restrictions and the like—and transnational actors such as oil companies have influenced US foreign policies, sometimes with results that in retrospect might have been politically unwise. Further, alleged exploitation, especially of poor countries' economies by multinationals, does not hold up under close examination for situations since World War II.[17] This latter conclusion by Raymond Vernon refers most likely to the amounts and qualities of capital, technology, and management skills brought into developing economies by the industrial states and the multinationals, which the affected nations were unable to duplicate on their own.

The political and strategic importance of the impact of foreign economic activities in affected states, especially in the poorer countries, is that effects which are beneficial economically can and often do have domestic political and social second-order consequences. These are often perceived negatively in the affected states, whether the results are intended or not by the foreign governments and firms. It seems plausible, writes Peter Evans, that "multinational corporations help transmit standards of consumption which may well represent a misallocation of resources from the point of view of the welfare of the community as a whole."[18] The weakness of local entrepreneurs leaves the state as the only entity with enough leverage to bargain with multinationals and as the only logical entity to try to mitigate their social effects. When the affected states' officials fear for their national autonomy and act to preserve it, democratic processes, if there are any, lose out to a centralized control which may or may not be what its citizens want as their way of political life. This applies to developed as well as developing societies.

One might argue from these transnational perspectives whether interdependence is the fitting rubric for modern international economic relations when their noneconomic effects are taken into account in poorer countries, whose desire for economic growth and development is so high that unwanted social and political consequences have to be risked. The situation might be better described as asymmetrical, or at least as a compound of dependence and interdependence which, as Waltz suggests, is quite different from a web of economic interdependence. He maintains in fact an "iron law"—that "high inequality among like units *is* low interdependence."[19] This is almost certainly true, with exceptions, between advanced and developing nations. Even for relations between developed nations, the effects of asymmetric economic power are politically important.

> We are at a moment in history in which increased economic interdependence among advanced countries looks close to inevitable. But it is a lopsided interdependence, one in which the United States is seen as gaining most from the continuation of the trend and losing least from its interruption. From a political and psychological point of view that is a dangerous situation.[20]

THE POLITICAL CONNECTION

Even in an essay concerned primarily with economic interdependencies and their political and strategic implications, interaction in the areas of the "higher politics"—security and prestige—cannot be ignored. North Korea has no substantial formal economic relations with South Korea, and US—USSR trade is minute compared to their size, but in neither case could we say that events in one do not affect the other. With modern communications and transportation leading to greater information about external events, "political decisionmakers in any given part of the system are far more sensitive [to these events] than was the case in the past."[21]

Economic power that resides in the compound of dependence and interdependence is attenuated or countervailed by this political interdependence to the degree that nations are willing to apply their political—coercive—power. (And of course it works the other way about—economic power attenuating political power.) All this is plausible enough in the arena of sovereignty against sovereignty. It is more difficult to make connections for national autonomy.

In respect to the effects of political and economic interdependencies on autonomy, there are at least two contexts worth our interest. The first is that entanglement of sovereignty and autonomy in which external events affect some nations directly and then affect other nations in turn because of their ties to the immediately affected nations, rather than to the sources of influence. An instance is the October 1973 War, the related oil embargo with its immediate effects on West

Europe, and its effects once removed on the United States. This is not to deny direct effects and direct interests for the United States; but in economic terms, one could say that the United States is relatively independent and therefore not subject to Arab political power through those economic means. The greater long-term political problem for the United States seems to be in its partnership with West Europe in economic, political, and security affairs. The United States is thoroughly involved and affected, more through its second-order connection with Europe than it otherwise might be, this stemming from an economic weapon.

The second context is more purely a problem of maintaining autonomy. The logic of political and economic interdependence yields the conclusion that central governments' tasks are enlarged and made more difficult to perform because of sensitivity to international affairs and because of the influence of these affairs on domestic society. We can argue that statesmen are more than ever pressured to consider the consequences of interstate relations on populations *within* states, and that these pressures narrow the margin of freedom to act in external affairs, while increasing sensitivity to external affairs circumscribes internal freedom of action.[22] An extension of this tendency is that traditional democratic processes, or inchoate democracy in some states, are weakened or retarded, sometimes in the name of national security, prestige, or other features of the higher politics. One could say that we have moved even further away from the New England town meeting model of democracy with each real or perceived surge of interdependence. At one extreme, the West German factory worker seems hopelessly far removed from a decision to use nuclear weapons in war, even removed from the choice of whether to have them around. Not only has he delegated his sovereignty to the Bundestag, and in turn to the Chancellor, but in turn again to NATO and ultimately to the US President, the United Kingdom Prime Minister, and the President of France, each of whom has control over nuclear weapons in Germany's behalf. Not that this author or the factory worker have better alternatives to offer. This extreme case is a fact of life, not a philosophical commentary.

Most of us may be willing to concede the short-term inevitability of this extreme case. Our concern is that the perception of interdependence affects activities, some traditionally domestic and private, which are not so clearly in the ambit of the administrators of the higher politics.[23] The possibility of sundered democratic processes might be the biggest danger from interdependence. We might worry about the inferences that could be drawn, and have been, about cause and effect, threat and intended harm, and about which so-called sacrifices we must make to meet challenges. The model is easily abused. In an economically interdependent world, actions taken or economic events occurring in one country affect other countries depending on the latters' sensitivity or dependence. Any economic act or event which affects others can be seen as having been *intended* to do so, and this perception is reinforced by the knowledge of the large role of governments in most economies. Effects from external sources seen as harmful are traditionally the concern of politics and national security. Even unintended effects too often might be seen as intended, that is, politically inspired, and therefore demand protective, retaliatory actions and greater centralized control over the national means of economic power. Will strategists see a communist or a capitalist, as the case may be, behind every change in factor prices, behind every attempt by poor nations to bargain for better terms of trade?

Even in a relatively clear case of political coercion by economic means, the Arab oil nations did not intend that poor oil-importing countries should be coerced or economically harmed by the oil export cutback and higher prices. Proper perceptions of intent can make a difference in choosing protective and compensating reactions on the part of affected nations. For those of us who doubt that we would fall victim to imputed harmful intent, we can test ourselves by imagining an economic event in Texas which has negative effects in "sensitive" Pennsylvania—say a rise in the price of beef. Would Pennsylvanians seriously impute malicious, political intent? An interdependent economic world is not unlike the American economy in this economic sense—other things equal! Yet would we see similar events originating beyond our borders as equally benign in intent?

Still, we can claim that the interdependence concept, being more realistic about economic relations than its major competitor—the state-centric view with its focus on power and its own susceptibility to teleologic reasoning—gives us a better understanding of the how and why of external events and their influence on our society. It gives us equal opportunity to say no as well as yes to assertions that acts were intended to do harm. The foundation of the interdependence concept, international trade theory, unlike some popular devil theories of international ideological conflict, rejects the concept that one's gain is another's loss; it is, in fact, its opposite.

TASKS FOR STRATEGISTS

Strategists see international events and developments in terms of conflict and their potential for conflict. The international system probably qualifies as politically and economically interdependent; perhaps more accurately it is a combination of dependencies and interdependencies, with asymmetry characteristic of many relations. The level of economic interdependence may be rising and with few barriers to the further convergence of factor prices, transnational flows of capital and skill, and international monetary linkages by common assent, it will probably rise further in the coming decade, at least for the industrialized subsystems. What does interdependence mean, especially rising levels of interdependence, for the likelihood of conflict between nations?

The jury is still out, mulling the theoretical claims. On the one hand, conflict between nations is held less likely because a "continuing pattern of cooperation and exchange" can create trust and lead to perceptions that the other nation is nonthreatening. While not a sufficient condition for peace, the likelihood of violence as a means to resolve conflict is less.[24] There is less tendency by the interacting nations to perceive threatening intent and to formulate black and white issues, and a greater readiness to communicate and seek accommodation. On the other hand, growing interdependence can be seen as the source of conflicts that could become violent for the same reason that a recluse has more opportunities for interpersonal squabbles when he ceases to be a recluse. Both positions require extensive theoretical explanation and empirical evidence that cannot be justly covered here, even if such existed. Logically,however, the concept of interdependence in terms of sensitivity imparts the opportunity for any actor to exercise power over others, but it says as well that *the costs of doing so also must be high.* As interdependence levels rise, the opportunities *and* costs also rise. Looking ahead ten to twenty years, if the Mideast oil exporters continue their domestic economic development, the costs to them of using economic means for political ends will rise, perhaps proportionate to their development. Clearly they must import to develop, and to that extent they become vulnerable—*interdependent*. And, the more economically egalitarian their societies become, the more sensitive they are likely to be to external economic and political events.

Another view is that as interdependence rises, the frequency of conflict will rise but the incidence of armed force as a means to resolve conflict will not rise proportionately. It could be a situation analogous to labor-management violence in modern US history. Since the legitimization of organized labor as a bargaining force—perhaps not truly accepted until after World War II—violence in bargaining disputes is less frequent although conflict is not and might in fact be more frequent. Yet, even today, on occasion, violence is associated with labor disputes.

That the costs of conflict rise with higher levels of interdependence speaks to competition-as-conflict more than to the conflict of clashing objectives. In terms of violent conflict, one is strained to believe that the United States is any more or any less likely to go to war against the nations of West Europe or with Canada, with whom we economically are the most interdependent. In cases where economic interdependence goes between nations with political antagonisms, one is tempted to say that violent conflict and other political means of conflict might be used less because they risk the loss of economic welfare through trade. Such generalizations will not satisfy the true believers on both sides, however, which is another way to say that the "intervening variable" of perceptions can make or break any of the theories about interdependence and the likelihood of conflict and war. The first task for strategists is this problem of trying to understand the influence of interdependencies on the probability and frequency of political conflict and warfare.

The second task of strategists is to hone discriminating abilities to distinguish political acts from economic decisions and events with political consequences. The 1973-74 Mideast oil developments are for the most part politically motivated; agricultural protectionist policies on both sides of the Atlantic are largely economic in rationale—they are not intended to harm or to coerce other producers or other nations for political concessions. In many cases, politics and economics are hopelessly entangled and it will be hard to tell who is doing what to whom and for what reason. In many other cases, the distinction should be easy to make.

Is this to say that intent is the sole criterion for decisions about protective action? The answer is no, for the good reason that unintended effects can hurt as much as intended effects; some might be intolerable. The question is, which events fall within the activities we think of as national security functions? Which events require the threat or use of force? Perception rears its metaphorical head again.

Suggestions that some centralized national authority akin to the US National Security Council should have enough authority and capability to "control" national economic policies so as to deter or defend against economic events not only miss the point about democratic processes, but reflect a kind of national security tunnel vision that can make a shambles of an economically interdependent world. To avoid war or serious political conflict on a lesser scale, interdependent nations must learn to live with the unintended effects of external economic events, compensating for undesirable ones with fiscal and monetary policies and by allowing free market adjustments when possible. This is expected of nations up to a point where the apparent irresponsibility of the affecting actor becomes intolerable to the affected actor in terms of the latter's autonomy. Obligations to others—the sense that what one does affects others, perhaps even does them harm—are most important in an interdependent world. The strongest are the most obliged. The United States is the strongest in terms of economic influence and will continue to be for some time to come.

Some of our more simplistic notions about the strategic use of potential influence will have to be further revised, although they are gone already from most mature strategic studies. One has in mind, however, the possibility of looking out at the interdependent world through the lens of "look at his capabilities, not at his intentions." Formulating foreign policies by this analog to tactical military problems is the antithesis of free trade, economic welfare through absolute and comparative advantage, and the mutual benefits of cooperation in general. If other nations adopt this tactical principle as opposed to acting on their rational self-interests, the United States would not have a trading partner in the world.

Teleologic perception—deducing intent from effects when, in this strategic context, the effects are judged to be harmful—is the handmaiden of self-fulfilling prophecies. Self-fulfilling prophecies in strategic studies start from the premise that we (whichever nation that is the standing place of the perceiver) have enemies who will do us harm with every opportunity to do so at little cost to themselves. If they are countered by our own power and influence from acting in one way, then they will act in other ways open to them. Expecting one's enemies to *cause* us problems in ways open to them, we are in danger of seeing effects as having that cause, even admitting that sometimes we will be correct.

An increasingly interdependent world offers unending opportunity for prophecy and teleology along most any lines one favors, the paranoid or the equally senseless idea that no one means anyone else harm—it's just the system at work. The task of discrimination is essential for strategists if their work is to have positive value to policymaking.

Indeed the profession finds its ultimate practical value only in governmental foreign and security policies. William Diebold asks, will governments make economic policy the handmaiden of foreign policy, "letting the ends of the latter dictate the means of the former?"[25]

> [P]olicies directed toward the long-run economic welfare have to come to terms with the world as a whole, while foreign policy measures more often than not have to deal with specific countries. Economic measures used to serve the latter purpose often seem contrary to the former. They are also likely to induce others to use economic influence in the same way. When this process gets going, we are only one step away from the rivalries of block-building, and rather far from the benign nationalism that is mainly concerned with domestic welfare.[26]

CONCLUSION

Available literature offers much more detailed and complex explanations of interdependence than have been noted here,[27] some which tend to make interdependence a more convincing reality and some which suggest we protesteth too much. My purpose has been to introduce it to strategists who might yet have missed it, and to remind them of the dangers of the Clauswitzian verb—when we recite that war *is* politics by other means, we sometimes make the historicist error of confusing Clausewitz' observation of what *was* with what *shall be*. I prefer the interpretation that war *could be* politics by other means until we raise "politics" to the status of a physical law.

If the interdependence view of economic and indeed political relations serves us as a realistic model for strategic study, it demands as well an awareness of its inferential pitfalls, most of which are carryovers from the state-centric model and cold war attitudes. Of course, the state-centric view still serves—the two models can live in peaceful coexistence. Who can deny that the United States and the USSR are clearly the two dominating military powers in the world, a fact unchanged by any claims for interdependence? Rather, the interdependence view is frustrating—a mark of its realism—precisely because so many events seem to be out of the control of nations in a world where nationalism is something of a secular credo. A thought from Richard Cooper says it best: most states will retain control over their policy instruments and will be able to pursue their objectives—they will be just less able to achieve them.[28]

TWO

Challenges to National Power

5

Lessons of Strategic Surprise: Pearl Harbor, Cuba and the 1973 Middle East Crisis

Kenneth E. Roberts

Strategic surprise succeeded for the "aggressor" at Pearl Harbor, in the Cuban Missile Crisis, and in the 1973 Middle East Crisis. The key to understanding the significance of these crises for future strategic planning lies primarily in an examination of the roles played by intelligence processors and decisionmakers rather than the failure of the intelligence gatherers or technology. Researchers in the areas of belief systems and decisionmaking such as Ole Holsti and Roberta Wohlstetter have long held that analysts seldom can review incoming information objectively. Instead, such information is often unconsciously fitted into preexisting intelligence positions and preconceived behavior patterns or else simply disregarded as irrelevant or erroneous. This article analyzes three key crises in an attempt to discuss, evaluate, and expand these conclusions, to briefly examine reasons for diplomatic successes and failures, and to identify relevant trends and commonalities upon which to base useful recommendations for improved US strategy formulation.

PEARL HARBOR, 1941

The United States and Japan began drifting toward conflict after Japan's invasion of Manchuria in 1931, but President Roosevelt anticipated continued resistance by China and growing impatience among the Japanese public and Navy with the sacrifices required for Japan's aggressive policies. During the winter of 1940-41, the situation became more serious despite continued opposition to war in the United States. Subtle warnings and attempts to negotiate were coupled with sanctions, but America's terms for peace were irreconcilable with Japanese interests and strategy.

A number of proposals for peace were considered and rejected between April 9, 1941 and November 20, 1941. After July 26, 1941, President Roosevelt froze all Japanese assets in the United States, closed all US ports to Japanese vessels, and proclaimed a strict embargo on the sale of American petroleum products to Japan. This action forced Japan to accept American demands for withdrawal from China and Indochina or obtain raw materials elsewhere. The Japanese desperately needed oil, scrap iron, bauxite, and other raw materials to expand their economy and to maintain their military forces. The world depression had already made it difficult for the Japanese to export their products abroad. The roots of the Pearl Harbor attack lay in a chain of events resulting from opposition to and misperception of these interests by the United States.[1] The United States could not accept the creation of a Japanese sphere of "coprosperity" in the Far East which Japan felt was so essential to her survival and economic growth. Successively stricter embargoes challenged rather than restrained Japan's aggressive policies.

The Japanese felt that US political power, based on democratic principles, was weak; consequently, they had little respect for it. US efforts to avoid "creating an incident" seemed to confirm these views.[2] They were cognizant of superior US military strength, but gambled the American people would decide against fighting a long war. Japanese strategy, therefore, sought to resist a counteroffensive as long as necessary in order to grind down US morale.

Roberta Wohlstetter has written perhaps the best study to date on the cause and impact of the intelligence failure at Pearl Harbor. She argues that the United States failed to anticipate Pearl Harbor because all the signals were imbedded in an atmosphere of "noise"—not for want of relevant information but rather because of overabundant, irrelevant data. In Washington, the signals from Pearl Harbor were competing with signals from Europe. In Honolulu, the competition was with signals indicating a Japanese attack on Russia and expectations of local sabotage.[3]

The data provided by American intelligence agents was "excellent," and the breaking of top priority Japanese diplomatic codes enabled US strategists to expect an attack. Although there were warnings that the attack would occur at Pearl Harbor, few diplomatic or military analysts anticipated such a bold maneuver. Intelligence resources available to the United States included top priority Japanese worldwide diplomatic and intelligence codes; radio traffic analysis which located the various Japanese fleets; economic and political analysis provided by Ambassador Grew in Tokyo; various military attaches and observers throughout Asia; results of British and other foreign intelligence; information provided by experienced businessmen, foreign correspondents, and newspapermen; the Japanese press; and intergovernmental personal contacts. Japanese intelligence operating from Honolulu also supplied military authorities in Tokyo with accurate, detailed information on US deployments in Pearl Harbor and advised of the likelihood of a successful surprise attack on the facility.

In late November, 1941, Ambassador Grew and US intelligence sources warned that a surprise aggressive movement might suddenly emerge from Japan. The United States intercepted a message from Japan to Ambassador Nomura in Washington on November 5, 1941 which stated that the deadline for diplomatic agreement with the United States was November 25; this deadline was later extended to November 29. A message intercepted on December 6 from Japanese intelligence in Honolulu advised Tokyo that the opportunity for surprise attack against Hawaii was good. The Japanese 14-Part Message, decrypted in Washington on December 6 and 7, 1941, convinced the President of the immediacy of war. Other well-known fragments of intelligence pointing to a Japanese attack included large troop and ship movements in Indochina and along the China coast, changes in Japanese naval call signs, and a radio silence in the Japanese Navy.[4]

Japan's decision to attack Hawaii first rather than move directly south was primarily a strategic gamble that a direct attack on the US Pacific Fleet in Hawaii would achieve maximum immediate destruction. It culminated an opportunistic foreign policy of probing for weaknesses, disguising aims, and moving cautiously in search of an expedient time to act. The United States was reluctant to go to war until given no alternative. By 1941, however, the strength of isolationism had diminished. The American people were generally aware that the talks with the Japanese were ending in the days before Pearl Harbor, but were not told the nation might soon be at war. The lack of

71

public belligerency perhaps contributed to the Japanese misperception of American will. The surprise attack, however, served to unify a previously divided American public behind the war effort.

CUBAN MISSILE CRISIS, 1962

American intelligence supplied Washington with accurate, fairly detailed information on Soviet actions in Cuba prior to the October 14 overflight which conclusively proved the existence of Soviet offensive missile installations. The quality of the photographs proved the validity of US charges. Timely discovery of the construction precluded a more serious crisis, inevitable if the United States had been faced with completed bases fully protected by surface-to-air missiles. US intelligence analysts and decisionmakers failed, however, to accurately evaluate Soviet strategy prior to the crisis. They either misunderstood or disregarded factors which might have led the Soviet Union to undertake gambles to improve its politico-military posture because of the persuasive belief that the Soviet Union would not deploy strategic weapons in Cuba.

Cuban relations with the Soviet Union warmed noticeably after Defense Minister Raoul Castro's visit to Moscow in July. Subsequently, refugee groups claimed that Soviet military "technicians" were arriving in Cuba in large numbers and later that these "technicians" were actually part of military units constructing bases in Cuba. Intelligence experts largely discounted these reports due to lack of definitive proof, a distrust of the motives of the refugees, the national policy of coexistence and its influence upon their perceptions, and the undependability of untrained observers.

As is now well known, Navy air reconnaissance photographed all ships visiting Cuba during the summer of 1962. High-level U-2 overflights were conducted, and by late September US intelligence had evidence of large numbers of Soviet military personnel, surface-to-air missile sites, and IL-28 light bombers in Cuba. Despite the fact that early reliable information on the number of Soviet troops and equipment was difficult to obtain, certain "signs" might have been detected earlier if American intelligence analysts and foreign policy decisionmakers had been more ready to intellectually accept the introduction of strategic missiles into Cuba. One such sign was that many Soviet ships arriving in Cuba were riding high in the water, indicating they were carrying space-consuming cargo.

In summary, refugees, press reports, foreign intelligence sources on the ground, and US reconnaissance and visual observation increasingly indicated that the USSR intended to install offensive surface-to-surface missiles in Cuba.[5] The Soviet Union claimed only to be interested in maintaining Cuba's sovereignty, but risked a carefully constructed policy of peaceful coexistence during the missile crisis to strengthen its hand in a global strategic sense. Like Pearl Harbor, the United States failed to anticipate the Cuban crisis and recognize the signals, not because relevant information was lacking, but because irrelevant data was profuse and American officials were predisposed to interpret the information in terms of certain expectations.

During the short decisionmaking period, the American public was generally aware that US relations with Cuba were becoming more strained, but were not officially told the Soviet Union had placed offensive missiles in Cuba. As soon as the American leadership and public became aware of the Soviet offensive buildup, many envisioned the possibility of another Pearl Harbor-type attack against the United States. Americans strongly supported the President's position once the nature of the crisis became apparent; those critical of his actions primarily felt stronger steps should have been taken. American public reaction undoubtedly served as one factor forcing Khrushchev to moderate his position on Cuba.

Khrushchev also seriously misjudged the leadership abilities and determination of President Kennedy, probably because of his failure to react forcefully to the Bay of Pigs crisis and to the Berlin Wall construction, and because of personal impressions gained at their summit meeting in Vienna. These impressions, combined with a general misunderstanding of the strengths of democracies during periods of crisis, led the Soviet Union to attempt to effect a major strategic realignment in Cuba.

The superior US military position in the Caribbean prior to the completion of the Cuban missile installations was well understood by Moscow. Soviet strategists were convinced that their secrecy and deception and the rapidity of construction would preclude any effective US response, however. This conclusion was strengthened by the US failure to respond to the previous buildup of conventional defensive weapons systems. When the nature of the threat became evident and the decision was made by the President to use force if necessary, various deployments were hurried to make US determination credible to the Soviet Union. The USSR had no real conventional military option with which to challenge the American threat once confrontation emerged. Neither air protection nor naval escorts were available to break the US blockade. Tactical nuclear weapons in Cuba may have offered some defense to the island, but the massive US preparations being readied for a possible invasion gave Khrushchev clear evidence of his military inferiority in the area.

Six alternatives were available to the United States as means of meeting the Soviet challenge:[6] (1) Do nothing; (2) Protest to the United Nations, to Cuba, or to the Soviet Union directly; (Diplomatic protest was used in conjunction with more direct, forceful action, to legitimize the US position.) (3) Make "surgical" air strikes on the missile installations; (4) Invade Cuba; (5) Enforce a maritime blockade of all traffic entering Cuban territorial waters; or (6) Enforce a quarantine to stop only those Soviet ships delivering missiles to Cuba. This latter policy was chosen as the primary US strategy because it could be implemented immediately, but permitted a more controlled military escalation and greater political flexibility; placed the burden of the next step with the Soviets; was viewed as moral and legal; was the most credible response least likely to escalate into nuclear war; and allowed time for strengthening US conventional forces.

The United States also utilized economic pressures to make it more difficult for the Soviet Union and others to supply Cuba. During September 1962, the State Department sought to persuade Western nations to reduce or terminate shipment of supplies to Cuba. The embargo denied US Government financing and cargoes to ships trading with Cuba; refused the use of US port facilities to the ships of any nation carrying military supplies to the island; refused entry into its ports to any ship delivering nonmilitary Communist cargoes to Cuba on the same continuous voyage; and banned all American ships and American flag ships from carrying supplies of any type to or from Cuba. The embargo presented a serious challenge since most shipping to Cuba was done in non-Communist flag ships. There is little indication that the embargo had any real impact on subsequent decisionmaking, however.

Thus, the United States skillfully combined diplomatic initiatives and military threats in a strategy to force a Soviet retreat in an unanticipated crisis. The Soviet Union, confronted with the American response and lacking a conventional capability in the area or global strategic parity, was forced to withdraw or face the unacceptable risk of nuclear war.

MIDDLE EAST CRISIS, 1973

The 1973 Middle East crisis is yet another example of misinterpretation of adequate, available intelligence. Few US or Israeli intelligence analysts and decisionmakers believed the Arabs were ready to risk another war. Despite warnings and signals of approaching conflict, the United States interpreted these in terms of preconceived notions, experience, and expectations. The national policy of detente with the USSR encouraged skepticism toward predictions of another Arab-Israel war. Misperception of European reaction also served to embarrass American "predictors," and time was lost in the resupply of Israel because improvised routes had to be developed.

A number of signals conflicted prior to the 1973 Middle East War, as prior to the attack on Pearl Harbor and the discovery of Soviet offensive missiles in Cuba, which, in retrospect, appear to be unmistakable warnings of aggression. In September, Egyptian and Syrian reconciliation with King Hussein of Jordan, after nearly two years of hostility, marked the initiation of a new phase of Arab rapprochement. King Faisal, on the other hand, began to indicate his desire to use oil as a political weapon by freezing current production levels unless the United States showed a willingness to revise its Middle East policy and follow a more even-handed approach in Arab-Israeli disputes.

The Egyptians moved large quantities of tanks, armored personnel carriers, guns, and trucks to within a few miles of the canal in late September. These movements were first viewed as a part of predicted training exercises which have been carried out annually by the Egyptian Army. Israeli forces were put on alert, but there was no general mobilization. A predicted Arab spring offensive had failed to materialize and most Israelis felt the danger had passed for the year. The indications of attack this time were clearer, however. Perhaps the strongest signal was the massive Soviet airlift from Damascus and Cairo to return home virtually all Soviet military personnel from Syria and Egypt during the few days preceding the outbreak of hostilities.

The primary impact of surprise in the October War was that the Israelis suffered a series of initial setbacks which were costly to reverse and were forced to recognize that their military security would be increasingly difficult and costly to maintain in the absence of an acceptable political settlement. Secondly, the confidence gained by the Arabs in these early victories helped eliminate some humiliation remaining from the June 1967 war. The assumption that the Arabs would be branded as aggressors and condemned by world opinion, as a result of the surprise attack, was not realized to the degree expected by the Israelis. Perhaps this was because much of the world perceived the Arabs to be attempting to regain their own territory occupied by Israel since 1967 or because of a desire not to be the target of the new-found Arab weapon of "petropolitics."

The primary US national interests in the Middle East at stake in the October 1973 War were the prevention of any single power or coalition of powers from gaining hegemony in the region and the maintenance of Israel's security and independence. The United States felt that the massive Soviet airlift of arms and equipment would upset the tenuous balance achieved in the region between the Arabs and Israelis. A resupply of Israel was therefore initiated to prevent her defeat or the loss of such territories as would endanger her existence in future wars or at the peace table. The stated Soviet intention to intervene directly in the fighting posed a serious threat to US interests. President Nixon, as a result, took both diplomatic and military action to warn the Soviet Union of the consequences of intervention.

The USSR has long desired to gain a foothold in the Middle East for geopolitical, military, and psychological reasons. Expanded influence there has strengthened Soviet credibility as a world power and rendered obsolete the old American policy of containment. Reports vary concerning Arab coordination with the Soviet Union prior to the attack, but the Soviet troop evacuation and the arrival of the Soviet sealift of new military supplies simultaneously with the outbreak of hostilities support the contention of foreknowledge and approval. When a direct confrontation with the United States became a danger, however, the USSR recognized no serious threat to Arab territories or any of its legitimate positions in the Middle East existed, and chose to accept UN mediation rather than pursue unilateral enforcement of a cease-fire and risk US retaliation.

President Nixon assigned an important role to military as well as political power in the resolution of the Middle East conflict by responding quickly to counter Soviet supply activities to the Arab combatants and by ordering a full worldwide military alert on October 25, 1973, to demonstrate US determination to oppose any unilateral Russian intervention. It appeared relatively certain that the Soviet Union was determined to put troops in the Middle East. Had the Soviets not perceived this reaction as credible, the political resolution achieved would have been endangered.

The US public, in general, is sympathetic to Israel and supports the policy of detente with the Russians and keeping the great powers in control of the situation. During the most serious hours of the crisis, the improvement in US-Soviet relations was a major factor in the avoidance of a confrontation between the two countries. Mutual interest in the preservation of detente, after the United States displayed its determination in a show of force, allowed a peaceful resolution by political means. Summits and special emissary exchanges were utilized to maintain communication with the Soviets and both sides of the Arab-Israeli confrontation throughout the crisis. Both the United States and the USSR modified their previous positions concerning Israeli withdrawal by jointly sponsoring the UN cease-fire resolution.

Thus, in the face of Arab and Soviet threats, the United States chose to match the Soviet resupply effort to the Arabs by stepping up delivery of previously ordered supplies to Israel and authorizing additional aid; to put in force military readiness preparations to counter possible Soviet unilateral intervention; and to initiate intense political and diplomatic action on all fronts. These actions represented the limits to which the US public and Congress would go without a more defined threat, but they served to warn the Soviet Union of American determination to protect its interests in the region.

The time for decisionmaking in the 1973 Middle East crisis was brief. The United States had to react quickly after the initiation of hostilities to prevent the Soviet airlift from upsetting the regional balance of forces. In the later stages of the crisis, quick American reaction was required to respond to the threat of Soviet intervention. It was necessary to insure that US intentions were well understood and to avoid being confronted by a Soviet fait accompli. In the final stages of battle, time became more critical as arrangements for a cease-fire attempted to keep pace with a fluid military environment. Time was important to the Israelis also because they felt that the world clamor for a cease-fire would quickly become irresistible. For both the Israelis and the United States, the surprise resulted in a reexamination of intelligence gathering and evaluation methods. It served to strengthen the mistrust many US decisionmakers have felt toward military intelligence since Pearl Harbor.

CRISIS CONSTANTS

Without a sound understanding of motivation and strategy in addition to capabilities, even the most accurate intelligence data on

77

economic development, technological sophistication, and military arsenals is useless. In all three crises, analysts and policymakers misread both the intentions of the adversary and his willingness to take risks. A comparison reveals a number of apparent constants which may be useful in future strategy formulation and crisis decisionmaking.

Each nation pursued its own national interests first. Prior to Pearl Harbor, both the British and the Dutch became disturbed because President Roosevelt consistently refused to state the conditions under which the US would enter the fight or supply assistance if their Eastern possessions were attacked. At Singapore, the United States and Great Britain were unable to agree on a common strategy in the Far East because of differing interests.

The United States reacted unilaterally at first in the Cuban Missile Crisis since vital security interests were threatened and since the need for secrecy and swift decisions for action made it impossible to hold prior consultations on a global scale. President Kennedy sought to retain control of decisionmaking, but realized that international organizations and diplomatic consultations could be very helpful in bringing about international understanding of the US position. That is why the US delegate to the United Nations promptly explained in detail to that organization the nature of the crisis, the US position, and why this country's actions were consistent with the UN charter, and, why the United States welcomed so strongly the support given this country by the Organization of American States. There is no evidence that Khrushchev sought the opinions of his Warsaw Pact allies before deciding to install missiles in the Western Hemisphere. Even during the actual crisis, the Soviet Union displayed disregard for Castro by failing to consult with him.

American allies in Europe generally viewed their primary interest in the Middle East as continued access to Arab oil; thus, not all of them cooperated with the United States. This disunity in the West limited the credibility of threats of possible counter-boycotts. European nations, especially France, criticized the United States because events in the Middle East were controlled by the United States and the Soviet Union without consulting other interested parties. The final cease-fire was arranged primarily by the two superpowers.

• Fears of encirclement and containment influenced action and reaction. Perceptions of an Anglo-American policy of encirclement against Japan in the Southern Pacific Ocean frequently appear in official Japanese documents and memoirs. Such a threat, whether real

78

or imagined, was certain to be taken seriously by an insular power such as Japan.

President Kennedy felt that the Soviet Union sought to encircle the West by subverting the world's developing nations. Cuba, of course, was the primary Soviet base of subversion in Latin America. Many American officials felt the Russians were simply reversing the old US policy of containment adopted by the State Department after the Second World War.

The US policy of containment sought to weaken the Soviet's viability as a world power by preventing the expansion of Russian influence to neighboring states. Greece, Turkey, and Iran were focal points of US efforts. Detente and increased sophistication and capabilities have allowed the Soviets to "leapfrog" this "line of defense" and attempt to establish a power base in the Middle East. Psychologically, militarily, and geopolitically, this was a natural, opportunistic move which led to their support for Arab demands against Israel. Influence in that region may also be viewed as part of a Soviet plan to encircle the Peoples Republic of China.

• Previous false alarms, alerts, and a numbness from facing repeated international crises served to dull reaction before agressive action was taken. In the weeks prior to the Japanese attack on Pearl Harbor, Admiral Kimmel and his forces in Hawaii investigated several false reports of Japanese submarines in the vicinity of Pearl Harbor. They doubted chances of a Japanese attack and viewed such alarms as serious irritants to their normal duties.

Likewise, Cuban refugees had been reporting Russian missiles in Cuba for more than a year and a half prior to the first official sightings. Stated goals of Cuban refugee groups and lessons learned from the Bay of Pigs invasion made American analysts particularly skeptical.

The Israelis had received various signals forecasting an imminent Arab attack for more than six months prior to the October War. Every time such a signal was received, the government had to make a decision on mobilization, which in Israel means disruption of the whole nation. The tense situation in general made all predicted attacks suspect.

• The role played by deception was always significant. Prior to Pearl Harbor, the Japanese gave shore leave to a number of Japanese sailors, issued false war plans to Japanese commanders, reinforced the northern border of Manchuria, engaged in false radio communications and negotiation, and utilized other methods of deception to hide their true intentions. They expected these tactics to confuse US intelligence analysts.

In Cuba, the Soviets used trees, tarpaulins, camouflage nets, paint, and mud to alter the missiles' natural shape. Cubans were kept from the docks while unloading was taking place and all movements occurred at night. As late as September, the Soviet Union continued to insist that there was no real need for offensive bases in Cuba since her nuclear arsenal possessed sufficient forces to destroy any foe. The Russians expected that the publicized defensive buildup would serve to shroud the introduction of strategic weapons into the Caribbean.

The Egyptians used sand colored netting to hide their equipment from Israeli aircraft and observation posts on the east bank of the Suez Canal in an attempt at secrecy. Prior to the outbreak of fighting, President Sadat of Egypt seemed to have embarked upon a new campaign of moderation; Soviet advisers were expelled, the Egyptian-Libyan unification proposal was abandoned, and new diplomatic initiatives were begun with Saudi Arabia and Jordan. A major policy speech by Sadat suggested moderation toward the United States, and a US firm, the Bechtel Corporation, was awarded the concession to build the new "Suez to the Mediterranean" oil pipeline. Significant indications had been received by Secretary of State Kissinger that the Arabs were ready to negotiate. It should be pointed out that Bechtel Corporation's relationship to the project was later changed to that of management for a fixed fee; under Bechtel supervision, an Italian consortium was awarded the contract in early 1974.

• Unexpected technological, tactical, and logistical capabilities facilitated surprise. At Pearl Harbor the United States failed to realize that the Japanese had been able to put fins on their torpedoes, thus making attack in shallow harbors feasible, and that the radius of the Japanese Zero fighter plane had been extended to 500 miles. Japanese pilot training, radar, and aircraft carrier capacity were also underestimated. The greatest military surprise the United States encountered in Cuba was the unexpected Soviet capability to build missile sites at such a rapid pace.

The effective Egyptian use of the surface-to-air missiles as a substitute for air cover was a surprise of comparable significance. The United States and Israel were impressed with Arab firepower and their seemingly unlimited ammunition and anti-tank missiles supply. Egyptian jamming, electronic countermeasures, and their nighttime and commando skills were also unexpected. Surprises in morale, degree of coordination, tactics, and toughness enabled Arab forces to make their initial gains.

• The presence of oil, embargoes, and economic pressure is important in all three crises. The Japanese strike at Pearl Harbor was directly influenced by increasingly stringent American embargoes of petroleum products, scrap iron, and other resources vital to Japan's economic growth. With these vital supplies halted, Japan was forced to look southward. Pressures in Japan mounted for war since time was on the side of the United States. Although US-British-Dutch boycotts of Japanese goods and embargoes on vital resources were aimed at forcing a change in Japanese policies, they had the effect of challenging Japan to regain her honor and economic self-sufficiency in whatever manner necessary.

It may be argued that US use of a comparable boycott aimed at Cuba prior to the crisis had a similar effect. It served to evoke a challenge to Fidel Castro and to insure that he would be forced to accept total dependence on the Soviet Union.

The United States is in a distinctly different position in the Middle East. This time "petropolitics" was used by the Arab nations against the West. The United States miscalculated the Arabs ability and determination to carry out their threats. The US reaction indicates that this embargo was also viewed as a challenge. It had no real military significance, and, by itself, affected no significant political or economic readjustments.

• Perhaps the most important constant is the role played by "behavioral surprise" or "apparent behavioral surprise" in each of these three situations. Research in decisionmaking theory and crisis diplomacy during recent years has made great strides toward analyzing strategic surprise. Ole R. Holsti developed the following hypothesis from his study of Dulles: "Individuals tend to assimilate new perceptions into a body of familiar ones and to interpret what is seen in such a way as to minimize the clash with previous expectations."[7] Klaus Knorr has developed a similar theme in his concepts of "technical surprise" and "behavioral surprise." "Technical surprise" is defined as "one not incompatible with the prevalent set of expectations. It occurs because the opponent was successful in concealing a particular capability." "Behavioral surprise," on the other hand, "occurs when the opponent's behavior is incompatible, or seems to be incompatible, with our set of expectations." "Behavioral surprise" occurs when the opponent acts highly irrationally or with unexpected irrationality; when intelligence is based more on stereotypes than objective perceptions; and, when an opponent's behavior is altered due to leadership or other important changes, and our expectations, though previously correct, do not recognize the shift.[8] Another condition which might also be added to Knorr's definition is a case in which an opponent acts with unexpected rationality.

The strategic surprises encountered at Pearl Harbor, in Cuba, and in the Middle East may be interpreted either in terms of "behavioral surprise" or "apparent behavioral surprise," a case in which one party adopts a course of action which seems to conflict with our set of expectations but actually does not. The US War Council concluded on November 25 that "the Japanese attack would fall on Siam, Malaya or the Dutch East Indies rather than the Philippines."[9] American policymakers felt that Pearl Harbor was really more of a deterrent than a target and that Japan would attack the British first. Evidence to the contrary given by an Army intelligence report in the fall of 1941 was dismissed by policymakers. Such a bold move by the Japanese was regarded as too radical a departure from normal behavior to be taken seriously.

Installation of offensive missiles in Cuba by the Soviet Union was likewise considered irrational and improbable. The Stennis Report on the crisis attributed the failure to predict Soviet moves to certain "preconceptions" of the intelligence community. A "substantial error" was noted in "the predisposition of the intelligence community to the philosophical conviction that it would be incompatible with Soviet policy to introduce strategic missiles in Cuba."[10] President Kennedy expected the Soviet Union to attempt subversion rather than direct confrontation.

The role of behavioral surprise is also important in the 1973 Middle East crisis. Terrorist attacks and sabotage were expected, but the Arabs were badly defeated in June 1967 and most US "experts" were convinced that no new full-scale attack would be launched in the near future. Stereotypes against the Arabs also led to mistaken conclusions about Arab fighting ability and Soviet willingness to aid them. Four categories of behavioral surprise emerge from the crisis:

• The individual Arab soldier was widely believed to be the weak link in the military organization.

• Politically, US and Israeli planners perceived Arab weaknesses as a result of their previous inabilities to coordinate among themselves.

• Although fairly accurate information was available on Arab equipment, the United States and Israel were surprised at the Arabs' ability to use it.

• Finally, we believed in Israeli superiority and felt the Arabs also recognized it and would defer any future adventures until in a stronger military position.

LESSONS LEARNED

The following conclusions appear valid, but should be repeatedly tested against the environment, events, and outcomes of other past and future crises. Although most of these propositions are not new, they have been revalidated by the conduct and outcome of the October 1973 Middle East War.

Political lessons.

• The advantage falls to the actor initiating the surprise aggression in diplomacy as well as in military strategy. The timing of initial use of force is primary.

• No "ultimate" intelligence resource is useful without sound political and behavioral analysis.

• In times of crisis, intra-alliance communication is subordinated to the national interest. The cost is high in terms of alliance unity, trust, and effectiveness.

• Direct and constant communication between national leaders during times of crisis reduces the potential for war. Despite secret Japanese pressure for a Konoye-Roosevelt meeting, the President followed the advice of Secretary Hull and Ambassador Grew and avoided such an encounter on the basis that it would only serve to further complicate the foreign policy situation and, if unsuccessful, would further the interests of Japanese militarists who were arguing that diplomacy's failure was inevitable. The Cuban Missile Crisis, due to improved communication, was marked by a new form of high-level, person-to-person diplomacy. President Kennedy and Premier Khrushchev discussed the crisis and proposed solutions in direct exchanges. At one point in the crisis, events were occurring at such a fast pace that diplomacy was conducted via ordinary shortwave radio in order to speed the exchanges. During the 1973 Middle East Crisis, Secretary Kissinger and Assistant Secretary Sisco went from capital to capital, first to Moscow and then throughout the Middle East.

• Ad hoc foreign policy decisionmaking is common during periods of crisis. In such situations, the power of the President generally predominates over Congress. Formation of key groups and consolidation of decisionmaking in the hands of a few are required to avoid bureaucratic formalities.

• Reputation and experience of decisionmakers and government officials can be determining factors in the conduct of crisis diplomacy.

Psychological lessons.

• Potential adversaries must be made aware of US bureaucratic and public will and determination through the maintenance of a flexible military force and the education of an informed, aware, and vocal citizenry. Diplomatic bluffs, official secrecy, and public silence invite strategic challenge.

• It is not often easy to discern the reasons for strategic surprise. We must therefore learn to live with uncertainty since crises seldom develop as predicted.

• Facts tend to be interpreted in terms of preconceived ideas and impressions.

• A tendency exists to overestimate the degree of actual common interest among nations.

• Past successes may lead to overconfidence which will cause a strong reaction when those earlier victories are not repeated or sustained and their achievements are threatened.

Military lessons.

• A counterproductive tendency toward overspecialization among intelligence analysts exists. This is particularly true of civilian analysts who have dealt exclusively with one country or region for many years and find it difficult to predict unusual or changing behavior which does not fit traditional patterns.

• Long-range planning is greatly needed. Such planning allows decisionmakers to perceive more options and grants more time for choice and commitment. If the choice proves wrong, mistakes can be rectified more easily.

• Military operations and strategy should be structured to provide opportunities for graduated options clearly identifiable to an opponent. Actions should be avoided which might be incorrectly interpreted as a precursor to large-scale warfare. Restraint and limited use of force, requisites of a measured response, should be valued.

• Military strategy should be coordinated and coupled with complementary political and economic strategies in an overall plan to achieve a limitation of crisis escalation. Military actions should clearly demonstrate US resolution to achieve whatever specific objective the President has chosen. If these actions are ambiguous, the adversary may conclude that the United States is seeking objectives greater than those stated or that there is a willingness to accept less than demanded.

• The requirement for quick action to meet sudden danger is necessary to gain time, develop options, and retain the flexibility to utilize or cope with further pressures.

• The necessity of maintaining forward deployed forces and strategic mobility remains essential to the protection and projection of military power.

• On-the-ground intelligence cannot be replaced totally by either aerial or electronic surveillance.

Economic lessons.

• Economic embargoes, though of increasing importance, are seldom successful and frequently counterproductive.

• The importance of economic interdependence is demonstrated during periods of political and military crisis.

One conclusion which may seem obvious should not be made—that Soviet pressure should be countered wherever it is met by approaching the brink of war and daring the Soviets to make a move. In Cuba, and to a lesser degree in the Middle East, the United States held certain advantages. This will undoubtedly not be true in all future crises, and the decision concerning the most appropriate action should be based upon each peculiar situation and the relative merits of the alternatives as they exist at the time.

TRENDS

Certain discernible international trends seem to emerge from an examination of these crises. These trends are both positive and negative:

• The analysis of these crises points to an increasingly important role for international diplomacy in future crises. The new emphasis on skilled statecraft has been precipitated by greater high level, personal diplomacy, the advent of the "hot line" and other improved methods of communication, and the extraordinary and improvised techniques of diplomacy exercised by Henry Kissinger.

• The great powers continue to show increasing responsibility in crisis handling.

• Continuing distrust of military intelligence by political decisionmakers appears to exist despite increasing dependence on intelligence estimates in selecting and implementing foreign policy.

• The strength of the current Soviet-American detente appears to be capable of weathering serious crises. Both the United States and the

USSR seem to be learning that they have more to gain by cooperation than by confrontation when opportunism appears dangerous. It is clear, however, that the Soviet Union intends to act like a world power with strategic parity.

• Economic diplomacy, boycotts, and embargoes are becoming increasingly accepted tools of "crisis management," despite past failures of these techniques and their tendency to evoke a reaction opposite from that intended.

RECOMMENDATIONS

Strategic surprise, as experienced in Pearl Harbor, Cuba, and the Middle East, will undoubtedly occur in the future. Analysts must be able to assemble seemingly irrelevant fragments of intelligence within a viable conceptual framework and act decisively to avoid escalation or to counter certain attack. Whether future threats involve nuclear destruction, limited conventional war, or merely confrontation and bluff, certain actions will be required.

There is a need to acquire greater diversity of viewpoints in the intelligence community and to encourage intellectual debate with nongovernmental scholars and specialists. Facts which seem to contradict "official intelligence policy" or "higher documents" should not automatically be dismissed or suppressed. The greatest danger to the effectiveness and utility of military planning documents is their tendency to inbreed. Related to this is the necessity of developing broader frames of reference, perhaps conflicting, in which to assemble, reassemble, and discard individual, unrelated bits of intelligence and in which to challenge the conventional wisdom.

While experience and some degree of specialization is essential, overspecialization in strategic intelligence should be avoided to reduce the tendency for "behavioral surprise." An analyst who has seen the Soviet Union or China consistently act a particular way will find it difficult if not impossible to perceive the unexpected. Frequent duty rotations and diversified training should therefore be encouraged, particularly for civilian Department of Defense personnel who may not have the enforced mobility of their military counterparts.

Information received from high-level overflights has been extremely valuable in collecting hard military intelligence. Although this information is basically valid and complete, it is frequently difficult to analyze. It does not always adequately inform decisionmakers of enemy strategy, perceptions, and intentions. Such data can best be collected by traditional, covert methods. Data collected in this manner is particularly relevant to probable future crises which will involve proxies; which will be played out in precise, defined limits; and which will, during the period of detente, involve personalized, high-level diplomacy rather than unlimited military conflict. Dependence on secondary sources and the information provided by the agencies of friendly governments may be useful, but problems of suspicion, context, bias, and special interest make analysis difficult. In such an environment, additional emphasis should be given to more traditional intelligence gathering techniques.

Interdependence and the increasing importance of embargoes in diplomacy dictate that major analyses be made to determine US dependency on foreign sources of vital raw materials and the potential for conflict, shortages, and blackmail. A commitment to develop substitutes for those endangered products or to develop the capability for synthetic manufacture to satisfy future military and civilian requirements should follow. This was done with rubber after the Japanese aggression, and important new fuel substitutes will undoubtedly result from the latest Middle East crisis. Anticipation of future needs and a major research and development program could give the United States a significant strategic advantage in future crises as well as perform a major scientific and economic service for the nation and the world.

Interdepartmental politico-military gaming should be expanded and should involve important officials as well as their staffs. This would serve to increase training for leaders at the highest levels of government in the delicate art of crisis management and would perhaps increase the recognition of signals and help head off future crises.

Finally, since misperception of US will is often a result of a lack of public awareness, increased attention should be given to avoiding unnecessary classification and official secrecy. Some progress has been made in this area, but many official military documents are still routinely overclassified.

SUMMARY

Pearl Harbor, Cuba, and the 1973 Middle East War were three very different types of crises, yet in their diversity certain commonalities and lessons emerge which can contribute to improved strategic planning. In all three of the crisis periods, the actors responded on the basis of their own national interests. Each crisis was preceded by numerous indicators which were incorrectly analyzed because of preconceived notions, stereotypes, and personal biases. Extraordinary and sometimes improvised methods of international diplomacy and communication were utilized in the search for solutions. Although fears of encirclement and containment influenced action and reaction, the importance of formal alliances was minor. The numbness which analysts felt in each crisis due to previous false alarms was exacerbated by enemy deception, restrictions on access to raw data, secrecy in decisionmaking, an abundance of irrelevant data, simple bad luck, delays, and technological and logistical surprises.

From these common elements certain lessons emerge. The importance of surprise, a credible deterrent, direct and constant communication among leaders, flexibility, deception, timing, and the maintenance of strategic mobility has been revalidated. While the importance attributed to alliances and their operation during crises has been shown to be exaggerated, it appears that the importance attributed to on-the-ground intelligence may have been unwisely minimized. No ultimate intelligence source is useful without sound political and behavioral analysis. Even then, we must accept that crises do not often develop as expected. This does not deny the proven need for long-range planning which allows the perception of more options and the time for more choice and commitment.

US national and popular will must be clearly demonstrated to ensure that American intentions are clearly understood by all potential adversaries. This objective can only be achieved by a strong military capability supported by an aware citizenry. Future crises similar to Pearl Harbor, Cuba, and the Middle East may be averted by such a demonstration of will. Frequent rotations of duty should be required to avoid overspecialization in strategic intelligence and improvisation should be encouraged in diplomacy and strategy formulation. A greater diversity of viewpoints should be encouraged and intellectual debate with nongovernmental scholars and specialists should be sought to challenge the conventional wisdom and limit inbreeding among intelligence documents. Also, increased attention should be given to the development of improved airlift and troop mobility capabilities and to the more traditional intelligence gathering activities. Finally, because of the increasing interdependence of economies and use of embargoes, a thorough analysis should be made of the sources of vital raw materials and the potential for conflict and blackmail. A major R&D effort should then be undertaken to develop substitutes and synthetics.

Trends indicate that while interdependence, detente, sophistication in crisis handling, and international political diplomacy are becoming more important, so are economic boycotts and embargoes and an increased dependence on intelligence estimates in selecting and implementing foreign policy. In this environment, better strategic planning is more critical than ever before.

6

Materials and the New Dimensions of Conflict

Alwyn H. King and John R. Cameron

The Middle East oil embargo of 1973-74 brought into focus the possibility of other strategic materials being used to threaten US national security or domestic well-being, and many observers are convinced that this lesson in economic warfare will not be lost on other materials supplier countries. Underdeveloped nations possessing strategically important resources could perceive opportunities to use economic coercion to achieve objectives which have not been adequately promoted through the traditional methods of worldwide economic cooperation and development aid.

A threat to US military sufficiency would be the most serious possibility. The current situation, however, suggests that short-term disruption of the US economy could result from a shortage of a critical material without seriously affecting the nation's war-fighting capability. In a peacetime environment, where a beleaguered nation's "ultimate recourse" is the diplomatic arena, political and economic coercion are increasingly important in the spectrum of conflict. An evaluation of US vulnerability to such coercion will provide a knowledge of relative strengths, weaknesses, and available alternatives; plans and policies can then be formulated to prevent or mitigate future threats.

Some of the fears expressed in current literature may seem

unrealistic. For example, it has been suggested that suppliers of bauxite might band together to enforce a bauxite boycott.[1] Australia, Jamaica, and Guinea together possess about 65 percent of world bauxite reserves; however, their recent participation in a meeting of the seven-country International Association of Producers of Bauxite ended with a moderate agreement which did not call for an embargo or price increase, but did establish a Secretariat and call for greater development and national control. Furthermore, with the exception of Australia, these producers need the hard currency that bauxite brings, and could ill afford to shut off this source of income. On the other hand, the bauxite industry, multinational in scope, could conceivably be dominated by a cartel capable of imposing a boycott or equally disruptive price increase for economic reasons. Any assessment of the implications of scarce resources must include an examination of political and economic factors as well as the military sufficiency aspect. The fact, for example, that over 70 percent of the world's tungsten reserves are located in the Communist countries—the People's Republic of China (PRC), the People's Republic of Korea (PRK), and the Soviet Union—seems to have been largely ignored, although a clear potential for future politically-inspired economic coercion is present.

Use of international economic coercion, in the form of withholding strategic materials from selected world markets, could be extremely serious. Not only could economic growth rates of the United States and other industrial nations be affected, but in the long term such action could result in a major readjustment in the distribution of wealth and economic and political power throughout the world. The possible danger of overdependence on foreign suppliers of strategic materials has long been recognized, yet US policies have not been developed to cope with the issue over the long term. In fact, present trends indicate increased dependence on foreign sources of many materials (including tungsten), and a substantial reduction in national stockpile objectives designed to protect the United States against such dependence in national emergency.

CRITICAL MATERIALS AND VULNERABILITY

US dependence on foreign sources for many commodities has become a subject of concern.[2,3,4] Based on a recent Bureau of Mines study,[5,6] Figure 1 shows the present and projected situation for primary minerals. The projected deficit for metals is larger (in terms of

1970 dollars), and growing at a more rapid rate than either nonmetallics or the energy-producing minerals. The April 1972 Interim Report of the National Commission on Materials Policy[7] presents further clear evidence; since shortly before World War II, this country has changed from a net exporter to a net importer of minerals.

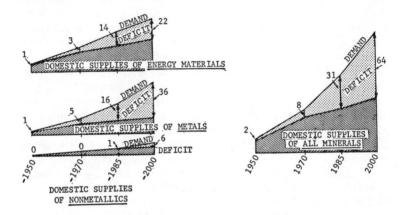

Figure 1. Developing Deficits: United States Primary Mineral Demand vs. United States Primary Mineral Supplies (Billions of Dollars, With 1985 and 2000 at 1970 Prices)

The fact that a large proportion of any given commodity is imported does not necessarily indicate a basic US dependence on foreign sources. Reasons for importing many materials are largely economic. Despite a plentiful resource base, domestic production may not be economically competitive with foreign imports because of higher extraction costs from lower-grade ores, higher costs of labor and capital, or domestic implementation of environmental protection measures. Serious implications for national security may result from those materials essentially unavailable within the United States, or from excessive foreign procurement which may severely erode domestic productive capability. The degree of our "dependence" on outside sources will hinge ultimately on the price we are willing to pay for self-sufficiency.

One important means of guarding against a dangerous dependence on foreign supplies, and possible vulnerability to coercion, is to maintain a stockpile of materials in short domestic supply, or whose availability may be severely curtailed in time of emergency. Such a stockpile has been accumulated in the United States under the authority of the Strategic and Critical Materials Stockpiling Act[8] and the Defense Production Act.[9]

In April 1973, the President issued guidance for establishing stockpile objectives for individual materials which provides assumptions that: the stockpile planning period shall be for the first year of an emergency; theaters of war will exist simultaneously in Europe and Asia; and imports of supplies will be available from all countries not in the war zone or not Communist-oriented. The most significant changes in establishing these objectives were: the reduction of the stockpile planning period from three years to the first year of an emergency; elimination of a safety- factor regarding availability of foreign supplies; and elimination of the Interdepartmental Materials Advisory Committee (IMAC) from the stockpile objectives planning function and computerization of this function under the General Services Administration (GSA).

These changes in policy resulted in a drastic reduction of total stockpile objectives from an estimated market value of over $4 billion as of December 1972 to approximately $0.7 billion as of June 30, 1973. The effect of this reduction on the stockpile availability of some of the materials included in the DOD list of Estimated Mobilization Requirements is indicated in Table 1, at the end of this chapter.

ASSESSING VULNERABILITY

It is feasible to identify in a qualitative way some of the more vulnerable critical and strategic materials. This procedure requires an inspection of determinants of vulnerability, such as availability of domestic reserves, availability of substitutes, number and location of foreign suppliers, ideology of foreign suppliers, and US stockpile objectives.

Such a qualitative vulnerability assessment has been made for the materials for which the United States imported 50 percent or more of its 1972 requirements. Those materials are the platinum group metals, mica, chromium, strontium, cobalt, tantalum, aluminum (bauxite), manganese, fluorine, titanium (rutile), asbestos, tin, bismuth, nickel, columbium, antimony, gold, potassium, mercury, zinc and tungsten. Although more than 50 percent of the US tungsten requirement was domestically produced in 1973, a rapidly decreasing production/consumption ratio and the unusual circumstance that the Communist countries possess about 75 percent of world reserves, warrant the inclusion of this metal in the assessment.

Of these 21 materials, ten were eliminated from further consideration because of favorable combinations of such factors as adequate US reserves, declining domestic demand, available substitute materials, availability of technology to process low grade ores, and proximity of foreign supplies. These ten are: mica, strontium, fluorine, asbestos, bismuth, columbium, antimony, gold, potassium, and zinc. Elimination of these materials should not be taken as grounds for complacency regarding their future status. In all cases, an adequate supply/demand ratio can be maintained only by continued emphasis on research and development of substitutes, exploitation of known resources, and continued exploration to discover new deposits.

The eleven materials for which the United States is considered to be most vulnerable to coercive pressures are aluminum, chromium, cobalt, manganese, mercury, nickel, platinum group, tantalum, tin, titanium, and tungsten. All exhibit a relatively unfavorable production/consumption ratio and are found in seriously short supply in the United States relative to known world reserves. Under normal conditions, the United States accounts for a large proportion of world consumption of all of these materials. In wartime, the consumption pattern of many of these materials would increase dramatically. Self-sufficiency in four of these minerals (chromium, manganese, tantalum, and titanium), as measured by the production/consumption ratio, is reported to have dropped from a small positive fraction to zero within the 1948-71 time interval.[10]

An assessment of relative vulnerability to economic, political, or military pressures for the eleven selected critical materials was performed making use of the five determinant factors previously mentioned. It is obvious that some factors should be weighted more heavily than others in this assessment, since a plentiful supply of domestic reserves, for example, would make any further consideration of foreign suppliers unnecessary.

Projections by the National Commission on Materials Policy indicate that our reliance on foreign sources for chromium and the other four most vulnerable commodities is not likely to diminish through the turn of the century.[11]

Relative vulnerabilities determined by this procedure are:

Material	Vulnerability Index	Principal or Major Exporters
Chromium	34	USSR, R. of S. Africa
Platinum Group	32	USSR, Canada, R. of S. Africa
Tungsten	27	Canada, Peru
Manganese	23	Brazil, Gabon
Aluminum	22	Jamaica, Canada
Titanium	20	Australia, Canada
Cobalt	20	Canada, Zaire
Tantalum	16	Canada, Brazil, Zaire
Nickel	14	Canada, Norway
Mercury	11	Canada, Mexico, Spain
Tin	6	Malaysia, Thailand

The above brief treatment is not intended to provide absolute vulnerability determinations for these materials. A comprehensive quantitative analysis based on this methodology would require the assignment of numerical intensity values to each of the factors influencing vulnerability, plus a quantitative evaluation of the specific conditions surrounding each material. With appropriate weighting of factors, this model could then be used for a more rigorous determination of a vulnerability index for any critical or strategic material. Vulnerability indices determined in this manner could then be incorporated into a simulation model such as that described by Nazli Choucri, M. Laird and D. L. Meadows[12] to provide an aid to policymakers in planning alternative future responses to resource problems.

A description of the eleven materials selected in this paper as most vulnerable demonstrates the characteristics that determine the index.[13]

Aluminum. This metal, which possesses many useful qualities including lightness, resistance to corrosion, electrical conductivity, and ease of working, has a wide range of applications, usually as an alloy. The military uses aluminum in aircraft, missiles, cartridge cases, bridging equipment, and electric power transmission cable. Copper, magnesium, stainless steel, and plastics offer limited substitution possibilities, but without identical results. Titanium, a more costly metal, may replace aluminum in certain temperature ranges. US aluminum production depends to a major extent upon bauxite imported from Jamaica, Surinam, Australia, Dominican Republic, Guyana, and Haiti, although some metallurgical grade bauxite is mined in Arkansas. Distribution of principal world bauxite reserves in long dry tons is: Australia, 4,700,000; Guinea, 3,500,000; Jamaica, 1,000,000; Greece, 700,000; and Surinam, 500,000.

Chromium. This metal, a very important ingredient in the production of stainless steels and other corrosion and heat-resistant alloys, has no completely adequate replacement. It may be possible to substitute for stainless steel, but some grades of stainless steel cannot be made without chromium. In World War II, steels containing boron were used as a substitute for the high strength chromium-nickel grades, but low fatigue properties caused many failures. During the period 1969-72, principal sources of chromium ore for the United States were the USSR, Republic of South Africa, and Turkey. Distribution of principal world chromite reserves in million long tons is as follows: Republic of South Africa, 1,050; Southern Rhodesia, 550; USSR, 21; Turkey, 5. US chromite reserves are negligible.

Cobalt. The principal uses of cobalt are in alloys, especially permanent magnets, high-temperature high-strength superalloys, and high-speed tool steels. Nickel can be used in place of cobalt in some alloys, but not enough is known of the possibilities of substituting other elements for cobalt in carbides or in some tool steels. The United States is the world's main consumer of cobalt. Principal import sources, 1969-72, were Zaire and Canada, with minor quantities from other nations. Principal world reserves of cobalt in short tons are as follows: Zaire, 750,000; New Caledonia and Australia, 740,000; Zambia, 383,000; Canada, 193,000; and the United States, 28,000.

Manganese. The bulk of the metallurgical grade manganese ore is processed into ferro-manganese, silico-manganese, and manganese metal. These products, in turn, are used to desulfurize and deoxidize steel and as a constituent of certain specialty steels to which they contribute toughness, deep drawing qualities, and resistance to shock and abrasion. No commercially economical substitute for manganese in steelmaking exists. The United States is almost wholly dependent upon foreign sources for its manganese ore. The principal US sources of ore are Brazil and Gabon, which together supply about two-thirds of requirements, and South Africa, Australia, India, and a miscellany of other countries supplying the balance. World manganese reserves are estimated at about 700 million tons; about 300 million tons in the Republic of South Africa, 200 million in USSR, 96 million in Gabon, and 46 million in Brazil. US reserves are about 1 million tons.

Mercury. Mercury is used in industrial control instruments, thermometers, barometers, batteries, switches, mercury vapor lamps, rectifiers, and as a cathode in the electrolytic preparation of chlorine and caustic soda. No completely adequate substitute for mercury exists although some substitutes are used in pharmaceuticals, disinfectants, fungicides, dyes, and other chemical applications. Generally less satisfactory substitutes for mercury are found in electrical applications. The United States produces some mercury; however, not enough to satisfy domestic demands. The principal sources of mercury for the United States currently are Canada, Spain, Mexico, and Italy. Principal world mercury reserves, in 76 lb. flasks, are estimated (1974) as follows: Spain, 2,600,000 FL; Communist countries, 1,160,000 FL; US, 380,000 FL; Mexico, 370,000 FL; Canada, 320,000 FL; and Italy, 260,000 FL.

Nickel. One of the most versatile of the alloying materials, nickel is predominately used in the production of stainless steels and various corrosion-resistant high nickel alloys capable of withstanding high temperatures. Alternate materials can replace nickel in most of its uses, but only at an increased cost and/or a loss in product performance. The United States produces approximately 10 percent of its nickel requirements. More than 80 percent of US imports come from Canada. Domestic known reserves, at 1972 prices, are estimated at 200,000 tons, but would increase to over 5 million tons at prices about 50 percent higher. Other important world reserves are located in New Caledonia, 15,400,000 tons; Canada, 6,300,000 tons; and Cuba, 4,200,000 tons.

Platinum Group Metals. Platinum, iridium, and palladium are used separately and in combination with each other and with other metals in the electrical, chemical, and dental fields and also in purification of hydrogen, photographic papers, automatic gas lighters, motors, and precision instruments. Platinum and palladium catalysts may find widespread use in reducing pollutants in automotive exhaust gases. There are no substitutes for platinum metals where their particular properties are required. Some metal salts can be substituted for catalytic purposes, and other less satisfactory alloys can be used for electrical contact points. The USSR, the Republic of South Africa, and Canada (in that order) account for most of the world's production of platinum metals. The major foreign sources for platinum and iridium are South Africa and Canada. Palladium is imported mainly from the USSR. Estimated world reserves of platinum group metals in million troy ounces are: Republic of South Africa, 200; USSR, 200; Canada, 16; Colombia, 5; and United States, 3.

Tantalum. This metal is in great demand for electronic applications, for chemical and corrosion-resistant equipment, as an addition to various alloys for high-temperature applications, and as the carbide for cutting tools. Other metals and materials may be substituted for tantalum, but usually at a performance or economic penalty. US imports of tantalum-mineral concentrates in recent years have been obtained from Canada, Zaire, Brazil, and Spain. Free world reserves amount to about 200 million pounds, with principal locations, in million pounds, as follows: Zaire, 80; Nigeria, 20; Brazil and French Guinea, 20; and Australia, 10. The United States has an estimated 6 million pounds of tantalum located in low-grade resources.

Tin. About 38 percent of the US tin requirement is used in tin plate for cans and containers. Other important uses of tin are in the electrical, construction, and transportation industries. Tin-free steel can replace tin plated cans and containers in some applications. Aluminum, stainless steel, and tinned copper tubing can be used in lieu of pure tin tubing. Principal world sources of tin ores are Malaysia, USSR, Bolivia, Thailand, and Indonesia. Principal US sources are Malaysia and Thailand. Principal world tin reserves, in thousand long tons, are estimated as follows: Thailand, 1,402; Communist countries, 715; Malaysia, 600; Indonesia, 550; PRC, 500; and Bolivia, 325.

Titanium. About 85 percent of the titanium metal consumed in the United States is used in aerospace applications including aircraft and guided missile assemblies, spacecraft, and turbine engines. The remainder is used in the chemical processing industry and in marine and munitions applications. The selection of titanium metal and its alloys over other materials in aerospace applications normally is made on a performance versus economics basis. High-strength, low alloy steel, aluminum, or other metals may be substituted for titanium in many structural applications; substitution usually necessitates redesign and may result in lower performance. The preferred ore mineral for the production of titanium metal and alloys is rutile, imported almost entirely from Australia. Principal world rutile reserves (titanium content about 50 percent), measured in short tons, are located in: Australia, 4,000,000; Sierra Leone, 3,000,000; Canada, 500,000; United States, 500,000 (low-grade); and USSR, 300,000.

Tungsten. Occupying a strategic position in industrial production, tungsten is one of the most dense of all metals, but when properly alloyed and worked is elastic and ductile. The major uses of tungsten are: carbides, mill products, pressed and sintered products, alloy steels and chemical uses. Titanium and other carbides and sintered aluminum oxide are used in some applications to replace tungsten carbide. Depleted uranium is being substituted for tungsten as counterweights for aircraft applications. The United States produces about 60 percent of its requirements for tungsten ore and concentrates. Current US import sources are Canada, Peru, Bolivia, Australia, Thailand, Argentina, Portugal, South Korea, and Burma. More than 55 percent of principal world tungsten reserves are located in mainland China. These reserves are distributed, in million pounds, as follows: PRC, 2,100; USSR, 475; North Korea, 250; United States, 238; and South Korea, 101.

The above information provides a basis for selection of the most important supplier countries, in terms of number of vulnerable critical materials for which each country is a principal or major exporter to the United States. This selection method would classify as currently among the "most important" critical materials suppliers: Canada, USSR, Republic of South Africa, and Brazil. The implication of this selection of most important supplier countries is that these nations should receive special attention in the consummation of trade agreements and development of economic interdependence, and, of prime importance, in the conduct of long-term political policy planning and analysis.

THE DIMENSIONS OF CONFLICT

The recent oil import situation resulted from an Arab-Israeli war in which the Arab countries demonstrated a higher degree of unity than they had previously, and in which the United States and a few other countries were seen as supporting Israel to the detriment of Arab objectives. For this and other reasons, Arab governments chose to impose quantity restrictions to importing nations and to raise basic prices in concert through the Organization of Petroleum Exporting Countries (OPEC). These events suggest new dimensions to the problem of assuring continuing supplies of critical resources. Traditionally, supply problems have resulted from interruption by war either through the sources falling under the control of hostile forces or through disruption of supply routes by overt hostile action. With the realization that the well-being of the economy and society are equal in importance to protection from direct military action, it becomes essential to consider the factors which could lead to action of a nonmilitary nature denying or interrupting normal peacetime supply patterns.

Resources contained in the soil of a nation are an essential attribute of wealth and sovereignty. The pattern of nationalization of foreign companies, usually engaged in extractive activities, is not new. The continuing growth of societies in the underdeveloped world, fed to a large degree by capital and credits from exploitation of resources, will increase awareness of the value and life of the resources, and the right or necessity to control them. The economic rationales for a nation allowing exploitation of its resources are that some nations have neither the technology nor the financial strength to support industrialization, and others require the monetary gains obtainable only by allowing externally financed development. However, as technology becomes more widespread and less expensive, the economics arguing for continued foreign exploitation diminish. As nations develop, the capital already secured approaches a point where they can rely less on foreign companies with whatever offensive political implications may be associated thereto. This capital also creates development in other sectors of the national fabric causing additional demand for increased revenues. The results may be nationalization of the particular resource, upward pressures on the price of the resources being extracted, or requests for credits backed by the threat of price or quantity controls.

A further dimension to be considered is the role of the multinational corporation. While the true relationship of the multinational corporation to the nation-state has not yet been defined, it represents a new factor in the control of and access to critical materials, and expands the opportunities that a state has to exert influence within the world system.

The final dimension of resources control has been intertwined within the preceding. States may choose to control the flow of resources to achieve some political objective either internally or within the world community, either as an adjunct to actual hostilities or as a substitute action. Resources may be controlled by a state, for example, to demonstrate to an internal political audience that it is sovereign and free of control by other states. Resources may also be controlled as a means of causing purposeful change in the policies of other states.

In summary, the flow of resources to the consuming country may be controlled through a variety of means and for a range of purposes. These dimensions must be considered in view of US dependence on imports to provide many resources needed to keep the economic structure in balance, and from the potential power which reliance on such imports represents for those seeking to influence US policy. Thus, the dimensions of conflict are expanded and new options may be evident to material-producing states.

NATIONAL SECURITY IMPLICATIONS

In a highly industrialized nation, requirements for energy-producing materials tend to grow steadily as a long-range trend while increased service orientation, miniaturization, technological sophistication, and improved secondary recovery techniques tend to reduce the requirement for physical structure materials per unit of output or product.

For nonenergy materials, there is no indication of situations developing in the foreseeable future of anywhere near the magnitude of the oil (energy) crisis. The unique circumstance wherein a small number of politically allied nations who, as suppliers, hold a dominant position in controlling a nonrecoverable resource for which there are no direct substitutes, is not found for any of the nonenergy materials. Nor are most producers of large quantities of raw materials in the enviable position of the oil "Big Three," Saudi Arabia, Kuwait, and Libya, who are prosperous enough to withhold their product for significant duration from selected portions of world markets in the interests of economic coercion. For some of the more critical resources, however, there is a distinct potential for more limited disruptions. In the absence of an increased emphasis on exploration for additional domestic supplies, improvements in extractive technology, and/or development of substitutes, this potential will increase.

This paper addresses, exclusively, the implications of shortages of nonenergy materials. Such a separation of energy-producing from nonenergy materials is not realistic however, since the extraction and processing of all minerals require some form of energy and in essentially all cases the lower the grade of ore being processed, the higher will be the energy requirement. Therefore, as high-grade ores are depleted and lower grade deposits become the only source, the cost and availability of the required energy may well become the determinant of whether or not a given mineral can be economically produced. Thus, one more degree of complexity is added to the implications of scarce resources.

US policy will need to balance needs for resources with a careful analysis of what pressures could be brought to bear upon the United States for economic or political advantage by producing countries. However, it should be recognized that producer states have limited

101

market possibilities and require the cash inflow generated by their production. To the extent that the United States could operate without a given resource longer than the producer without the cash inflow, the United States could endure price or quantity disruption over at least the short term. Policies designed to insure supplies from one nation may prove counterproductive with respect to assuring supplies, or supplies at responsible prices, from another nation.

It is extremely difficult to separate military-related requirements from those of civilian industry. For example, we might estimate that 10 percent of US stainless steel production is used in military-related applications. In the event of a 90 percent reduction in available chromium supply, it may not be economically feasible for industry to produce the 10 percent military requirement of conventional stainless steel and simultaneously convert to some substitute material for the remaining 90 percent. Any significant shortage of a critical material therefore may be expected to have some impact on defense-related applications.

The impact on the war-fighting capability of the United States is dependent on the context in which the resource shortage occurs. If shortages are incurred in a nonhostilities environment and last longer than a brief period, the war-fighting capability would be affected to the extent that the stockpile was inadequate or not used to support military procurement, that the force structure was not adequately manned and initial supplies provided, or that the ratio of civilian-military production was not modified. In this environment, public and Congressional support could be difficult to secure to achieve militarily necessary adjustments. Beyond this general comment, three situations should be considered: a general war involving nuclear exchange, a large-scale conventional war, and a limited war with or without active US involvement.

The first of these might be of such short duration or result in such widespread destruction of industrial capacity that continuity of materials supplies would be unimportant. In the event of continuing hostilities following the nuclear exchange, an adequate stockpile of certain critical materials would be a necessity to maintain the nation's war-fighting capablity in the face of the inevitable cutoff of foreign supplies of some materials. Even this would be effective only in the case of a relatively short war, with popular support, and with no requirement to furnish supplies to allies.

In the case of a large-scale conventional war of significant duration, an adequate stockpile would again be a necessary, but probably not sufficient factor to maintain military effectiveness. Because of the complex nature of the US economy, a great deal of prior planning, which has not yet been accomplished, would be required to ensure that development of alternative sources, increased use of substitutes, and reallocation or rationing of critical materials in short supply could compensate for the interruption of supplies from foreign sources. The nature of the war in terms of domestic support, industries affected, and materiel required is crucial to this situation. The development of alternative sources or the procedures of rationing, while feasible, depend not only on the mechanics but even more on the political decisions necessary.

For a limited war, foreign suppliers are sufficiently numerous and geographically located so that most nonenergy materials would not likely be cut off from all sources of supply. Possible exceptions are chromium and, in the future, tungsten. If a sufficient stockpile of these materials is maintained to allow time for conversion, substitutes could be used for most important applications of both, and shortages would not seriously interfere with military capability. Consideration must also be given to the probabilities that quantities could be decreased by nations wishing to appear aloof from the conflict (for example, to avoid cessation of aid or trade programs by a direct or indirect participant in the conflict) or to support a party to the conflict by further exerting pressures on the United States or on other nations on which the United States depends for processed or finished products. The limited war situation appears as the most critical contingency to be considered from the viewpoint of maintaining popular support. The Vietnam War illustrates the difficulties in securing the necessary support for critical decisions. For example, reserve forces were not called upon during the Vietnam buildup for what were generally accepted as domestic political reasons. Hence, in any given situation of a general or specific material crisis, the domestic political, as well as foreign political, implications will be significant and the former may well be controlling.

ECONOMIC IMPLICATIONS

Although the immediate war-fighting capability of the United States may be maintained by stockpiling to allow time for adjustment, the potential for economic difficulty will still exist. Withholding of critical supplies may be envisioned for any material for which principal resources are limited to relatively few countries, for which control rests with a few companies, or which are controlled by nations not firmly supportive of the United States. Such withholding could be either economic or political in motivation, and the impact on the United States could range from mild annoyance to serious economic disruption depending on the duration of the embargo, the size of available stockpile, and the ability to convert to substitute materials.

US war-fighting strength depends heavily on the economic strength of the nation. If resources needed for defense production are available but at higher prices, military budgets will rise with a series of economic consequences including lessened social sector support or increased taxation. If the resources are not available, significant diversion of existing supplies from the civilian to the military sector would be necessary with negative consequences in price systems and in public support of the defense effort.

Such diversion would be much more difficult and less effective than it was during World War II because of the dramatic changes in industrial and military levels of technology. Applied to the materials situation, the implication is that there will be an increased level and intensity of competition between the civilian and military production sectors. Where before it may have been relatively easy to reallocate critical materials to defense production, the same case may not exist today based on such aspects as the sophistication of business and personal life, the complexities of the large service sector of the economy, and changed patterns of manpower training requirements.

IMPLICATIONS FOR US STOCKPILE POLICY

Self-sufficiency in all important materials is neither physically nor economically possible, and valid economic reasons exist for not maintaining an excessively large materials stockpile. For these reasons, a method of assessing relative vulnerability should be useful in determining which materials must be stockpiled, or where other efforts should be concentrated to reduce the overall economic and political vulnerability of the US critical materials supply.

The weighted vulnerability index method outlined above suggests that, currently, chromium is one of the most vulnerable critical materials. For example, a closer look at the chromium situation reveals that, at present stockpile objective levels, a six-month interruption of supplies of this material could precipitate a serious shortage (stockpile objective quantities are used here rather than total stockpile quantity since surpluses may be disposed of at any time by Congressional disposal authorization). This could conceivably lead to significant price increases for some steels, because of the use of more expensive substitute alloying elements, or increases in price of some products due to costs of redesign and retooling to use alternate materials or configurations. With main sources of chromite supply in Africa and the USSR, and a negligible domestic supply capability, economic or politically-motivated coercive pressures must be considered. This and the other vulnerable materials must be closely examined to determine where and to what extent corrective measures are required. In this regard, the conclusions and recommendations of the National Commission on Materials Policy are pertinent.

> We conclude that . . . in the interest of national security, it is unwise to become dependent on specific strategic commodities for which the United States lacks a resource base and which are obtained mainly from a small number of countries which may choose to restrict or cut off the flow of supply.

> We recommend that . . . where problems are foreseen, the United States should: foster the expansion of domestic production; diversify sources of supply; develop special relations with more reliable sources; find substitutes or develop synthetics; increase the dependence of supplying countries upon continuing US good will; and allocate the existing supplies through a priority use system.[14]

The value of the US stockpile of critical and strategic materials has been a subject of considerable controversy since its inception in 1939, and has been criticized on technical, political, and economic grounds. Historically, the concept of maintaining a stockpile of certain scarce materials is valid. In the early stages of World War II, an impressive German stockpile (in addition to economic and military pressure on suppliers) permitted the Nazis to wage successful aggressive warfare in spite of an effective naval blockade during much of the period.[15] This study of critical materials suggests that today's stockpile planners may, in some cases, be underestimating its importance as a tool in helping to ensure national military and economic sufficiency. The 1973 reduced stockpile objectives for 17 critical materials, including titanium and tungsten, do not meet the DOD direct mobilization requirements. (See Table 1.) Although stockpiling has been criticized in the past as "preparing to fight the last war over again," today's planners may be "fighting the last war" in a different sense, in assuming, in their hypothetical first year of a war, US control of the oceans and no interruption of supplies from friendly overseas suppliers. In previous years various interested department representatives participated in stockpile planning. The importance of a review of stockpile objectives by this Interdepartmental Materials Advisory Committee, with its broad background of interests and experience, has apparently been overlooked in the new computerized methodology, and the Committee is no longer active.

MITIGATING OPPORTUNITIES

The US materials position could obviously be enhanced by an increased emphasis on research and development. New methods of exploration, improved metallurgical processes, development of substitute materials, and increased secondary recovery all depend on research and development. Since funds for such activities are not unlimited, the method outlined here could be developed to quantitatively assess materials vulnerability to assist realistic establishment of priorities.

Contingency planning is necessary in two new areas. First, it is increasingly necessary to determine what production and/or processing capability exists within the United States or in alternate countries to those now providing vulnerable resources, and then to determine what potential exists for a new variety of disrupting factors. A broad range of economic contingency plans should be prepared which include modification to the US stockpile program and conversion to domestic production and/or processing.

Second, it is increasingly necessary to determine, in consideration of the threat to the United States, these new dimensions which have heretofore been ignored as inconsequential. Consideration of resources and vulnerability will have wide implications regarding intelligence community assessments. Contingency planning could then be initiated on a rational and case-by-case basis toward measures designed to preclude harm to the US economy or security. Such planning must combine political, psychological, and economic approaches to cover a range of options from alternative sources to coercive measures, as well as ways to meet the desires of producer nations.

As recommended by the National Commission on Materials Policy, the United States should work closely with international organizations to foster cooperation between consumer and supplier nations. Unilaterally, the United States could overhaul and improve the present system of developmental aid to reduce the negative aspects of economic nationalism, to discourage collusion among supplier states, and to promote interdependency between the underdeveloped and industrial areas of the world.

This large and complex task has been the subject of much discussion but little action. As early as 1959, astute observers were noting that: "Aid also aims at developing political and economic conditions abroad that will reduce, and eventually eliminate, the variety of nonmilitary dangers that either now exist or that present trends portend."[16] Today, some of the nonmilitary dangers are even more imminent, in the form of an increased potential for materials-related economic coercion by materials supplier nations.

Many recent studies have recognized the risks involved in the current trend toward increased dependence on foreign sources. Recognition of a problem, however, is often not followed by effective corrective action. The dangers inherent in excessive reliance on foreign oil were recognized before 1959, as evidenced by establishment of the Mandatory Oil Import Control Program by President Eisenhower in March of that year.[17] Fifteen years later, it is painfully obvious that corrective action in that case was less than adequate.

To a large extent, US dependence on foreign extraction and/or processing is the result of economic pressures; it is cheaper to buy a commodity than to produce it in the United States. In this sense, dependence on foreign states is to US advantage and at the same time to the advantage of the selling state. Again, this serves US advantage to the extent that the selling states purchase US technology and goods. In addition, selling states do not have unlimited markets and are dependent on the purchaser which, if the United States, is also to the US advantage. In an economic sense, dependence on foreign suppliers may be a net gain situation for all sides.

When the issue is addressed from the strategic military viewpoint, dependence on foreign suppliers takes on negative connotations by providing opportunities to the selling state for coercion, disruption, or stoppage. Even here, however, the United States can provide substitutes from stockpiles and other sources or technologies given time to do so. Strategically, dependence is a problem of the potential exercise of capabilities, since the motivations for materials coercion can be met by political and economic policies in situations short of general nuclear war or hostilities cutting off supplies. Clearly, the capability for materials coercion exists, but US interests may not be served best by policies designed to achieve complete self-sufficiency, but rather by recognizing and making use of the two-sided nature and the potentials of the situation.

Material	Unit	DOD Estimated Mobilization Requirements (April 1973)	US Stockpile Objective (July 1973)	Vulnerability Index (This Report)
Antimony1	Short Ton	733	0	-
Asbestos (Amosite)	Short Ton	58	0	-
Beryllium (in BeCu)	1000 Lb	26	0	-
Chromium2,3	1000 Lb	3,397	0	34
Columbium2	1000 Lb	51	36	-
Iodine	1000 Lb	1,260	0	-
Magnesium	Short Ton	25,612	0	-
Manganese (Battery Grade)				23
Natural	Short Ton	11,099	10,700	
Synthetic	Short Ton	13,413	0	
Molybdenum2	1000 Lb	457	0	-
Opium	1000 Oz	1,195	0	-
Quartz Crystal Blanks	1000 Oz	4,856	3,340	-
Rubber, Natural	Long Ton	18,950	0	-
Titanium Mill Products	1000 Lb	14,806	0	-
Tungsten2,3	1000 Lb	1,801	0	20
Waterfowl Feathers	1000 Lb	1,127	0	27
Waterfowl Down	1000 Lb	431	0	-

TABLE 1. Comparison of DOD Mobilization Requirements and US Stockpile Objectives for 17 Critical Materials

NOTES:
1. Requirement covers flameproofing uses only.
2. Content of nonferrous materials only.
3. Stockpile objective includes 4,234,000 Lb of tungsten ores and concentrates, and 444,710 Short Dry Tons of metallurgical chromite ore.

7

Oil and US Policy

Robert L. Day

Until recently, the United States met virtually all of its energy needs from domestic sources. This self-sufficiency gradually eroded as our domestic energy production failed to keep pace with our rising energy consumption. US demand for all forms of energy has reached an annual growth rate of nearly 5 percent.[1] At the same time, our domestic production of crude oil, gas, and coal has leveled off or begun to decline. As a consequence, our new energy needs of recent years have been met through imports—primarily petroleum. Of total US energy consumed, oil accounts for about 46 percent. During the 1960's, our oil imports increased only 6 percent per year, but since 1970 they have risen 18 percent annually.[2]

In 1973, US oil imports were 36 percent of total oil consumption; by 1985, imports are expected to rise to 57 percent of total consumption. More importantly, the United States may become increasingly dependent on Middle Eastern oil. For example, in 1973 the United States imported only 1.8 million barrels per day (bpd) from the Middle East, or 10 percent of its oil consumption.[3] In 1985 it may import 11 million bpd or 42 percent of its total oil consumption from the Middle East. The steady increase in oil imports to the United States from Nigeria and new discoveries in Mexico could alter these estimates.

This paper sets forth certain international dimensions of the energy problem—supply, security, cost, domestic alternatives. It is impossible to look at political, economic, or military aspects of US policy in the Middle East without considering this area's vast reserve of petroleum resources. The availability of Middle East oil will be a prime determinant of US policy for the remainder of this decade and perhaps well into the next.

ENERGY CRISIS—FACT OR FICTION?

Since 1972, concern in this country about an impending energy crisis has been growing. Thousands of articles, studies, and conferences have warned of an absolute worldwide shortage of oil. Adding substance to this rhetoric have been regional shortages of gasoline and heating fuel, exacerbated by the Arab oil embargo. Yet, there are sufficient proved oil reserves to meet the industrial world's growing demands for some time—at least through the end of this century and probably well beyond. Nevertheless, the United States and its allies are facing energy shortages of varying degrees of severity. It is a question of whether those who have the oil will produce it, mainly to please Japan and the industrialized North Atlantic Treaty Organization (NATO) nations whose 23 percent of the world's population consumes almost 70 percent of the world's energy.[4] The answer might well be "no." Western Hemisphere suppliers, for reasons of self-interest, are placing limits on the amount of oil they will produce and export. The large Eastern Hemisphere Arab producers placed limitations on the amount of oil they would produce for political reasons, and embargoed oil to the United States. Of greater concern, however, is the likelihood that these major producing nations, in the years ahead, may permanently limit their production—not for political reasons, but simply because they could not use nor absorb the revenue this production would generate. By 1985, many Arab leaders believe that oil in the ground will be worth more than dollars in the bank.[5]

At present, this nation has an abundance of fossil fuels. Although we are using domestic oil and natural gas at twice the rate we are finding new sources, we have sufficient reserve of these fuels to meet our energy needs through 1990. More importantly, we have sufficient reserves of low sulphur coal to meet our energy demand for another century or more. Thus, we are less concerned with the size of our reserves than with the lead time and cost of developing them.

Our present predicament is the legacy of two decades of inattention to developing problems: belated recognition that US demands were rapidly outstripping supplies; over-zealous environmental legislation and controversies; and a failure to develop long-term programs. National long-run interests have been sacrificed to secure immediate objectives such as unrealistically low prices for the consumers.[6] At a time when we should have been intensifying efforts to find more oil and gas, we have reduced depletion allowances, imposed price controls, delayed development of arctic and offshore reserves, and enacted legislation which almost precludes the use of coal—our most abundant resource. Public policy and local resistance have also discouraged the building of new refineries and nuclear power plants, and delayed the development of deep-water ports and terminals to enable the use of larger and more efficient supertankers.[7] Recent shortages of refined petroleum products reflect primarily a lack of domestic refining capability rather than a lack of crude oil.[8] Additional refining capacity is only now being built which will add 20 percent to existing capacity, but completion is not expected before 1976. In the near term, however, the imbalance in the supply and demand for petroleum products will grow, and this deficit must be met with imports—primarily from the Middle East.

What is needed today is a comprehensive energy program. Such a program will face long-, mid-, and short-term problems—all of which demand solutions if we are to avoid future crises of mammoth proportions.

The long-term phase concerns the development of nonfossil fuel energy—the utilization of energy sources, not now economically or technologically possible, which will be the ultimate substitutes for our fossil fuels sometime in the next century. The solutions to this problem are not immediate, and lie in research and development financed by large-scale federal subsidies on a planned and continuing basis.[9]

Unlike long-term solutions, the remedy to our mid-term ailments requires immediate decisions. This has little to do with the depletion of fossil fuel reserves, but rather how we can develop these reserves as rapidly and as effectively as possible. These decisions involve changes in legislation concerning environmental standards, measures to promote oil and gas exploration, development of oil shale technology, economic liquefaction and gasification of coal, and expanded use of nuclear reactors.

In the absence of alternative sources of energy, the United States by 1985 will be dependent on imported oil for approximately 29 percent of its total energy requirements.[10] This degree of reliance, on essentially Middle East oil, could well represent a security problem for the United States in that: producer countries will likely charge higher prices, causing not only balance of payments problems, but also accumulating vast foreign exchange reserves which would be used against our national interests; the Middle East is politically unstable and oil supplies ·from there have suffered frequent interruptions; most of the Middle East governments have used oil as a political weapon; and many producer countries for reasons of self-interest may well restrict exports to the United States. Given our nation's security interests, a prudent course of action is to develop our own alternate energy sources—*the extent to which we rely upon these new domestic sources vis-a-vis imports may well depend on the action taken by the oil producing nations over the next few years.* But the important point is that we have these alternative sources developed and ready to go by 1985.

Lastly, there is the short-term problem which is the most difficult. What do we do between now and 1985? Whatever the government or industry choose to do will not alter the fact that the United States must rely on Middle East oil to meet energy requirements through the early to mid-1980's. Even if prices continue to rise, investments are increased massively, and environmental standards are completely scrapped, it will be too late to overtake the growing gap between supply and demand. The lead time to effect new technologies, explorations, and ideas is simply too great. Like the Europeans and Japanese before us, we now must pay for increased oil imports and take those actions which guard against oil stoppages.[11] *The solution to the short-term problem cannot be sought in technology but rather in politics*—adjusting our international political arrangements to minimize supply interruptions and recognizing that we have interests throughout the Middle East and not just in one country. US interests lie not only in Israel but also in nearby oil producing nations, and we should continue to apply diplomatic and economic pressure on both Israelis and Arabs to move toward peace. The United States should demonstrate that Israel and the Arab countries have full support for existence as nation states, but not for each and any policy decision, particularly if such policy would show promise of prolonging hostility in the area counter to primary US interests.

A second short-range course of action is energy conservation. We should provide incentives for mass transit systems, revise electric rates to promote conservation, and encourage the use of better insulation in the construction industry. Finally, the federal government must have a comprehensive standby rationing program in the event of long-term supply interruptions.

The era of low-cost, clean-energy sources is ending. Hereafter, energy options will bear significant costs. Such may be retail, balance of payments, environmental, and discomfort costs, or combinations of these. Irrespective of the above, the United States will import increasing amounts of Middle East oil in the near future. The outlays associated with such imports will not be of crisis proportions if we act intelligently now, and make plans that hedge against the uncertainties of the future.

WORLDWIDE SUPPLY AND DEMAND

At present rates, the world will use as much oil in the next decade as it did in the previous 100 years. By 1985, total energy requirements will almost double in the United States and Western Europe, and go even higher in Japan. Crude oil is expected to meet 52 percent of these requirements, and the free world countries at that time will need approximately 65 million bpd. Of this amount, 66 percent or 43 million barrels daily will come from the Middle East.

If current trends are allowed to continue, the import demands of major consumers will develop through 1985 as shown in Table 1.[12]

	1973	1975	1980	1985
United States	6	8	12	15
Western Europe	15	17	19	22
Japan	6	7	10	16
Other	6	7	10	12
TOTAL	33	39	51	65

TABLE 1. Oil Import Demand (Million bpd)

The mid-range estimate for the next 11 years projects an increase of US imports from 6 to 15 million bpd. Japan, almost totally dependent upon imported oil, may experience a threefold increase by 1985 while Western Europe's imports increase by roughly one-half. More importantly, our allies who rely on oil to provide a larger percentage of their total energy requirements,[13] are also much more dependent on imported oil, and have fewer, if any, domestic alternatives than the United States. This dependency on oil imports is shown in Table 2.

	1973	1975	1980	1985
United States	36	42	49	57
Japan	100	100	100	100
Western Europe	99	97	90	85

TABLE 2. Imports as Percent of Oil Consumption

As a percentage of total oil consumption, Europe's dependence upon imported oil may decrease slightly to about 85 percent of total consumption as the North Sea reserves come into production. Within Europe, only the United Kingdom and Norway have significant oil production potential. Other major consumers will remain heavily dependent on imports. Western Europe and Japan will also be looking to the Middle East to meet their growing requirements.

RESERVES

The world's proved oil reserves are more than adequate to meet the huge and growing demands expected well beyond 1980. Cumulative world demand for 1973-83 is estimated at 270 billion barrels against proved reserves of about 570 billion barrels.[14] But this oil is neither evenly distributed nor equally accessible. The 13 states comprising the Organization of Petroleum Exporting Countries (OPEC)[15] now control more than 75 percent of the world's proved reserves and produce most of the oil entering world trade. This situation will not alter to any significant degree in the years up to 1980. The 26 percent of proved reserves lying outside of OPEC includes 43 billion barrels in the Communist countries and 109 billion barrels in non-Communist countries, of which 35 billion are in the United States.

While new discoveries continue to add to reserves, such additions are not likely to be large enough to considerably influence the present geographic distribution. The discovery rate of new reserves in recent years has been declining outside of the OPEC countries and the Soviet Union. Recent significant onshore discoveries have been limited to Alaska, Ecuador, Peru, and Siberia. The best prospects for the discovery of new deposits lie in the offshore areas, especially in waters up to 200-300 meters. Even if major finds are made, however, production in the 1970's would be relatively limited due to the time needed to develop necessary facilities. In sum, it is highly unlikely that large oil deposits will be found in areas that would substantially reduce the world's dependence on present suppliers in the period before 1985.

Hence, the vast bulk of the world's reserves will continue to lie in present OPEC countries, particularly those around the Persian Gulf. Saudi Arabia, Kuwait, and Iran possess nearly half of the world's current proved oil reserves. As the price of oil increases, additions to the world's proved reserves are likely to come from technological advances that will increase the amount of oil that can be recovered from the presently discovered fields in the Persian Gulf, where today's proved reserves allow for the recovery of only 25 to 30 percent of the oil underground. Thus, the share of the world oil production needed to meet the demand forecast through 1985 will come from fields already producing oil or in the process of being developed.

SOURCES OF IMPORT

Although some diversification could be effected in obtaining oil supplies from other than Middle Eastern sources, these alternatives would not meet the combined requirements of the United States, Western Europe, and Japan. At the present time, there is no substitute for Middle East oil. As noted in Table 3, production from the Middle East countries will become more important as we move into the next decade.[16] Between now and 1985 the amount of oil in world trade will about double, and approximately 87 percent of this increase will come from the Middle East. For the United States, the policies of four nations, two Western and two Eastern Hemisphere suppliers, are of particular importance.

	1973	1975	1980	1985
Saudi Arabia	7	10	15	22
Iran	6	7	8	9
Iraq	2	2	3	4
Kuwait	3	3	4	4
Libya	2	3	3	3
Other Middle East	3	4	6	9
Nigeria	2	2	4	4
Venezuela	3	3	3	3
Indonesia	1	1	2	3
Others	4	4	3	4
TOTAL	33	39	51	65

TABLE 3. Principal Sources of World Oil Production
(Exports in Million bpd)

Venezuela. For years, Venezuela has been the Western Hemisphere's largest oil exporter, but for all practical purposes her production has peaked. Venezuela is not running out of oil, but the Venezuelan government has put increasing pressure on the oil companies to redress what it regards as earlier wrongs. This, plus the fact that US companies have been told that their concessions will not be renewed after they expire in 1983, has caused the oil companies to curtail new investment. As a result, exploration has dropped off and the discovery of new reserves has lagged. The Venezuelan government, which has stabilized exports at about 3 million bpd (Table 3) and is not likely to expand production, is mainly concerned with maintaining the country's income. In one official's words: "Venezuelan policy is not to increase production abruptly, but rather to insure stable, gradual growth."[17] This expression of economic nationalism has cast a pall over new investment plans, which include development of the Orinoco heavy oil tar belt [18] believed to have reserves in excess of 700 billion barrels of oil. US officials have proposed long-term arrangements for the hard-to-extract Orinoco oil. Venezuelan officials have been reluctant to respond to this offer and it now appears that high investment costs and political uncertainties may delay the development of these reserves indefinitely.

Canada. The other nearby desirable source of petroleum for the United States is Canada. Its oil industry is young and undeveloped offering a considerable potential. Although proved oil reserves are only about 10 billion barrels (less than 2 percent of the world total), some experts believe this could expand greatly with Arctic Shield exploration. In addition, the Athabasca tar sands of the prairie provinces could yield up to 300 billion barrels of oil. Once again, the investment cost would be enormous.

The United States is intensely interested in obtaining Canadian energy, but Canada is much less enthusiastic. Canada, although self-sufficient in oil, has severe transportation problems between the oil fields and refineries in the Western provinces and the major consuming areas in the East. To solve this problem, Canada has imported one million bpd to the East Coast, and has exported about the same amount from Western oil fields to the United States. This was a good arrangement when imported oil was inexpensive, but now that its own demand has grown and the cost of imports has increased, Canada is not interested in the US market. Canada is concerned about her own self-sufficiency in fossil fuels, and is presently forecasting an oil deficit by the mid-1980's. In addition, Canadians are well aware of huge

American investment north of the border and the government will likely resist any economic arrangement on energy where she will again be the junior partner to her "corpulent neighbor."[19] The turning point in Canadian-American relations may have occurred in March of 1973 when the Canadian government announced a temporary limit on crude oil exports to the United States of approximately 1.2 million bpd. With Canada's announced policy of retaining at least 25 years of reserves, the political climate is not conducive to the development of Canadian resources for US use. The prospect is that Canada will place further restrictions on exports, and will remain a static source of oil for the United States at about 1.0 million bpd or even less.

Saudi Arabia. For the United States and the world, Saudi Arabia is the key country in the oil world of tomorrow. Saudi Arabia has 25 percent of the world's oil reserves and is the world's largest exporter of oil. Most importantly, she will likely be the world's largest oil producer by the end of 1975.[20] Production increased from 6.5 million barrels in January 1973 to 9 million barrels in June 1973, fulfilling expansion plans well ahead of schedule. In other words, Saudi Arabia has added more than "another Libya" to world oil production in one year,[21] and will do so again by 1975. Saudi Arabia is particularly important to this country as *90 percent of its production is through the Aramco consortium, where foreign participation is wholly the United States'.* The world's energy planners are banking on Saudi Arabia to meet its announced plan of 15-20 million barrels a day by 1980 and 22 million barrels a day by 1985. Aramco officials, who have been investing $500-$800 million annually to make these goals possible, are concerned that their ambitious expansion plans will be curbed.

King Faisal is undoubtedly still convinced that continued close cooperation with the United States is in the best interests of his country. However, under political pressure in a very brief war, he embargoed Saudi oil not only to encourage Washington to change its Middle Eastern policies, but also to emphasize the future importance of Saudi oil. As the Arab-Israeli negotiations have progressed, it is encouraging to note that King Faisal has resumed the flow of oil and agreed to increase production to 11 million bpd in 1975. In addition, he has hinted at a lowering of the price.

A totally unrelated factor which may limit future production is simply an economic matter. Should the Saudis expand production to meet world needs, they will accumulate money they cannot spend. In 1973, the Saudi government spent only 60 percent of its $5 billion plus in oil revenues. At present prices, its oil revenues will be approximately $20 billion this year, and $45 billion by 1980. Some influential members of the Saudi royal family believe that their government does not need and cannot use this extra revenue and should freeze production at about 11 million bpd. Should Saudi Arabia limit production to these levels, it would have a severe impact through 1985. By that time, it is estimated that one in every five barrels of oil then used in the United States will come from Saudi Arabia alone. The Saudis are expected to provide 75 percent of the growth in Middle East production from here on in.

Iran. The Shah has striven consistently to establish his country as a reliable supplier in contrast to his more mercurial Arab neighbors. The Shah hopes to maximize Iranian revenues over the next decade or two in order to accelerate Iran's economic development program and pay for his sizeable military forces. Iran, with a population of 32 million, will have no trouble spending its oil income. Now producing about 6 million barrels per day, Iran will reach a peak of 8-9 million barrels in 1977 when a plateau on production will be enforced so as not to dissipate the country's reserve (approximately 10 percent of world's total) too rapidly. Most of that oil is already committed to Western Europe and Japan and *could not be shifted to the United States* in a crisis, except at the expense of America's allies.[22] Thus, Iranian oil, while important on the world scene, is not a substitute to the United States for Arab oil in the years ahead.

Other Producers. Aside from Iran and Saudi Arabia, seven Eastern Hemisphere countries can be classed as major oil producers: Kuwait, Libya, Nigeria, Iraq, Algeria, Abu Dhabi, and Indonesia. Taken together, these seven are vital to an adequate supply of oil on world markets, producing at the end of 1973 about 23 percent of the world's oil supply. None of these nations produce more than 6 percent of the world's total, and the vast increases of output expected from Iran and Saudi Arabia in the 1970's will diminish their relative importance in the total world oil picture.

FINANCIAL IMPLICATIONS

The price for imported oil increased almost threefold during the period January 1, 1973 to January 1, 1974. These prices have now been completely divorced from factors such as costs and return to capital and are largely determined by producer governments. For example, the

Saudi government revenues of $7.01 a barrel are about 70 times the 10 cents per barrel production costs.[23]

The drastic increase in oil prices will have a significant short-term impact on the domestic economies of all nations and on international economic relationships. The dollar value of world oil imports will jump from $46 billion in 1973 to about $120 billion in 1974. Western Europe's costs will increase from $22 billion to $56 billion; Japan's from $6.6 billion to $18 billion; and the United States from $9.3 billion to $21 billion.[24]

Predicting the net impact of rising import costs on the overall balance of payments is complicated by the inability to accurately forecast the quantity of funds that will flow back into the United States and other countries; however, little likelihood exists that, as a group, the overall payments position will be balanced. The United States is relatively well insulated from the most serious effects of soaring oil prices because it is about 85 percent self-sufficient in relatively low-cost energy sources and possesses a variety of alternative energy sources.[25] In contrast, Japan is dependent on high-cost imports for about 95 percent of its energy needs, and almost totally dependent on outside sources for oil. Europe also receives about 85 percent of its oil from other nations.

Over the long run, the US balance of payments will be less severely affected than those of other industrial nations. This is not only the result of its degree of energy self-sufficiency, but also that it enjoys about 25 percent of the Arab import market, and that US financial institutions are already handling the majority of Saudi and Iranian funds. In any balance-of-payments analysis, the United States must retain its share of the Arab import market, and maintain or expand exports to other nations. In this respect the outlook is very good. US products, because of their low energy cost, will become increasingly competitive on the world market. In addition, US expertise and advanced technology in energy related products—such as deep-sea drilling equipment, gas liquefaction plants, coal mining equipment, nuclear power plant equipment and cryogenic tankers—will provide the United States with expanded export opportunities.[26]

Similar analyses for Japan and Western Europe show that oil will represent a sizeable balance of payments outflow, which sales to oil countries will not offset. To pay for oil, the Europeans and Japanese *must* sell their goods elsewhere—to each other, to the United States, and to the world at large. Japan, in particular, will be challenged to new export efforts. The biggest danger is that these countries, faced with overwhelming costs for oil, will engage in competitive and destructive trade wars: providing export incentives, imposing import barriers, or devaluing their currency to handle part of the problem. All of which will provoke retaliation by other countries.

Unfortunately, the less-developed countries will be most seriously affected by rising oil prices. The non-oil producing, less-developed countries face an increase in their collective oil import bill of nearly $10 billion this year.[27] The effect will be reductions in their growth rate or living standard either because of reduced energy supplies at higher prices or because of a reduced capacity to import goods or services other than oil. In turn, this worsens the worldwide situation as these developing nations will gradually dry up as a market for the industrialized nations.

A secondary impact of rising oil prices is soaring fertilizer prices, which in turn has reduced the food output of many developing nations just beginning to edge into the benefits of the "green revolution." These countries become more dependent on grain imports, and these imports must come primarily from the United States. In this connection, it is interesting to note that while we Americans have expressed moral outrage at the Arabs for tripling their oil price during the past year, we have been, at the same time, congratulating ourselves on being able to finally balance our foreign trade account—*primarily by raising the price of American wheat threefold over the past year and a half.*[28] From the viewpoint of countries unlucky enough to need imports of both food and fuel, it is probably difficult to see much difference between Arab and American export policies. Obviously, oil-rich Arabs and food-rich Americans should agree to help the poor countries, but neither seem very interested. US help in the "Food for Peace" program in 1973 dropped to one-third former levels. Moreover, the United States, based on GNP, has dropped to 14th place among the 16 rich donor countries who aid the less-developed countries; and the United States has further isolated itself by refusing thus far to join in the fourth replenishment of funds for the International Development Agency. As Americans, we too must remember that the energy problem does not stand in isolation of other major trade, economic, monetary and defense considerations. Although in an advantageous position, any lasting solution will depend on increased cooperation among nations and not on protectionist policies leading to isolationism and autarky.

The sheer size of the revenues accruing to the oil producing countries in the years ahead has become an intriguing subject of speculation and worry by many foreign exchange specialists. Exporting countries' revenues will increase in 1974 to nearly $100 billion or three-and-a-half times the 1973 level. As shown in Table 4, the Arab states will receive about half of the total revenue increase, with Saudi Arabia showing the largest gain. By 1980, assuming present price levels, oil revenues will approach $160 billion annually.[29]

Most producers will be able to spend only a portion of their increased revenues on foreign goods and services. Even before the recent price increases, the earnings of Saudi Arabia, Kuwait, and the other small Persian Gulf states exceeded their absorptive ability.[30] Their imports and aid disbursements will grow substantially in the years ahead, but cannot keep pace with the increase in earnings. Other Arab producers have a greater current need for oil earnings to finance their economic development and military programs, but even in these countries the magnitude of the revenue increase and the normal delays in planning make it virtually impossible to spend the accumulated revenue this year.

The major non-Arab producers—Iran, Indonesia, Nigeria, and Venezuela—will find it somewhat easier to expand imports immediately. These countries have larger populations and greater opportunity for economic diversification than do most Arab producers. Nevertheless, the revenue increases are bound in the short run to outstrip the ability of even those countries to absorb foreign goods and services. In sum, oil producing countries will probably have extremely large surpluses to invest or deposit abroad.

	1973	1974*	1980*
TOTAL	27	95	153
Arab	15	51	95
Saudi Arabia	5	20	43
Kuwait	2	8	12
Libya	2	7	9
Algeria	1	3	5
Iraq	2	6	9
Other	3	7	17
Non-Arab	12	44	58
Iran	4	18	23
Indonesia	1	4	6
Nigeria	3	8	12
Venezuela	3	11	12
Other	1	3	5

*Estimated.

TABLE 4. Revenues From Oil Exports (Billion US $)

The question is whether the Arab oil exporters, particularly Saudi Arabia, will use their reserves to create chaos in the international monetary market, buy up the world's gold, and speculate against the dollar or other currencies. Under present regimes, these courses of action seem doubtful. First, the Arab countries have been ultraconservative investors, preferring US banks and gilt-edged bonds.[31] This preference does not seem likely to change, and the sheer magnitude of future revenues will steer investments toward the industrialized West and Japan. No other investment areas are large enough to accommodate such massive holdings. Once these investments are placed, movement into or out of dollars is a slow process. In this connection, it should be noted that during the recent dollar devaluation Libya, Saudi Arabia, and Kuwait—the three large holders of foreign reserves—held their dollars and took losses totaling nearly $300 million.[32] Second, to expect Saudi Arabia to cut off the hand that feeds her underestimates her political and economic sagacity. It is doubtful that the Saudi government will engage in financial manipulations designed to upset the currencies of the nations where her funds are invested, and to which oil must be sold. During the Middle East fighting, Colonel Qadhafi called for the Arab oil nations to withdraw their financial reserves from US banks and institutions. Although the oil producing nations did curtail oil shipments to the United States, no immediate move to displace their financial investments was made. This would likely occur only if the Israelis are completely intransigent in the ongoing cease-fire negotiations, and their position is visibly supported or tacitly condoned by US policy.

In addition to a strengthening dollar, the United States will have another major advantage vis-a-vis other consuming nations in attracting the surplus revenues of the oil producing countries. Our large and relatively secure capital market will present attractive investment opportunities. In the near term most of their excess funds will probably go into short maturity assets—such as Euro-dollars—and dollar deposit accounts. Over the long term, much of this money may go into direct investment or securities. The question of direct foreign investment in the United States has attracted a great deal of attention.[33] In spite of a $2 billion increase in 1973, concern over the volume of foreign investment in the United States seems unwarranted when compared with domestic investment. The direct foreign investment in the United States is $14.4 billion, less than 1.5 percent of US gross private domestic investment.[34] In sum, the United States will be able to absorb large amounts of surplus oil money through portfolio holdings, real estate acquisitions, and other direct investments.

In the present energy situation, the United States stands to emerge the best of any major consuming country, regardless of future Arab policy. But the United States cannot prosper in the midst of a world depression. It would be illusory for anyone to think that because the dollar is strong, the United States can ignore and insulate itself from the worldwide effects caused by the energy problem. There is a need for national awareness that the United States, or any other nation, cannot isolate itself from any major world problem. Thus, while the monetary problems generated by Middle East oil should be manageable, they must be considered within a much larger framework. If the United States is to successfully solve its energy crisis, it must be done by cooperation with our major trading partners, and with assistance to less developed countries.

INTERNATIONAL OIL COMPANIES' CHANGING ROLE.

Recent negotiations between the OPEC and the international oil companies clearly reflect the dual goals of the producing nations. They wish, first, to maximize their revenues in this "sellers" market; and, second, to control the one resource so vital to their economic future. The major producing nations want equity control of their oil resources and still have cooperation of the oil companies. By 1980 it is anticipated that most, if not all, oil producing countries will have equity control of their oil resources. The choice of cooperation and participation, rather than nationalization, is a clear recognition by the major producing countries of the advantages to be gained by working with the large oil companies. These companies provide irreplaceable technical and managerial skills, and an integrated transportation, refining, and marketing system able to dispose of the vast quantities of oil now being produced. More importantly, nationalization would eliminate the oil companies as intermediaries in oil negotiations, and result in "country-to-country" negotiations between producer and consumer, tending to "politicize" the problem.

Historically, US policy has been strongly against any form of bilateral arrangement for oil with producer countries. Several factors signal this policy may be reversed, however, with the Federal Government playing a much stronger role in international oil negotiations. Such a role may be necessary to prevent excessive price increases and preclude destructive competition for scarce supplies.

First, a number of the European countries and Japan are actively seeking bilateral arrangements to ensure a required flow of oil in the future. Second, as the producing nations gain equity-control of their oil resources, the bargaining power of the oil companies is correspondingly reduced. Third, and most important, is a growing recognition that the energy problem cannot be separated from other problems of cooperation among the major world powers. Serious strains in our relations with Europe and Japan in the past indicate the need to negotiate international problems such as international monetary reform and trade protectionism. This type of comprehensive cooperation and negotiation is far beyond the realm of international oil companies. As the oil company negotiating position continues to erode, the role of the Federal Government will likely expand. We can expect broad bilateral government-to-government arrangements, within which the multinational oil companies can provide advice and assistance. The companies will still play a major role, but primarily as contract operators of oil fields, suppliers of technical expertise, and long-term customers rather than owners of oil.

The relationships and arrangements between the producing countries, the international oil industry, and the consuming countries are changing rapidly. Present negotiations on participation and equity-control will result in new, but as yet unclear, patterns. Irrespective of the patterns, the Middle East countries will still need to sell the oil, and most of the rest of the world will still need to buy it. But the terms of sale, technical assistance, and means of marketing may be determined by political factors rather than pure economic merit and historical precedence.

The international oil companies have come under the close scrutiny of Congress: in 1973, 14 of 21 House Committees held hearings on energy legislation. The news media and many politicians have focused a great deal of attention on the size of individual petroleum company profits, causing greater public awareness. Coupled with the current shortages of petroleum products, all the publicity relative to earnings has created the impression that petroleum companies are engaged in profiteering. That belief is doubtless shared by many representatives of government, and many obviously believe punitive actions against the industry are therefore necessary. But punitive actions are not in the public interest, and will only jeopardize our national efforts to obtain adequate supplies of petroleum products.

The impulsive rush toward governmental interference in the oil industry seems to be motivated primarily by the growth of petroleum company profits in 1973. When considered superficially, a 71 percent increase in profits appears excessive, but an analysis limited to a single year comparison is grossly misleading. If petroleum companies are to serve the expanding needs of consumers, they must make long-range investment plans based upon the average growth of profits over a long period of time, not just the increase of a single year. For the past 10 years, the annual growth in earnings of the 30 largest (4 foreign) oil companies has averaged 9.9 percent.[35] At that level, it was substantially below the return for most other industries. The average increase fell far short of the growth required to provide capital funds needed to keep pace with the expansion of petroleum demand. The Chase Manhattan Bank estimates that the capital investment needs of the petroleum industry in the 1970-85 period are expected to amount to $810 billion—a staggering sum compared with the $215 billion invested between 1955 and 1970. Together, borrowed capital and capital recovery are expected to satisfy about half of the petroleum industry's financial needs between 1970 and 1985. The other half, however, will have to come from net profits. If required profits are to be generated over that 15-year period, they will have to grow at an average annual rate of 18 percent—more than double the rate of the preceding 10 years.

A fixation on a 1-year profit increase tends to mask other pertinent facts as noted in the Chase Manhattan report:[36]

Why Profits Increased So Much: Devaluation of the dollar had the single greatest effect. Indeed, nearly one-fourth of the worldwide increase in profits can be attributed to devaluation alone. About one-sixth of the profit gain was brought about by the increase in the value of inventories following the progressive firming of petroleum prices in most of the world's markets throughout the year. As explained earlier, the price changes were the result of both economic and political forces. Historically, the profitability of both the petrochemical and tanker operations of the companies has ranged from extremely poor to extremely good. It is unusual, however, for both operations to stage a strong recovery in the same year, as was the case in 1973. Because these activities did recover at the same time, they also contributed substantially to the expansion of the group's profits. The growth of demand for oil continued unabated in 1973. Worldwide needs were 3.2 million barrels per day larger than in the year before. And, with that much additional oil moving to market at price levels that averaged higher than in the previous year, a substantial increase in profits was a perfectly normal consequence.

Of the total growth in profits, the great bulk—more than 85

percent—occurred in operations outside the United States. The next table compares the actual amount of profits in both areas in 1973 with the net earnings in the year before: 37

Profits	1973	1972	Change from 1972	
	Million Dollars		Mill $	Percent
United States	4,354	3,656	+ 698	+ 19.1
Rest of World	7,368	3,204	+4,164	+130.0
Worldwide	11,722	6,860	+4,862	+ 70.9

In 1973, taxes increased more than profits in both domestic and overseas operations. In fact, taxes have increased more than profits for many years. The following table shows the degree of increase from 1968 to 1973: 38

	1973	1968	Change from 1968	
	Million Dollars		Mill $	Percent
Profits	11,722	6,664	+ 5,058	+ 75.9
Direct Taxes	20,845	7,276	+13,569	+186.5

In the United States alone, total direct taxes rose by 33 percent in 1973 compared to a 19 percent gain in domestic profits. Income taxes were up almost 73 percent.

In addition to the $20.8 billion paid in direct taxes in 1973, the companies also transfer to governments an enormous amount of money in the form of excise taxes. In 1973, these taxes amounted to another $26.4 billion. The total taxes taken by governments as a result of the group's operations in 1973 amounted to $47.2 billion—$13.5 billion in the United States and $33.7 in the rest of the world. Of the total taxes paid, the major portion went to governments of the petroleum *importing* nations. Over the past 5 years, governments took $172.7 billion dollars in taxes. The companies' profits over the same period were $39.2 billion dollars. Clearly, governments are benefiting far more from oil company operations than the companies themselves.

In the past five years, the oil companies invested nearly two-thirds more money than they generated in profits. And in the United States they spent nearly twice as much as they earned. In fact, well over half of their worldwide investment was made in the United States even though their profits were larger in the rest of the world. The companies were able to invest more than they earned only because they could obtain part of the money they needed through the mechanism of capital recovery and another part by borrowing.

None of the above should be construed to give the oil companies a carte blanche in their pricing policies or operational practices. The American public should expect that oil company operations be conducted in a responsible manner—and unfortunately oil company spokesmen have not always articulated their case very well. But to consider governmental regulation or restrictions because the price of gasoline has risen rather dramatically tends to ignore two basic facts: first, it was the oil producing countries—not the companies—that tripled and quadrupled the price of crude oil; and, second, the price of gasoline in this country is less than 50 percent of the median price in Europe.

As for an alternative to the oil companies, do we want to replace free enterprise with governmental control? Do we want to see the type of governmental control over the oil industry that we have in natural gas? Do we want to see private oil companies broken up into small parts, fragmenting their expertise, on the basis that smallness is good and more efficient? Do we want to see legislation passed which would reduce the incentive to search for new oil supplies? Perhaps, but just as we expect responsible actions from oil executives, we should also expect the same degree of responsibility from Congress. Because this nation's economic and social well-being is highly dependent upon an adequate supply of petroleum, we cannot afford political expediency or legislative ignorance that would jeopardize that supply.

DOMESTIC ALTERNATIVES

Our future vulnerability to oil cutoffs or shortfalls could be eliminated in the longer term by developing North American energy sources as a substitute for oil imports. The United States could probably meet almost all of its needs by the late 1980's if a major and costly effort were made to develop nuclear power, coal, and oil shale. A major political commitment to overcome environmental objections would be required. The development of these alternative energy sources would also partially alleviate the economic and political problems that may arise as Middle East oil production expands to meet the needs of our Allies who have no domestic alternatives. A key issue is whether the increased economic and environmental costs of developing self-sufficiency are justified by the threat to our national security associated with importing. Further research is necessary before we will adequately comprehend the economic and environmental costs of all the alternatives, but the following seem the most likely to provide substitution for foreign oil by 1985.

Increased Domestic Oil Production. Present proven oil reserves, to include Alaska's North Slope, are estimated to be 35 billion barrels. Increased domestic oil production, both onshore and from the continental shelf, offers considerable possibilities. It is estimated that there are 417 billion barrels (about 200 offshore) of undiscovered oil which would be producible under current technology.[39] However, adequate price and exploration incentives must be provided on a long-term basis. Exploration offshore will be expensive, but less so than developing the North Slope of Alaska, and offers a larger potential. This exploration will meet strong resistance from environmental groups, and once reserves are located their development will take a minimum of 5 years. As the domestic price of oil increases, significant additions to US domestic production could be forthcoming from secondary and tertiary means of recovery. Today, the average recovery rate from oil fields is about 30 percent. As prices increase and technology improves, it is estimated that recovery will increase to 37 percent by 1980; 42 percent by 1990; and 60 percent by the year 2000. This alone will double US reserves.[40]

Nuclear Options. Nuclear power is expected to increase sharply as a major source of energy in the future, rising from today's level of about 2 percent of total domestic supply to about 15-18 percent in 1985.[41] A total of 44 nuclear power plants were operating in April 1974; 54 were under construction and 105 others planned.[42] The technical capability exists to make major additional increases in nuclear power generation. The National Petroleum Council and Atomic Energy Commission (AEC) estimated that nuclear power could be expanded, beyond that presently programed, saving the equivalent of 6.9 million barrels of oil a day by 1985.[43] But such decisions must be made immediately as the lead time to site and build nuclear reactors is about 9 years. Today's nuclear reactors are of limited long-term value, as they use uranium-235 which constitutes less than 1 percent of all available uranium, and the AEC estimates this material will be exhausted in about 20 years.

The AEC is now developing a fast breeder reactor to convert U-238, which makes up the other 99 percent of all uranium, into fissionable plutonium, and in the process will produce more fuel than it consumes. In this technology the United States lags well behind the USSR and

Western Europe. Russia and France will soon put their first breeder reactors into operation; the first US prototype will not be ready until 1982, if then. It will be at least 1990 before these can be placed in operation. Of course, nuclear reactors of any type have two serious technical drawbacks that will limit their utility. First, large quantities of waste heat must be dissipated requiring vast amounts of water and effluent disposal. Adequate sites are limited, and there is increasing community resistance concerning the siting and safety of these facilities. Second, radioactive byproducts retain their potency for hundreds of years and, while they can be disposed of in many ways, any disposal procedure leaves a long-term potential hazard.

Reconversion of Coal. Coal, the most plentiful domestic source of fuel, is also the most promising source for future development. The United States has approximately 150 billion tons [44] of recoverable coal, enough to meet US energy needs for hundreds of years—certainly until technology opens up the other possibilities now foreseen. The use of coal is a matter of price and investment to develop technologies either to liquify and desulphurize coal for use as petroleum; desulphurize coal for electricity generation; use coal to produce hydrogen, which can then be burned cleanly; or to gasify coal into methane, the basis of natural gas. The Federal Government is already investing in some coal technologies, but only a limited scale. The use of coal on a larger scale runs head-on into increasingly restrictive pollution and environmental standards, plus the social cost of strip mining and the spoilage of lands used for this purpose. Desulphurization of coal and renewal of land is possible—but once again at a price.

Use of coal for synthetic gas holds great promise for easing our dependence on foreign sources of energy in the long term. The National Petroleum Council estimates that with a maximum effort and some relaxation of environmental standards, the use of coal as an energy source could increase by about 50 percent in 1985 over that projected.[45] This could reduce oil imports by 7 million bpd—almost 50 percent—by 1985. This effort would require sustained and massive government assistance.

Oil Shale. The oil shale deposits of Colorado, Utah, and Wyoming are estimated to contain over two trillion barrels of oil—several times greater than the world's proved oil reserves. But oil shale development has been delayed because of uncertainties in extraction technology, production costs, and government policies. Under existing technologies, for each barrel of oil produced, one and one-half tons of rock must be processed and vast quantities of water used. Again, the environmental costs would be great, and an investment of $3 billion would produce only about one million barrels a day by 1985.[46]

Solar Energy. The direct use of the sun's radiant energy could be practicable on a large scale for space heating by 1990, although solar energy for generating electricity is much farther off. Solar energy is already used in home heating in some places and has proved economical. Experts believe that solar heating and cooling systems could supply up to one-half of the energy now needed for residential and commerical heating and air conditioning, which together account for 20 percent of the energy consumption in the United States.

Many observers at home and abroad contend that we are the world's most wasteful users of energy. Per capita, our consumption is six times the worldwide average—four times more than the Japanese, two and one-half times more than the West Germans, and 30 times more than the two and one-half billion people in the developing nations.[47] The effectiveness of any energy use policy in the United States will depend upon greater awareness that limiting demand is important, either to restrain energy costs, meet problems of pollution, or reduce problems of supply. Thus far we have concentrated almost solely on increasing the supply of energy—which involves less political and social pain—than restraining demand for energy. This approach is likely to continue, unless outside factors force a major change in attitudes.

An energy conservation program could significantly reduce domestic consumption—some authorities claim we squander 40 percent of total energy consumed. Conservation efforts would bear results far sooner than initiatives aimed at building domestic production capabilities. An Office of Emergency Preparedness (OEP) study has estimated that strict conservation measures could reduce energy demand by as much as the equivalent of 7.3 million bpd by 1980, cutting imports by 60 percent and limiting them to about 25 percent of total oil consumption (today's level).[48] To achieve savings of this magnitude would require an intensive energy conservation effort with high public visibility and acceptance, direct presidential support and, in many cases, Congressional action.

There is no reason why the United States cannot become independent in energy. In addition to developing domestic resources, we should also diversify our international sources of energy to the greatest extent possible. But we should not rush into these programs pell-mell, or attempt to achieve self-sufficiency in an unrealistic

131

time frame. The various programs and alternatives must be well planned, and the costs—social, environmental, and in dollars—carefully weighed.

SUMMARY

During the remainder of this decade there is little that can be done, short of widespread conservation measures and stringent Federal rationing programs, to avoid the increasing dependence on imported oil. Over the longer term, our policy alternatives will broaden, and it may be possible to develop sufficient domestic production or alternative energy sources so that imports could be limited. As the situation evolves, we will learn more about the feasibility of domestic alternatives, and at what cost in dollars and to the environment. A choice can then be made between maintaining or limiting our dependence on oil imports. The main task now is to insure that the proper steps are taken to provide a carefully hedged domestic program that will insure the maximum development of options and, in the interim to pursue those political policies which will guarantee sufficient stable sources of oil imports. Uppermost, the energy question must be kept in its proper perspective—it does not stand in isolation from the major monetary, trade, environmental, and security issues facing this nation. Oil is perhaps only the first of a number of commodities that the United States will have to import from abroad in increasing quantities. If necessary, and at great cost, we could become self-sufficient in energy only to find ourselves increasingly dependent on other countries in a number of other areas. Any lasting solution to the energy problem must be sought in the wider context of our evolving relations with other countries. Growing competition in trade, the multinationals, our traditional alliances, and a wide range of economic and monetary problems leave us no alternative to interdependence with other nations. As stated by Robert E. Hunter, "We cannot have a Fortress America economically any more than we could have it militarily."

8

Ocean Space
and National Security

John G. Pappageorge and Donald M. O'Shei

Nearly all nations of the world have painfully felt their dependence on Arab oil resources. Considering that the Arab countries have a long history of inability to act in concert, they have done remarkably well in orchestrating a slowdown in oil deliveries to achieve political objectives. Similarly, as members of the Organization of Petroleum Exporting Countries (OPEC),[1] they have been able, through monopoly practices, to quadruple oil prices to a point where the mechanism of supply and demand as a means of determining economic value no longer applies.

Unfortunately, some wrong conclusions are being drawn from the current situation. The term "energy crisis" itself implies that we are running out of things to burn which simply isn't true. Four times as much oil was discovered in 1970 as was pumped out of the ground.[2] The crisis is really that most of the non-Communist world is becoming increasingly dependent upon Middle Eastern oil. The important lesson to be learned is that even an abundant resource can become the basis for an international crisis if enough of it can be monopolized by a relatively small number of countries. US planners concerned with economic and national security matters have cause for alarm when they note, for example, that almost 75 percent of the world's known tungsten reserves are located in the Soviet Union, Communist China and North Korea.[3]

Countermeasures to economic coercion in the form of withholding resources are well known. One is to develop and use substitutes for the materials that have been denied. Another is to discover and develop (in parts of the world outside the control of the original supplier) alternate sources of the denied resource. Such solutions, however, may be difficult to achieve, either because the technology to develop substitutes is lacking or is too expensive, or the newly-developed supply source may subsequently attempt economic coercion. The possibility of using economic coercion or military force in return exists; however, it tends to be counterproductive in that it may lead to escalatory countermeasures which in fact decrease the flow of resources in question. The dilemma created by resorting to force to secure a critical war reserve resource, for example, can be summed up as, "I am willing to go to war to get the oil I might need in case I have to go to war."

Considering less traditional solutions, two developments will have a dramatic effect on how nations solve problems of resource allocation—the growing awareness of the riches of the sea and the expanding technological capability for extracting those riches from ocean space. The term "ocean space" is chosen rather than the term "seabed resources," often the terminology used when dealing with petroleum reserves or hard mineral deposits, because the question of equitable apportionment of the mineral and petroleum resources found beneath the sea cannot be discussed in isolation. The sea's riches are so varied that conflicting views on their use must first be reconciled among foreign and domestic interest groups that feel they have a stake in the final decision. Ultimately, US policy decisions must treat seabed resources as only a part of the whole. Compromises in a number of areas will be necessary in order to arrive at a balanced US position.

In any discussion of US policy with respect to the use of the sea, one must understand the magnitude of the issues at stake. The first requirement is to define the nature and scope of available sea resources and the promises they hold for the future. Traditionally, the sea has been used as a means of cheap transportation, for national defense purposes, and as a food source. Important future usages may include the extraction of fresh water; the mining of minerals; prediction and control of the weather; and the conversion of sea wave energies into other forms of power.

Man's long use of the ocean surface as a transportation medium will increase as world commerce expands. Moreover, developing technology now offers the possibility of huge nuclear-powered submersibles to carry large quantities of cargo (perhaps even passengers) rapidly and efficiently at depths where surface turbulence and storms create no problem. Another technological possibility is the use of "surface effect" ships which ride on an air cushion above the water at speeds up to 100 knots.

Similarly, use of the ocean for military purposes is also well established. Indeed, it is possible that man's greatest expenditure of manpower and resources with respect to the sea has been for national defense purposes. Developing technology has increased man's capability to use the ocean for military purposes. Witness in particular the nuclear submarine's capability to move stealthily through the ocean depths with almost complete invulnerability, ready to launch its nuclear-tipped missiles, assuring a second strike nuclear capability. Much research conducted on the military use of the sea is highly classified, but it is easy to imagine the enormous technical efforts being made by the more powerful maritime nations in such vital programs as antisubmarine warfare, underwater stations, more sophisticated nuclear submarines and, of course, the development of better surface ships.

The use of the sea as a source of food, primarily fish, needs little elaboration. However, it is growing increasingly possible to derive huge quantities of protein from sea plants and animals to feed that half of the world's population that is consistently protein short. Monies spent for research on protein extraction and for further development of ocean farming (or aquaculture) can have a multiplier effect. First, they will obviously increase the world's total food supply. Additionally, new methods given over to underdeveloped countries will increase their capability to feed themselves and hence reduce their need for foreign aid.[4]

One of the most plentiful ocean resources is water itself. Although presently very costly, desalinization plants are already converting sea water into drinking water. With time, technology can be expected to further increase man's capability to extract fresh water from the sea at a reasonable cost.

Technology is rapidly unlocking the secrets of extracting minerals from the sea floor and beneath, giving the most immediate promise of new wealth and power from the oceans. The potential is impressive. One hundred years ago (1872-76) the oceanographic expeditionary ship HMS Challenger discovered that the Pacific Ocean floor appeared to be covered with lumps of phosphorite and manganese compounds.[5] These nodules, irregularly spherical in shape, vary in size from a quarter of an inch to almost a foot in diameter. Additional explorations have confirmed their presence throughout the Pacific and other oceans as well. By current estimates, about 20 percent of the Pacific Ocean floor is covered with nodules, in some cases found in very heavy concentrations of up to 100 pounds per square yard of ocean floor. Their mineral composition varies widely, offering the promise of many mineral resources. The following table indicates the magnitude of some mineral resources that appear to be available:

Mineral	Amount (Billions of Tons)	Land Reserves* (Years)	Sea Reserves* (Years)
Aluminum	43	100	20,000
Cobalt	5.2	40	200,000
Copper	7.9	40	6,000
Manganese	385	100	400,000
Molybdenum	.75	500	30,000
Nickel	14.7	100	150,000
Zirconium	1	100	100,000

*Based on 1960 rates of consumption

TABLE 1. Partial List of Estimated Mineral Reserves
of the Pacific Ocean (From Nodule Formations)

In addition to the minerals listed above, the nodules are estimated to contain 207 billion tons of iron, 25 billion tons of magnesium, 1.3 billion tons of lead, 10 billion tons of titanium and 800 million tons of vanadium.[6] Further resources are found in metalliferous muds containing copper, gold, iron, lead, manganese, silver and zinc; also red clays containing aluminum, copper, iron and manganese; as well as calcerous oozes similar to limestone and siliceous oozes similar to diatomaceous earth.[7] It is also reasonable to assume that the lands beneath the sea contain rich veins of gold and other minerals.

When one considers that the figures in Table 1 apply only to the Pacific, the worldwide potential is staggering. In fact, mineral deposits are forming on the ocean floor faster than we are consuming them on land.[8] Not only does the mineral content seem high but the supply appears inexhaustible, even at consumption rates much higher than today's.

Further riches, natural gas and oil reserves, are found beneath the seabed. Estimates of world petroleum reserves under the seabed keep growing. In 1947 they were considered to be 1,000 billion barrels; by 1966 the estimate had risen to 2.5 trillion barrels.[9] Within the last 10 years, oil and gas production facilities have been established off the shores of 22 nations and exploration conducted off the coasts of at least 75 countries.[10] It appears that offshore petroleum revenues can be expected to exceed those of any other mineral extracted from beneath the sea in the foreseeable future.

The oceans may also hold the key to future weather prediction and perhaps even weather modification. The movement of the surface waters is affected by subsurface factors such as earthquakes on the ocean floor, movement of currents, and water characteristics such as salinity and temperature, and greatly affects the air column above and consequently the world's weather. Better understanding of the ocean together with adequate monitoring of the changes that occur within it offer possibilities of savings and increased efficiency in those industries such as agriculture, where advanced knowledge of weather conditions is important. Similarly, the ability to minimize the effects of hurricanes and tidal waves will also increase as more becomes known about the seas.

Lastly, tremendous energy is contained in the ocean resulting from the continuous movement of its waters. While the potential energies in tidal movements are well understood, the potential energies in waves themselves tend to be overlooked. In a rather technical article on ocean waves published in *Science and the Sea,* Willard J. Pierson concluded with the following:

Just how much of the wave energy in deep water is ultimately destroyed by breaking at a beach, how much by whitecaps and turbulence in deep water, and how much by friction against the bottom in shallow water is not known. Barber and Tucker of NIO estimate, however, that a run-of-the-mill ocean swell—perhaps 2m high in deep water—contains 5 X 10^6 ergs of energy per cm^2 of sea surface. If the period of this swell is 10 sec, its group velocity in deep water is about 7.8m/sec, which means that the swell is transmitting energy at the rate of 3.9 X 10^9 ergs/sec for *each* cm of length along the crest. When this swell reaches a coast this energy is nearly all spent in turbulence in the surf or breaker zone. It amounts to approximately 40 kw along every meter of shoreline. And how many meters are there along the shorelines of the world?[11]

Having surveyed the principal uses, wealth and power that the oceans can offer to mankind, we must ascertain what stake the nations of the world already have in the resources of the ocean. This will assist in determining what maneuver room remains for developing future American policy on ocean space.

US INTERESTS IN OCEAN SPACE

Three factors complicate consideration of US interests with respect to ocean space. The first is that so many actual and potential uses of ocean space exist that it is difficult to establish common reference points from which compromise positions can be derived that will satisfy different interest groups. The second, which follows, is that uses of ocean space will vary in importance to the United States with time. Navigational rights, primarily the straits issue, are currently most important. They rate special emphasis today—so much so, as will be seen later, that the US position with respect to a general international agreement on the law of the seas will hinge on certain minimum conditions beyond which the United States is unprepared to go regardless of concessions proferred in other areas. In the future, however, the straits issue could decline in relative importance, perhaps, in relation to pollution or seabed resources issues. The third factor is the realization that almost every use of ocean space—actual or potential, relatively important or not—has military significance.

Various interest groups tend to view US policy in the law of the seas from a different perspective. US fishermen, for example, fall into two groups. Coastal fishermen would prefer that US jurisdiction extend far enough out to sea to protect their commercial interests in a particular species of marine life against exploitation and depletion by other nations' fishing fleets. Conversely, US distant-water fishermen would prefer very narrow jurisdictional limits by coastal states in order to assure their ability to fish the high seas in such lucrative areas as the Humbolt Current off the coast of Peru.

Petroleum and mining interests, represented mainly by larger US-based multinational corporations, would seek the best of three worlds. First, they would prefer to deal with only one country in each instance. Off the US coast, they would prefer exclusive US jurisdiction to extend far enough to cover the entire continental margin. Off the coasts of other states, they would still prefer to deal with only one country. However, they would like international sanctions invoked against any state that seeks expropriation or cancellation of original contract terms. In high seas areas, they would like minimum interference in their operations with guaranteed US protection rather than dependence on international jurisdiction. Thus, in terms of their own self-interests, it makes good sense for US-based mining and petroleum interests to seek contract arrangements with only one country in each instance; to seek US protection and guarantees in their high seas operations; and, to seek international assurances to buttress their position off the coasts of other nations.

The maritime industry probably has the most clear-cut interest of all—that territorial sovereignty be limited as much as possible to insure minimum interference with ocean shipping, especially through constricted areas such as straits and canals. Overseas airlines would also prefer narrow limits and overflight rights for the same reasons.

The scientific community would prefer maximum freedom to explore the wonders of ocean space, with the earliest possible exchange of information amongst all the oceanographers of the world.

Environmentalists, while agreeing on ultimate goals, are split according to their confidence in the ability of an international regime to properly protect ocean space. Some with high confidence would set international pollution standards from shore to shore of the world's oceans, while others would establish less ambitious initial objectives. Canada's declared 100-mile pollution zone off of her shores above 60 degrees North latitude is an example of this latter approach.[12]

The US Navy would, in all probability, prefer to operate under conditions of complete freedom of the seas. Exceptions to that freedom would be due to *military* treaties like the recent one which precludes the emplacement of nuclear weapons on the ocean bottom. The Navy is keenly aware that the center portions of some 120 straits throughout the world will change from high seas to territorial status if territorial sovereignty is extended universally from 3 to 12 miles. Overflight rights for US military planes are also threatened. While it is generally true that the US Navy would prefer that territorial seas be narrowly defined, one Navy element would prefer much broader territorial limits. The antisubmarine warfare element would gain much by keeping enemy submarines, especially submarine launched ballistic missiles (SLBM's), at a greater distance from US shores.

NAVIGATIONAL RIGHTS

A number of functional dimensions to a regime for control of the seas exists. Such rules impinge on fisheries, scientific research, pollution control, and the exploitation of mineral and petroleum resources and the other uses of ocean space discussed earlier. From the national security standpoint, however, especially for a global power like the United States or mercantile nations such as Great Britain and Japan, no aspect of the oceans' use is more important than as an avenue of transportation. The threat, real or imagined, to commercial and naval communications posed by changes to the law of the sea must be rationally and discreetly assessed before the United States enters into an international agreement. It is important, therefore, to organize, in layman's terms, some of the key considerations that bear on such an assessment.

For the last two and a half centuries, the ships of all nations have been free to transit any region of the high seas subject only to rules of the road and noninterference with another's use. The type of ship, naval or commercial, its cargo, and its mode of travel on or beneath the surface have been irrelevant to this right. With the advent of aircraft, the right of free transit was extended to the airspace above the high seas.[13]

As with most general doctrines, the right of free transit has from its inception been subject to certain reservations. Most, such as the naval blockade, are quite specialized and of limited impact. One, however, the concept of the territorial sea, has been of substantial and continuous importance. The historic tendency was to concede to the sovereignty of the coastal state those waters that could be continuously dominated. The "cannon-shot" rule, a distance of a marine league—3 nautical miles—which was the approximate range of a seventeenth century shore battery, was a practical distance used to establish the line of demarkation between the "proximate" and the "outer" seas.[14] Landward of this line, the right of a foreign vessel was limited to "innocent passage," a complex term which will be subsequently discussed in its modern context. The right of innocent passage has never applied to aircraft overflying territorial seas.[15]

In 1945, Pandora's Box was opened with regard to territorial sea limits, ironically by the United States. In his now famous proclamation, President Truman unilaterally extended US jurisdiction to "... the natural resources of the subsoil and seabed of the continental shelf beneath the high seas but contiguous to the coasts of the United States."[16] Although subsequent US announcements have pointed out that no navigation or overflight rights were affected by the Truman

Proclamation, the limited unilateral extension of control by the United States tended to legitimize more ambitious claims that others subsequently made.[17] The next few years were marked by a plethora of such actions, including several that asserted sovereignty to an offshore distance of 200 nautical miles.[18]

Attempts have been made to resolve the confusion. In 1958 a Law of the Sea Conference held in Geneva clarified a number of issues. Conspicuously unresolved, however, was an agreed upon dimension for the breadth of territorial seas.[19] A two-thirds majority necessary to adopt such a rule was probably precluded by the politicization of the argument dominated by the US 3-mile and the Soviet 12-mile positions.[20] Another try was made in 1960, but the Canada-US compromise proposal of a 6-mile limit and an additional 6-mile contiguous zone in which fishing would have been under exclusive coastal state control failed by one vote of being adopted.[21] The search for an accord continues.

The traditional 3-mile limit is no longer a point of departure for discussions. Of the 120 coastal states only 50 claim territorial seas of less than 12 miles, 58 claim 12 miles, and 12 claim greater distances up to 200 miles.[22] It is apparent that a general agreement, if it is to be reached, will involve significant extensions of coastal state jurisdiction beyond that presently recognized by US views of international law. From the standpoint of national security, some of the extensions being considered are very significant.

Breadth of Territorial Seas. It has been calculated that the global application of a 200-mile territorial sea would convert 30 percent of the high seas into territorial waters. Some Soviet authorities place this estimate closer to 50 percent.[23] While no one, including the mostly Latin American "200 mile club", can really expect adoption of such a rule, the dimensions are applicable to 200-mile resource zones, fishing zones, pollution control areas and other contiguous zones that are being seriously discussed. A 12-mile limit, on the other hand, involves substantially less than one-half of one percent of the ocean's surface, all in close proximity to shore lines. It is difficult to identify any serious impact that a shift from a 3-mile to 12-mile coastal sea would have on navigation or air traffic. Additionally, weapons technology is such that the buffer zone feature of territorial waters has long lost any substantial offensive or defensive significance. There are, however, a large number of choke points through which international traffic passes that, unlike the typical coastal margin, present problems under a 12-mile regime.

The International Straits. On the order of 120 straits in the world would revert from a high seas to a territorial waters character if a 12-mile limit were adopted.[24] Some quarrel with this statement, pointing out that a number of these straits are not used much by naval or commercial shipping. Moreover, many are bordered by nations which are allied with, or at least friendly to, the United States and therefore their use by US traffic would not be restricted. Such arguments seem shortsighted. Population, industry, and sources of raw materials change with time. A little used strait today may straddle a major trade route 50 years from now. Further, a cursory glance at the shifting patterns of alliances and antagonisms of the relatively recent past makes it clear that a rule of international law may well outlive even the closest bilateral relationship. In any event, included in the 120 are such waters as Dover, Hormuz, Gibraltar, Babel Mandeb, the entrances to the Gulfs of Finland and Bothnia, and passages through the Philippine, Indonesian, Lesser Antilles, Japanese, and Kurile Island chains, most of which are of inarguably strategic importance.[25] Their change in status to territorial waters would directly involve US security interests in several ways:

• Since there is no legal right of innocent passage for aircraft, overflights above the straits could be proscribed.[26] For example, with Gibraltar closed, it would no longer be legally possible for US aircraft to enter Mediterranean air space without the permission of at least one other nation. During the October 1973 War, clearance for US aircraft manifested for Israel was, with the exception of Portugal, not extended even by long-standing allies.[27] It is not difficult to envision a future scenario with a similar result. The United States would then be faced with unpleasant options of modifying its courses of action, violating air space—Soviet style—or submitting to whatever concessions that Spain or another nation might demand in exchange for overflight rights. The present international air corridor down the center of the Gibraltar Strait represents an enormously preferable situation.

• Submarines could not legally transit the international straits while submerged.[28] The seriousness of this restriction to US naval operations is difficult for the layman to assess. It seems obvious, however, that a potential enemy could more easily keep track of the limited number (44) of submarine launched ballistic missile (SLBM) boats currently authorized the United States under Strategic Arms Limitation Talks (SALT) I if they were to surface while transiting straits. It appears probable that some might transit Dover or Gibraltar into the

Mediterranean, the Kurile Straits into the Sea of Okhotsk, the Tsugaru Kaikyo into the Sea of Japan, or the Lombok and other straits through Indonesia into the Indian Ocean. Additionally, routes through the Philippine archipelago into the South China Sea would be affected. One author sums up this aspect of the question as follows:

> It is certainly possible that some combination of missile range and vital target location would require access to some of the bodies of water mentioned... The possibility exists, however, only so long as one postulates targets on the Euro-Asian mainland. It is virtually impossible to find any suitable missile launching areas adjacent to the North American continent where access is significantly affected by a 12-mile limit.

> Accordingly, it appears then that a 12-mile limit with its accompaning ban on submerged transit through international straits could constitute a serious impediment in certain areas to the mobility of US strategic nuclear deterrence systems. Whatever degradation of undetectability would result, either from surface transit through affected straits or increased concentration of submerged traffic through a reduced number of unaffected straits, would occur at a most disadvantageous point, i.e., entry by the submarine into the relatively shallow and confined waters of a vital launching area.

> An expanded territorial sea limit does not appear to present the Soviets with the same degree of difficulty with respect to their submarine missiles systems. Nowhere is their access to patrol area within range of their assumed targets on the North American continent impeded to any significant degree. The classic Soviet strategic problem of maintaining adequate access to the open oceans is also not rendered significantly more difficult by a 12-mile limit. The net result then may be an alteration, unfavorable to US interests, in the current strategic power balance and resulting nuclear stalemate.[29]

• The right of all vessels, commercial or naval, transiting the straits would be limited to innocent passage. By implication, as long as the vessel is engaged in legitimate activities it may proceed unmolested. Unfortunately, it may not be that simple. The currently operative definition of innocent passage is extremely vague: "Passage is innocent so long as it is not prejudicial to the peace, good order, or security of the coastal state."[30] Notable is the clear statement that it is the passage, not the conduct of the particular ship engaged in the passage, that is subject to analysis. Secondly, the presumed adjudicator of innocence is the coastal state, unilaterally. Thirdly, what is "prejudicial to the peace, good order, or security" is undefined; the determination may be made on a subjective basis. Some coastal states believe that a warship, by definition, does not qualify for innocent passage.[31] Another view is that a large tanker, which as a source of spillage necessarily poses an ecological hazard, is barred.[32] The same reasoning has been applied to nuclear powered vessels which, following a catastrophe, could be sources of pollution.[33] The destination of a vessel and its cargo have been challenged in attempts to limit shipments to an adversary—amounting to a "paper" blockade long forbidden by the law of the sea.[34] In short, probably no practical limits to such interpretations exist. They may be made on pragmatic, political, ideological, emotional, economical, or, for that matter, whimsical grounds.

> If you are faced with a situation where each party is free to state and interpret the law as he sees fit, in accordance with his own interests, and there is no way of settling which of conflicting statements is the law, then by definition none of the interpretations is necessarily authoritative or binding on anyone. In such situations, which is the international situation, you cannot say with certainty what the law is, or even that there is any law in a meaningful sense. All you can do is assert your opinion.[35]

The United States, in evaluating this question, should bear in mind that, although the law of the sea is couched in legal-sounding terms, there is no practical procedure for enforcing one's opinion (other than the US Navy). As a practical result, a ship claiming innocent passage has the rights that the coastal state chooses to give it. To accept such an arrangement for the international straits would be naive at best. It has been said that "International law is the law that the wicked do not obey and which the righteous do not enforce."[36] The United States does not want to take on a continuing requirement of enforcing its legitimate rights to innocent passage. The alternative, if the 12-mile limit were accepted, would be to trust to the good faith of the riparian states, an unacceptable concept. As Mr. John R. Stevenson has pointed out,

> We doubt whether any state would wish to subject its sea communications or defense preparedness to the consent or political goodwill of another state. Accordingly, it should be apparent that new rules of international law that might have the effect of reducing mobility cannot be expected to enhance international stability... This would increase, not diminish, the chances for conflict.[37]

The Archipelagoes. A question that raises similar issues to those posed by the international straits is treatment of the archipelago nations. Traditionally each constituent island has been considered a separate entity with its bit of territorial sea measured from its low watermark. A number of archipelago states, now take issue with this procedure, contending that because of their specialized geography, they are largely dependent on the intervening waters and that such waters comprise a legitimate and inseparable part of the national domain. An appropriate rule, representative of this thesis, would be to circumscribe the outer shores of the outer islands with a single base line which would function as the border of the country. Inside this boundary, waters would be regarded as internal, under the total control of the archipelago state. To the seaward would be measured the territorial sea. Indonesia, the Philippines, Iceland, Equador (for the Galapagos), the Faroes, and Fiji have advanced variations of this proposal, although all except the Philippines and Indonesia appear willing to renounce ambitions to control navigation through what are now treated as high seas passages.[38]

The net effect of the archipelago doctrine could create substantial barriers to navigation. The Philippines and Indonesia are astride strategic straits. If the rule were to be applied universally, many other island groupings might be eligible including Britain, Japan, Hawaii, those islands north of Canada and the USSR, the Kuriles, various Caribbean chains, and any number of Pacific groupings. Further, since the proponents of this policy are impatient with land area to water area ratios, maximum inter-island distances, and other objective techniques proposed for determining what constitutes an archipelago,[39] larger political groupings such as the Trust Territories of the Pacific Islands could conceivably qualify.

An acceptable archipelago regime would, from the perspective of freedom of navigation and overflight, have to be characterized by very specific definitions and guarantees. To forestall "creeping jurisdiction," such agreements specifically ought not be couched in terms of concessions by the sovereign archipelago state to the international community, but rather in terms of specific rights granted to the archipelago state with all others reserved to the international community.

Contiguous Zones. Some claims to control over contiguous zones do not amount to claims of sovereignty. One is the "patrimonial sea" concept, advanced by a number of Latin American countries, which would allot to the coastal state full sovereignty out to 200 miles but would preserve international rights of free transit and overflight beyond 12 miles.[40] Such an approach to the "internal" waters formed by application of the archipelago has, as mentioned, been proposed. Canada's 100 mile pollution zone is another example.

Some aspects of these schemes are probably irrelevant to the problem of maintaining open seaways, but not all. A state that has the power to unilaterally impose pollution standards on transiting vessels has the power to control navigation. The administration of such systems could involve unreasonable inspection procedures, and the standards themselves could impose infeasible requirements on vessels. A ship attempting to negotiate a long journey, even under a reserved right of free transit, might encounter as many varying antipollution codes as coastal states. It would have no assurance that objective compliance with even the most rigid standards would protect it from the vagaries of inequitable enforcement. Considering that most contiguous zone proposals refer to a 200-mile limit which, it may be recalled, would cover a third to a half of the ocean space and, obviously, all of the straits in the world, the potential for mischief can be appreciated.

No reasonable nation or agency is unmindful of the need to limit pollution of the seas, but the proposed establishment of zones for unilateral national enforcement of standards, however established, is not constructive. In the first place, the vessel in transit is not a major source of pollution compared to ships entering and leaving port in waters that are territorial even under the 3-mile standard.[41] Secondly, such an arrangement, will break down under the weight of proliferated standards, procedures, interests, and attitudes. To expect substantive results to emerge from such chaos is unrealistic. A system must employ objectively derived international standards, administered and enforced by an objective international agency, to be effective. To this end, ocean space under control of coastal states should be as limited as possible so as to maximize the jurisdictional area of international pollution control.

To review briefly, a major objective of the United States with respect to a new law of the sea is to preserve the freedom of movement through the oceans and air space of the world essential to its national security and well-being. To this end:

• A territorial sea breadth of 12 miles is acceptable and probably represents the only basis for a general agreement.

• The right of free transit over, under and through international straits is a nonnegotiable requirement for any treaty.

• The treatment of archipelagoes must be such that the concept does not result in a proliferation of barriers to communication.

146

• Coastal states must not be delegated authority in contiguous zones that would have the practical effect of empowering them to unilaterally control navigation.

The United States should not be too optimistic about the prospects of selling its position. An initial and necessarily awkward step is to disavow statements and offers made by US representatives at the 1960 Geneva Conference. At that meeting the United States proposed a 6-mile limit with no provision for retention of free transit rights through straits. Since such a measure would have caused 54 straits, including Gibraltar, to revert to territorial waters, the consistency of US logic can obviously be questioned.[42] A graceful finesse does not appear to be available. It should simply be made clear that the previous proposal no longer represents an acceptable basis for discussion.

Additional problems result from the fact that the United States has played an unusually open hand in international discussions. A series of statements, announcements, and draft treaties have rather clearly illuminated the US position on most aspects of a law of the seas regime. It is clear that:

• President Nixon regarded the current law of the sea to be "inadequate to meet the needs of modern technology and the concerns of the international community."[43]

• Further, "If it is not modernized multilaterally, unilateral action and international conflict are inevitable."[44]

• The United States will accept a 12-mile territorial sea subject to free transit and overflight rights in international straits.[45]

• The United States will agree to the expansion of exclusive national fishing rights at least over nonmigratory species.[46]

• The United States will agree to an international regime for the exploitation of seabed resources "beyond the point of national jurisdiction and would agree to regard these resources as the common heritage of mankind."[47]

• The United States will agree to "substantial" sharing of revenues from such exploitation "particularly [for] economic assistance to developing countries."[48]

Thus, the United States is on record as not only attaching crucial importance to reaching an agreement, but also has stated, in advance, major concessions it is willing to make. A substantial danger exists that other parties regard the announced concessions as already "in the bag" and consider them to be mere points of departure for escalated demands.

The United States should take the position that no agreement is better than a bad agreement—and stick with that position. It would be unfortunate if the United States were to be characterized as the nation that blocks a final agreement. It would, however, be more unfortunate if it permitted fear of being so characterized to drive it into accepting an arrangement which failed to support national security interests. Secure in the knowledge that no sovereign state can be legally bound by a treaty without its consent, the United States can, if necessary, continue to apply its own standards in the hope that the passage of time will demonstrate the wisdom and value of its views. The conceded potential for acrimony and conflict inherent in this procedure might be worth accepting in preference to institutionalizing a system that would deny to future generations the freedom to travel freely the surface of the globe. Regardless of the specific outcome, a number of other national security issues of lesser immediate import must be addressed now considering the long lead time needed to develop the requisite organizations and equipments to support US policies.

OTHER SECURITY IMPLICATIONS

Stated succinctly, the US Navy's task has been to use the sea as a means of promoting national security and economic strength, a task that should not change in the coming years. What will change, however, is the way in which that task is carried out.

To be sure, the traditional causes of military confrontation, to include questions of sovereignty over resources and people, are coming to the fore as greater attention is given to ocean space. The current controversy over ownership of petroleum and mineral rights in the Yellow Sea and the East China Sea is an example. At the center of the argument is each party's definition of the continental shelf's edge and its relationship to the Okinawa trough, some sea mounts and some islands in the area. Stakes are high and dangers are great. Four states—China, Japan, Korea, and Taiwan—confront each other with their conflicting claims to the Northeast Asia seabed. Japan, Korea and Taiwan have issued overlapping-all concession areas to a number of the big (mostly US-based) multinational oil companies.[49] Thus, the controversy over oil and seabed rights grows in an area of the world where the interests of four of the five major power centers (China, Japan, Russia, and the United States—Western Europe being the fifth) intersect. In another important area of the world the age-old hatreds between the Greeks and the Turks might be rekindled over

148

attempts to delimit oil and mineral rights in the island-dotted Aegean Sea. Similarly, the discovery of an estimated $2.5 billion of rich mineral deposits in the middle of the Red Sea between Sudan and Saudi Arabia could also lead to a conflict situation.[50] In short, a number of very knotty questions "over who owns what" could lead to conflict.

The reason for developing these points has been to describe a probable environment wherein the increased use of ocean space should lead to increased US economic strength. But the means used to increase US economic strength will perhaps require new forms of military security, which must be articulated so that subsequent efforts to develop any special doctrine, organization and equipment can be undertaken.

As an example, a recent advertisement in *The New York Times* asked, "Why not have gas and oil wells off the Atlantic coast—*out of sight of land*?"[51] The argument that followed was very compelling. Even the environmentalists are not fighting the proposition too vigorously. On March 22, 1974, the Council on Environmental Quality implied that drilling at distances of 30 to 50 miles offshore would be environmentally acceptable.[52] No doubt drilling rigs will eventually appear 100 miles or so offshore. The only question is how soon.

At the same time, the mining industry is lobbying for a bill in Congress that will guarantee US investments in seabed exploitation regardless of the final outcome of international discussions. Three US-based companies are known to have already invested over $100 million in deep-sea mining technology.[53] Howard Hughes' Summa Corporation seems to be in the lead, and his ship, the Glomar Explorer, is picking up manganese nodules in the Pacific on an experimental basis. Others, notably the French, Germans, Japanese, and Russians, are also pushing their seabed mining programs.[54]

Seabed mining operations will be characterized by large investments concentrated in a few, highly complex facilities—mainly ships, port facilities and processing plants. According to Mr. Leigh Ratiner, until recently an ocean resources expert in the Department of Commerce, just three mining operations each processing about 10,000 tons of nodules a day would give the United States "12 percent of the manganese it now imports, 41 percent of the copper, 54 percent of the nickel and three times current imports of cobalt."[55] He maintains that this could be a reality by the end of this decade.

Even as the United States solves the problem of overdependency on others for raw materials, the petroleum rigs and hard mineral mining ships that are the alternate supply source are far out to sea and represent a new kind of vulnerability. An oil rig, firmly attached to the sea bottom, is an easy target for any type of "smart bomb" or, more properly termed, precision guided munition (PGM). The rig, along with the pipeline leading back toward shore, would also be highly susceptible to sabotage. Would we be willing to drop depth charges on what we believed to be a foreign submarine parked on top of, and causing damage to, the pipeline? Similarly, a very expensive and not easily replaced hard mineral mining ship, dragging a 10,000 foot metal tail, would be an easy mark for PGM. Superports and processing facilities, while closer into shore, present the same type problem. For lack of a better name, it might well be called the problem of "pinpoint sovereignty."[56]

The present law of the sea allows for only a 500 meter zone for protection and safety of the installation, perhaps adequate for defense against sabotage during peacetime. In wartime, of course, it is not. For comparison, President Roosevelt felt · he could protect all US installations during World War II by declaring a 10-mile war zone around US territory. The Navy is faced with the problem of developing the doctrine and the operational capability (to include unique types of training and equipment) for defending certain critical pinpoints of sovereignty. It is not evident, at least in open literature, that the Navy's present missions of strategic deterrence, sea control, projection of power or naval presence specifically address this issue.

As a correlative question, what should be the Department of Defense advice regarding a recommendation to draw down land-based war reserves in favor of increased dependence on reserves lying on the ocean floor? This could be especially attractive if it resulted in savings which could be used for other governmental purposes, including defense. Assuming that the choice is to go to war reserves on the ocean floor, what forces, now scheduled for other missions, would be needed to protect the line of communications from the designated pinpoint back to the United States?

In addition to problems of military protection, pinpoint sovereignty creates a delicate socio-political-economic problem. Pinpoints can become hostages to threats from potential adversaries because the implication, in today's environment, is that any of them could be destroyed or sabotaged without creating a serious enough incident to go to war. They are too remote, and too few people, if any, would be hurt to have much effect on the body politic. "Remember Texaco Rig 417"

150

is not likely to mobilize and solidify public opinion as did the term "Remember Pearl Harbor." Many might prefer to accept the economic loss and the attendant risk of intimidation by the threat of further loss during the next diplomatic exchange.

Yet another problem pertains to the exchange of information. The precise bathymetry, geomagnetic and sub-bottom seismic data of a given location are not classified unless they describe an ideal spot for a submarine-launched ballistic missile launching. Years from now when most ocean space has been mapped, that kind of information will, of course, be unclassified. In the meantime, the Navy must continue to collect a great deal of apparently unclassified data that it should not share with others. This affects the US position regarding scientific research and cooperative scientific expeditions with other nations. At the same time, any limitations on the freedom of Navy ships to collect the data they desire may seriously jeopardize the US security posture.

On the other hand, the US Navy may find it difficult to justify withholding information on national security grounds if it enters into an arrangement with a US interest group for an information exchange which enhances US security but at the same time gives the US group a competitive economic advantage over similar groups in other countries. The California tuna fleet, for instance, is among the users of the thermal structure predictions that are disseminated by the Antisubmarine Warfare Environmental Prediction Service. One fishery official reported that this kind of information was responsible in one case for a fourfold increase in the fish catch. The Bureau of Commerical Fisheries, in return, is conducting joint sonar experiments with the Navy to develop identification of species (nondefense) and false target (defense) classification of sounds.[57] A trade-off may be necessary between defense and commerical interests to insure that the overall US position on the law of the seas remains internally consistent.

Ocean surveys today create the greatest problems for antisubmarine warfare (ASW) operations.[58] Additional monitoring problems will be created because more ships will be coming into use, to eventually include cargo and passenger submersibles. More ocean traffic will not only complicate the identification and monitoring problem for the Navy's ASW elements, but also increase traffic safety problems. To illustrate, a diving submarine effectively occupies a column of water 10 miles in diameter. Warned of a dive, other submarines give the area a wide berth.[59]

At some point, for reasons of safety, international negotiations must devise means of avoiding interference and collisions between ships. These rules, as perhaps the mandatory use of internationally coded sonar impulses for all ships, will have a definite effect on the US security posture. Again a trade-off dilemma may face US policymakers as between the guarding of certain procedures for national security reasons and the exchange of certain information for safety reasons. The drafting of necessary safety rules can become quite delicate.

Increased ocean traffic is having its effect in more mundane ways as well. Each year the Navy's Pacific missile range schedules over 20,000 launch and support operations. More than 5,000 require clearance of some part of the sea test range.[60] While not particularly dramatic in themselves, various types of interference with naval operations—in the form of hazards to navigation, acoustic and electronic interference, presentation of false targets to Navy sensors and the disruption of weapons exercises by the appearance of inadvertent targets—are cumulatively detracting from the Navy's ability to use ocean space for purposes of national security.

In summary, most countries best equipped to exploit ocean space are also most concerned with ocean space as their first line of defense. The United States is a prime example. And yet, while much has been said—as it must—about more immediate national security concerns as embodied in the straits issue, little has been said about the special national security problems bound to emerge with the growing use of ocean space. Moreover, these problems should not be buried under some sort of "security classification." The potential problem areas must be articulated and addressed publicly. Otherwise, our political leaders might be faced with other "Pueblo" type incidents where the US capability to respond is severely limited to a body politic stunned into slack-jawed amazement because no earlier public discussions on alternative courses of action had taken place. Even recognizing that certain aspects of the use of ocean space must remain classified, it is still important to articulate potential problems more widely within the government. In short, it may be later than we think. It's time to expand the dialogue—publicly whenever possible—on how we might handle the national security problems that may evolve from the increasing use of ocean space.

THREE

The Changing Face of Europe

9

Observations on US-USSR Detente

Martin J. Slominski

We read about and hear of "detente" nearly every day, yet it is difficult to know precisely its purpose or how we are to achieve it. Some persons interpret the current state of "detente" differently than the dictionary definition of "an easing or relaxation of strained relations and political tensions between nations." Part of the ambiguity of "detente" was indicated by General Creighton W. Abrams, Chief of Staff, US Army, in a speech delivered on October 22, 1973.

> 'Detente' is expressed by some as a fact. It is applauded by others as a policy. It is saluted by still others as a new era... Detente is an idea, a perception of intention among countries. As such, it is not an objective fact. It can change as quickly as perceptions change. But we must deal in facts—in the reality of power, of capability, of strength—when we are addressing the nation's strength—when we are addressing the nation's security.[1]

The US Government position on detente was given by former President Nixon in his State of the Union Message on January 30, 1974.

> We take another giant strike toward lasting peace in the world—not only by continuing our policy of negotiation rather than confrontation where the great powers are concerned, but also by helping toward the achievement of

153

a just and lasting peace in the Middle East. . . We will pursue our relations with the Soviet Union in the climate of detente established two years ago in Moscow.2

A few days earlier, Secretary of State Kissinger had also considered the subject.

Let me explain what we understand by detente. We do not say that detente is based on the compatibility of domestic systems. We recognize that the values and ideology of both the Soviet Union and the Peoples Republic of China are opposed and sometimes hostile to ours. We do not say that there are conflicting national interests. We do say that there is a fundamental change in the international environment compared to any other previous period, a change which was expressed by President Eisenhower more than 20 years ago when he said, 'There is no longer any alternative to peace.' Under conditions of nuclear plenty, the decision to engage in general war involves consequences of such magnitude that no responsible statesman can base his policy on the constant threat of such a holocaust and every leader with a responsibility for these weapons must set himself the task of bringing about conditions which reduce the possibility of such a war to a minimum and, indeed, over any extended period of time reduce this possibility to zero.3

Through detente, the US Government is striving for a decrease in defense expenditures, an arms race moratorium, an exchange of people and ideas, and interdependence between Communist and other economies to give the Politburo a vested interest in peace.

In the United States, there is acceptance for a world at peace regardless of what the policy is called, but there is less accord on attaining or proceeding toward that goal through detente. A former briefing officer for Admiral Elmo Zumwalt believes detente is "frayed," in need of a "demonstration of good faith on both sides," and an appropriate US action would be a "unilateral decision to postpone procurement of certain strategic weapons for a limited period. . . "4 Related opinions were discerned at a US-USSR trade conference held in Washington on February 27-28, 1973. There, American spokesmen told their audience that better defense lies not in military action, but rather in economic accord; both governments must develop economic collaboration as a force that will diminish military confrontation; dealing with the USSR is not as complicated or lengthy as suspected; and US exports to the USSR could reach $2.5 billion annually within three years. Contrary views on enhancement of detente are held by Senator Henry Jackson, many in the Congress and the Government

Accounting Office with particular respect to the emigration of Jews from the Soviet Union, granting of most favored nation treatment and financing foreign trade. These views seek more reciprocity in the US-USSR detente. For views at the opposite end from unilateral disarmament, we can turn to those who endorse Dwight D. Eisenhower's remarks that "Now you are thinking about war, about victory in war or better, keeping us out of war."[5] For like-minded persons detente will be heightened and war will be avoided only if the United States has both the will and the ability to fight for its interests.

THE SOVIETS AND DETENTE

In the Soviet Union, different views regarding detente can be discerned. General Secretary Brezhnev, in a report to the 24th Congress of the Communist Party of the Soviet Union, on March 30, 1971, reflected the major points of foreign policy for his country. In describing US-USSR relations he said:

> An improvement of Soviet-American relations would be in the interests of the Soviet and American peoples, the interests of stronger peace. However, we cannot pass over the US aggressive actions in various parts of the world. . . The frequent zigzags of US foreign policy, which are apparently connected with some kind of domestic political moves from short-term considerations, have also made dealings with the United States more difficult.[6]

Speaking on the 50th Anniversary of the USSR some 19 months later, Brezhnev said: "The Soviet Union is prepared to develop relations with the United States of America. . . At the same time, the Soviet Union will always firmly oppose the aggressive actions of the United States and the policy of force."[7] He spoke optimistically of the US-USSR agreements reached in Moscow in May 1972, and then criticized those who view Soviet actions as "designed to 'contain' or 'encircle' China" for Brezhnev envisages "the Republic of China would become an equal partner. . . "[8] For the Soviet Union, some members of the Politburo would like to achieve, through detente, massive infusions of Western technology, a neutral United States in the event of conflict with China, a diminution of the risk of a two front war, an acceptance of the territorial status quo in Eastern Europe, and the exercise of internal control without foreign comment.

A Washington columnist opines that Brezhnev does not have

unanimous support in the Politburo, writing "the Washington squabbles between hawks and doves have overflowed into the Kremlin."[9] He continues "Grechko's Army paper *Red Star,* takes aim at Brezhnev himself in barbed comments ostensibly directed at 'Western' loose thinking about the nature of nuclear war and how to prepare for it" but really aimed at the supporters of strategic arms limitations. Malcolm Mackintosh also believes "Marshal Grechko's promotion to the Politburo in May 1973 may mark a new departure in Army-Party relations and in the system of checks and balances hitherto maintained by the Soviet political leadership."[10] Further, he writes "some Soviet military figures were initially skeptical about the strategic arms limitation concept and the desirability of negotiating with the United States" but this attitude changed to one of support when "the military realized that its requirements were going to be met..." Other observers of detente report a repetition of the same Soviet military opposition to Strategic Arms Limitation Talks (SALT) II as existed at the beginning of SALT I.[11]

Andrei Sakharov, the physicist credited with an important role in developing the Soviet hydrogen bomb and currently a member of the Academy of Sciences, holds another dissenting view. He opposes the present course of detente believing its terms are too favorable to the USSR. In his view, technological aid from the United States and other countries only will help the Communist Party solve domestic economic problems and free other resources to augment military strength with dire consequences for the non-Communist world.

Possibly representing a constituency of one, Khrushchev in his later years advocated a more extreme method for halting the international arms race and reducing expenditures. In papers published in 1970, he wrote "even if a Soviet-American agreement on bilateral reduction in military spending is impossible, I keep coming back to my own feeling that we should go ahead and sharply reduce our own expenditures, unilaterally."[12]

I believe a different and important obstacle to detente can be fathomed from what Soviet citizens and observers of the Soviet scene are not saying about the topic, as much as from what they are saying. Admittedly, it may fall within the category in international affairs that Secretary Dean Rusk once described as "picayune anxieties" which should be disregarded so we can get on with the broad concepts. However, experience in negotiating with the Soviets and their Russian predecessors supports an opinion that no minor details exist when dealing with them.

What may have seemed to be a "picayune anxiety" could turn out to be an "Achilles' heel" after negotiations are completed. The late Philip Moseley brought this out most vividly in his description of 1945 discussions on the location of sector boundaries in Berlin. Only after arguments within the American delegation which General Henry H. Arnold, Commanding General, US Army Air Forces had to resolve, was it agreed to refuse slight modifications in the line the Russians desired. Had we acceded to this Soviet-requested change, the Red Army would have been positioned so closely to Templehof Airfield runways that minor construction in its sector would have blocked every air approach, a fact which convinced General Arnold of the need for his personal intervention in the discussion among US delegates. The Berlin Airlift of 1948 would have been impossible had the Soviet army been as able to control air approaches to Templehof as effectively as it controlled canal, road, and rail routes to Berlin.

Our current negotiations with the Soviet Union should be as farsighted. With a notable exception, basic to sound negotiation, there is reason to believe they are. This exception is the failure to establish a joint, factual basis for negotiation. Although this is a major problem in our negotiations with the Soviets, we do not conclude agreements unless we have our own information which we regard as authentic and unless we can verify by our own means whether the agreements are being fulfilled. Let us study this problem in further detail however. Interestingly the SALT I agreements were most specific about systems that, in large part, are nonexistent and probably will never be built, but less specific about systems which are supposed to exist and, therefore, could have been described in greater detail. This does not mean that the Soviet government has violated or will violate any agreement, but the absence of agreement on real facts can lead to misunderstanding and later charges of deliberate deception. Recalling SALT I, the most obvious recollection may be the charts showing the number of antiballistic missile (ABM) sites and launchers, intercontinental ballistic missiles (ICBM), long-range aircraft, and submarines capable of launching nuclear weapons agreed upon. The Russian version was far different from what the American saw most frequently. *Pravda* on May 28 and *Izvestia* on May 30, 1972, printed their versions of the complete texts of the Antiballistic Missile Treaty and the Interim Agreement on the Limitation of Strategic Offensive Arms. While accurately mentioning 100 ABM launchers and 100 ABM missiles at each of two authorized sites, those official Soviet papers said nothing about limiting the Soviet Union to 313 modern large ballistic missiles (SS-9), 1096 other ICBM launchers, or 950 submarine launched ballistic missile (SLBM) launchers as emphasized in US analyses of the interim agreement.[13] It should be noted those are US figures for the offensive weapons systems, not Russian agreements! The term SS-9 is our expression, not the Russians'. The Soviet delegates never provided even the weapon systems' nomenclature, much less their numbers and characteristics from which we would negotiate. Accounts of SALT I negotiations tell of American negotiators teaching their Russian civilian counterparts the technical and physical characteristics of Russian weapons sytems. This is almost incredible since V. S. Semonov and others on the USSR team have been representing the USSR in international negotiations for years, while the Politburo consists mainly of persons who hold engineering degrees,[14] who have been involved in such technical details as determining the caliber of principal weapons systems used by general purpose forces.

Equally disconcerting is the Soviet handling of details in the Protocol in the Interim Agreement which concerns submarine launched missile systems. This sensitive matter was resolved by former President Nixon and General Secretary Brezhnev only hours before the signing. Our communications media and official publications detailed this Protocol; I have yet to see it in the Soviet press. *Pravda* on May 28 and *Izvestia* on May 30, 1972 omitted this most significant agreement. A matter resolved by the two heads of government is not a picayune detail that can be brushed aside when thinking about where we and the Russians go from here in detente.

Turning to Mutual Balanced Force Reduction (MBFR), what is one fundamental issue? For us, it appears to be the idea of a balanced military force reduction in central Europe which takes cognizance of asymmetries in the force structures of North Atlantic Treaty Organization (NATO) and Warsaw Pact countries. At the World Peace Congress on October 26, 1973, Brezhnev said the cutback "should not upset the existing balance of strength in central Europe and in the European Continent generally." You and I can know in great detail from open US and NATO sources what we and our NATO allies have stationed there in numbers of divisions, brigades, aircraft, tanks, and personnel. What do the Warsaw Pact countries have there? Herein lies the significant distinction. For the purpose of MBFR negotiations, the Warsaw Pact countries have forces stationed in Europe based on estimates provided by open and official US and NATO sources.

However, these NATO estimates are what one widely quoted Soviet authority on MBFR, labeled "proizvolniye"[15]—arbitrary figures prepared for solely NATO defense budget purposes. More recently General of the Army A. Yepishev wrote "a story about a Soviet threat has been concocted . . ." to distort the "patriotic and international mission" of the Soviet Armed Forces.[16] He was describing the estimates by NATO member countries. In fact, while the Russians have proposed an initial reduction of 20,000 troops in 1975, they have not disclosed any details on their divisions, regiments, aircraft, tanks, and numbers of personnel from which we and they might proceed to negotiate a mutual and balanced force reduction. In effect, the NATO countries seem to be negotiating among themselves, for the Warsaw Pact countries have not yet openly committed themselves to a factual basis for negotiation.

What may we anticipate after concluding an MBFR agreement? We may expect Soviet statements and demonstrations to the effect that the "First Tank Division" of the "Sixth Motorized Rifle Army" was withdrawn from the German Democratic Republic. To which NATO order of battle specialists will say the "First Tank Division" never was in the area and there is no such organization with the nomenclature of a "Motorized Rifle Army." We should expect movements of people and equipment in such ways that the same person may appear to leave the area several times. The amount of equipment actually withdrawn also will be unknown. These Soviet counterintelligence measures may be of little significance when the USSR declares a unilateral reduction in force, but when the deception is applied against an official agreement it can produce a political disaster at the US and West European polls for a political party connected with the negotiations. Lack of disclosure by the USSR may not be a bar to the conclusion of an MBFR agreement, but it can destroy the basis for mutual confidence that is essential to the achievement and furtherance of detente.

As we turn to SALT II, what appear to be crucial issues? One is the matter of US forward based nuclear delivery systems. Soviet sources cite numbers of US nuclear weapons and delivery systems stationed in central Europe. Have you ever seen any figures provided by the Soviet government or even an admission that the Soviet Union has nuclear weapons and delivery systems stationed in central Europe and deployed in positions from which they can be launched against central Europe? Once again the US delegates find themselves teaching Russian delegates our intelligence estimate of the situation.

Our purpose in the conference on Security and Cooperation in Europe (CSCE) negotiations is to achieve a freer exchange of persons and ideas with the USSR and Eastern Europe. As the Federal Republic of Germany (FRG) Foreign Minister Walter Scheel put it, "We should make it clear that detente implies an improvement of human contacts." Speaking at the World Peace Congress in Moscow October 26, 1973, Brezhnev rhetorically asked: "What do we expect from the conference?" His answer was "the territorial integrity of all the European states, the inviolability of their frontiers, the renunciation of the use or the threat of the use of force in the relations between countries, noninterference in each other's internal affairs and the promotion of cooperation in diverse fields." The Russians seem to be operating on the principle that what is ours can be theirs and what is theirs will remain theirs. French Foreign Minister Michel Jobert was among those skeptical of the Soviet proposals for the CSCE and noted that the conference could mislead public opinion by making false assurances.

OTHER NATIONS AND DETENTE

Concern over detente extends beyond the United States and the Soviet Union. Governments throughout the world have indicated, by words and actions, their appraisals of the detente concept and its products, such as the ten agreements reached in Moscow, the agreement on the prevention of nuclear war, and the on-going discussions on SALT II, MBFR, and CSCE.

China's leadership appears opposed to the course taken by the US-USSR detente, believing the USSR is doing just what Brezhnev in his 50th Anniversary speech said it was not doing. Chou En-Lai condemned SALT I as a sham. "The ink on the agreements was hardly dry before one announced an increase of billions of dollars for military expenditures and the other hastened to test new-type weapons. . . The agreements marked the beginning of a new stage in the arms race rather than attempt to curb it," he said.[17] He viewed the United States and the Soviet Union as sources of world disorder when he spoke at a public banquet for Zambia's President Kenneth Kaunda on February 21, 1974. However, he also saw this disorder as an opportunity to be exploited by the developing countries with China's support.[18] On the other side of the world, the European governments have their own views on detente.

An ambivalence exists in Eastern Europe. Detente, by its very definition, means a relaxation of tensions which should lead to fewer controls and more freedom of action. The fact that all the talk of detente in international affairs has not improved life noticeably for the individual Soviet citizen concerns the peoples of Eastern Europe who believe that detente could lead to tighter controls by their own Communist parties and lessen the probability of a change for the better.

Governments and peoples in Western Europe appear more optimistic than their brethren in the East. In general, they are behaving as if detente is a fact in their political and economic relations and are shaping policies accordingly. True, there is concern that the CSCE is not leading to a freer exchange of ideas and easier movement, that MBFR may weaken NATO militarily more than the Warsaw Pact countries, and that other on-going US-USSR negotiations will result in decisions that are important to European security but without European voices in the decisions. Despite such possibilities the attitude in Western Europe has reflected the confidence of individual nations in their ability to cope successfully with any Soviet political and economic challenge so long as the United States keeps the military posture in balance.

Japan, the Organization of Petroleum Exporting Countries (OPEC), and other nations in various stages of economic development all have a stake in the US-USSR detente. However, their relations amongst themselves and the superpowers have changed since the SALT started. Governments in Western Europe have fallen as a result of economic and political crises, new financial centers are arising in the OPEC, the dependence of Japan's economy on foreign raw materials appears to be a greater vulnerability than previously recognized, and hardly a country escapes the impact of these and other changes, all of which are outside the influence of detente but impinge on US-USSR relations. Every indication points to further political, economic, and financial changes. This new environment cannot but have some effect on the two superpowers and their relations with other governments.

DETENTE's POSITIVE SIDE

Despite hopes, fears, and actions that seem to work against detente, the list of accomplishments to date is impressive. It includes the May 1972 Summit Agreements on bilateral relations, limitation of strategic armaments, commercial and economic relations, maritime matters, and cooperation in science, technology, space, health, and environment.

161

During Brezhnev's visit to the United States in June 1973, agreement was reached on joint measures aimed at the prevention of nuclear war. Currently the CSCE, MBFR, and SALT II negotiations are part of both the military and political aspects of detente.

Both sides have made public commitments to reach a permanent agreement on offensive weapons. G. A. Trofimenko, writing in the magazine *S Sh A* states that mutually satisfactory formulas could be found to insure the security of both sides, while taking into account existing asymmetries in the strategic relationship.

An economic or business detente is well underway. At the previously mentioned trade conference, the Russian delegates made the prospects enticing and the American participants were more than hopeful. Soviet spokesmen reported that major industrial countries other than the United States are expanding trade with the USSR at annual rates ranging from 18 percent to 35 percent, and indicated a willingness to modify the USSR Five-Year Plan to produce goods for the US market providing there is sufficient economic justification to do so and a need for more support by the US Government exists. You and I will finance gigantic projects in the USSR which are beyond the resources of even the largest US corporations or else risk losing out to the Japanese, Italians, French, and German entrepreneurs. The Soviet Union has not yet been granted the most favored nation treatment which it expected and the Government Accounting Office in March 1974 temporarily halted further extension of credit to the USSR through the Export-Import Bank. On balance, however, it has benefited from economic arrangements without having to make any significant political concessions to the United States.

In another area, the Soviet Minister of Power and Electrification reported favorably on cooperation between the United States and the USSR in power engineering.[19] A few alert signals have been raised about technological exchange. Dr. Malcolm R. Currie, Defense Research and Engineering Director, spoke of "the long-term danger both to our security and to our world economic position if the US export of technology is not conducted with more restraint."[20] To date the flow of technology appears to be alleviating USSR economic problems in exchange for expressions of Soviet goodwill.

Detente also appears to be working in health care. The Soviet press carried accounts of a "telex line between the USSR Ministry of Health and the US Department of Health, Education, and Welfare," a visit by Secretary Caspar Weinberger, and a determination of areas for further cooperation.[21]

A general West European assessment holds detente as an operational policy for the United States and USSR by which neither superpower believes the situation to be "the result of affection and trust but of the recognition that the two will have to live together."[22] Under these circumstances "contact and goodwill are more important than concrete agreements."[23]

SUMMARY

Detente, with its popular connotation of an easing or relaxation of strained relations and political tensions between nations, represents the attainment of goals which have long been accepted by US leadership and the general public. But this popular meaning overwhelms the precise significance of the word. For detente is not a fixed goal or objective which the United States can reach by an easy approach and then rest. On the contrary, detente is dynamic and ambiguous, to be met and endured through application of coordinated political, economic, and military policies. One difficulty lies in the establishment of these policies by US national leadership and continuing support for them by the electorate. In the foreseeable future, there is something to be gained by making American citizens more aware of the process of detente because they have become more critical of political leadership and less willing to accept any result as the best that our leaders could have achieved. On its part, the USSR has created an array of Potemkin villages behind which it has hidden the realities. Detente to the Politburo has not been important enough to justify the exposition of types of information commonly available in the United States and which are essential to form a basis for negotiations. While this secrecy is most noticeable in military matters, there is reason to believe it carries over into business detente as well. Differences between the United States, the Soviet Union, and other nations will not be resolved by talk alone although that is an indispensable first stage. Finally, any long-range expectations from a US-USSR detente should anticipate changes in the political situation in the Peoples Republic of China (PRC), the economy of Japan, every aspect of Europe, the OPEC financial reserves, and elsewhere throughout the world which can frustrate the most honorable intentions of American and Russian agreements in the name of detente. We have come a long way since General deGaulle first spoke of detente and the Johnson Administration prepared for limitations on strategic arms. It is worth our attention and effort to continue moving along those directions, laying a sound foundation for a longer lasting freedom from armed conflict.

10

Western Europe and Atlantic Relations

James E. Trinnaman

The events of 1973, the "Year of Europe," and their continuing and intensifying aftermath, have filled newspapers and journals with articles by those currently or formerly involved in policy formulation, both in the United States and Western Europe. Many writers have despaired over the deterioration of the relationships underlying the Atlantic community concept and the manner in which the impetus toward Western European integration apparently failed to survive its first serious challenges. Others, on both sides of the Atlantic, have cast recriminations at the failures of their respective partners in Europe and the United States. Future Western European integration and the nature of its relationship to the United States are unclear. Considerable effort is being expended on both sides of the Atlantic to explore the range of problems and opportunities to be encountered by both sides and what the future may hold, depending on the success or failure of all parties in meeting these challenges.[1]

This paper proposes to examine briefly these events and the extent to which they have exposed the fundamental rationales underlying US and Western European interests and policies, and to suggest some critical parameters for the continuing process of determining US security interests in Western Europe in an era of high risk and uncertainty. The term Western Europe, as used in this chapter, refers only to the NATO European powers. It does not include Sweden, Finland, Eire, Austria, Switzerland, and Spain.

In the World War II aftermath and the onset of the "cold war," the United States determined that the reemergence of a politically, economically, and militarily revitalized and stable Western Europe was vital to its own security interests. The last 25 years attest to the success of those economic and military institutions created to promote these interests. Through this period the United States also gradually constructed a set of assumptions regarding the feasible and desirable future of Western Europe.

• Western European states would be economically prosperous and increasingly willing and capable of integrating and orchestrating their wealth of natural resources and productive manpower through an expanding European Economic Community (EEC) and other institutions. At the same time, this economically integrated community would be largely reinforcing of and complementary to US economic and industrial might.

• In the military area, Western European states would share the US view of the Soviet/Warsaw Pact threat and, therefore, be prepared to assume increasingly the burden of defense of Europe against a broad spectrum of conventional threats. Western Europe would also continue to rely on US assurances to meet the range of required nuclear deterrence, tactical and strategic.

• Although less certain of the specific character of political integration which would emerge, the United States anticipated that these economic and military institutions would gradually encourage political development which would also preserve and reinforce the Atlantic orientation.

Recent events have cast doubt on these assumptions by jeopardizing earlier progress toward Western European integration upon which these assumptions are based. The major aspects of these problems are as follows.

THE ECONOMIC PROBLEMS

Economically, Western Europe since World War II has been highly successful in recovery and in the degree of integration and institution-building achieved. In combined figures, Western Europe approximates the United States in Gross National Product (GNP), is the world's largest trading entity, and accounts for over 30 percent of US foreign investment and about 25 percent of US imports and exports. It also possesses combined reserve assets of about $68 billion (the United States has $14.6 billion).[2]

At present, most West European countries are preoccupied in dealing individually with the negative aspects of this dramatic rise to economic prominence. Their economies are suffering from serious inflation; only the Federal Republic of Germany (FRG) is now experiencing an inflation rate of less than 10 percent per year.[3] Western European governments are attempting to adjust their economic growth rates downward, and deal with substantial unrest among students and labor. An especially complex problem, foreign and migrant labor, developed as a result of excessive internal industrial demands for labor and a general unwillingness to export technology, financing, and factories outside national boundaries as opposed to importing foreign labor.

Within the EEC, problems surrounding the establishment and operation of the Regional Fund to deal with development in the residual less-developed corners of Western Europe, and the expressed desire of the new labor government in Great Britain to renegotiate its accession agreement to the EEC, are causing fairly severe strains on European political institutions. Continued failure to arrange some mutually satisfactory system of coordinating monetary policies among the states further aggravates the problem of inflation control.

The economic area has also imposed strains on the Atlantic relationship. The United States interpreted such policies as the Western European countries' rush to drop trade barriers among themselves; to protect the basic exchange earning sectors of the economies of some member countries (especially agriculture in France); and to negotiate most-favored nation treatment with other states as being undertaken at the expense of US economic interests.[4] Undoubtedly, some in Europe saw these policies as necessary protection of European economic capability in the face of powerful and efficient US production. Others took satisfaction in developing economic policies independent of the United States, and if "independent" turned out to be "in competition with," so much the better.

Many Europeans are also concerned over the growth of US ownership and control of some basic European industries and the increasing strength and importance of US-owned multinational corporations in the European economies. Resentment of this perceived inequity is likely to continue for some time.[5]

There have been many signs of US concern with emerging Western European economic competitiveness and growing inability of the Atlantic community's mechanisms to forestall divergent policies through consultations and negotiation. One sign came in 1971 with US Treasury Secretary Connally's imposition of selective import taxes to rectify in part EEC discrimination against US agricultural exports, and also to relieve the US balance of payments deficit.

The extent of this deterioration became apparent only during the oil crisis in late 1973. The states of Western Europe are heavily dependent on Arab oil, variously between 70-85 percent, and a continued and increasing flow of Arab oil is vitally important to their economies. The crisis had multiple effects on the EEC. It divided the member states on ways to assure the continued flow of oil, which included a brief period of individual negotiations with the Arab countries best characterized as "every man for himself." It was one of the important reasons causing France and then Italy to withdraw from the narrow track system of controlled EEC currencies fluctuations (the so-called "snake"). It also created a continuing controversy over ways to meet the increased oil costs and to adjust financial institutions to deal with the monumental problems of absorbing monetary dislocations anticipated to be on the order of $50-60 billion annually.

The problems of the oil crisis were compounded with US irritation over lack of European support for its efforts in the Middle East, first to support Israel and subsequently to press for disengagement and search for a settlement. Secretary Kissinger complained that European negotiation with the Arabs, economic aid offers, and favored-nation trade treatment without prior consultation and coordination with the United States seriously endangered the delicate efforts to arrange a settlement without further Soviet encroachment in the Middle East.

THE POLITICAL PROBLEM

Most Western European states are governed increasingly by left-center/socialist coalitions, perpetually threatened by the flood of internal problems. Preoccupation with these problems has contributed to an environment in which efforts to construct European political institutions have been secondary and slow to evolve. European popular opinion, reflecting a wide spectrum of social malaise and discontent, generally holds Western European governments in relatively low esteem, and characterizes most political leaders as mediocre and without vision, vitality, or nerve. These are generally regarded as governments of technicians firefighting each day's problems.

The West European states have reconfirmed recently their intent to pursue political integration by 1980, partly in reaction to the disruptive effects of the oil crisis on the existing policy coordination mechanisms. It also responds to the perception of the progressive deterioration of relations with the United States over lack of timely consultation and divergent, potentially conflicting policies on dealing with the Arab states.

Western European states are not agreed on the nature of a "politically integrated" Europe or the relationship it would have with the United States and the Soviet Union. It is generally recognized, however, that whether "political integration" in the 1980's emerges as a loose confederation of independent states with limited central powers, or simply a group of independent states with efficient consultation and policy reconciliation mechanisms, the final resolution will be influenced in part by the respective US and Soviet interests.[6] For some time to come, the Western European states will wrestle with the challenge posed by Secretary Kissinger in April 1973[7] and again more forcefully in March 1974: How does Europe intend to conduct itself in the world as a "distinct and original entity"? What will this mean for the Atlantic community, the relations with the United States, and the defense of the Western World?[8]

THE MILITARY PROBLEM

The North Atlantic Treaty Organization (NATO), together with US guarantees of a credible nuclear deterrent against the Soviet/Warsaw Pact threat, have been the backbone of Western European defense for 25 years. Even in better days, NATO required immense expenditure of political and diplomatic energy to maintain the delicate and changing balances of concepts, policies, and strategies more or less satisfactory to the member nations. For some years now, these balances have been so delicate that any major recommendations of change or modification are regarded as potentially damaging to the alliance.

In general, Western Europe's perception of the Soviet threat increasingly diverges from that of the United States.[9] Despite continuing enlargement and refinement of Soviet military capabilities, already generally regarded as more than sufficient to control Eastern Europe and meet any NATO challenge, most Europeans perceive the threat of actual warfare as considerably reduced. They also see a greater desire in Moscow to pursue its aims through other avenues.[10]

Europe fears a progressive erosion of US interest in European security, weakening of US determination to maintain the nuclear umbrella over Europe, and the possibility of a unilateral reduction of the 300,000 US forces stationed there. In the extreme, Europeans see this as leading to Western European disintegration and possibly a rush of governments individually to Moscow to make whatever accommodation might be offered. Paradoxically, continued strong assurances of US defense support permits European governments to maintain relatively small defense budgets (the average EEC country budget for defense is 4.2 percent of GNP, while the United States maintains 7.8 percent),[11] and to pursue, independently of the United States, some limited diplomatic and economic accommodations with the Soviet Union and Eastern Europe.

Continued US-Soviet negotiations for Mutual Balanced Force Reduction (MBFR)[12] are part of the same paradox. One would expect greater European recognition that success in these negotiations, as well as in the broader Strategic Arms Limitation Talks (SALT), could contribute substantially to European security and forestall the increases in European defense burden already too long delayed. However, most European reports see instead the institutionalization of Western defense inferiority, the progressive withdrawal of US defense assurances and, worst of all, the decoupling of US strategic nuclear capability from the defense of Western Europe. In this sense, Western European governments have always harbored a belief that the only real deterrence in the military equation was an automatic linkage whereby any military adventure into Western Europe triggered a US-Soviet nuclear exchange. This may explain, in large part, Western European reluctance to take up the burden of a credible conventional defense, and misgivings over strategies calling for graduated steps from conventional response, to tactical nuclear weapons, and only then to consideration of strategic weapons. The idea of the United States buying time to explore means of terminating some conflict in Western Europe short of strategic nuclear exchange between the United States and the Soviet Union, while Western Europe is being subjected to major devastation, is not a strategy likely to please many Europeans.

The new declaration for NATO, which President Nixon called for as a culmination of the "Year of Europe," was signed belatedly in June 1974. The declaration was intended to revitalize NATO on its twenty-fifth birthday and to act as a guide for the alliance through the next quarter century. The common defense and the dependence of the alliance on US security forces was reaffirmed and the declaration contained the promise of timely consultations on common problems within and outside NATO. However, the 14 months of negotiation to prepare the declaration still failed to reconcile the allies on such basic differences as the amount of defense Western Europe needs; each member's "fair share" contribution to that defense; and the long-term goal to maintain, reduce, or withdraw US forces in Europe. Some delegations were also openly skeptical of the promise of timely consultations, suggesting that only time will tell whether or not all parties will make a serious effort in this regard. On balance, the new declaration is a hopeful sign, reestablishing the foundation for a new sense of alliance; but the vitality of NATO will depend on the day to day workings of the organization, the continuing demonstration of commitment of member states to work toward the common interest.

Recent agreement with the FRG to offset some costs to the United States of stationing forces in Europe (about $2.2 billion for 2 years through arms purchases) will relieve the immediate pressure from Congressional sources for unilateral troop withdrawal. Also, recent signs of French willingness to participate more actively in NATO suggest that France may gradually reconsider its 1966 troop withdrawal, and generate some cautious optimism. However, despite continued assurances, Europe will continue to worry over US determination and be acutely alert to signs of weariness and pique.

THE WESTERN EUROPEAN VIEW

The Western European press complains with regularity that the United States no longer listens to its European allies, fails to appreciate their problems, and shows little insight into those conditions which delimit their energies and initiatives. The following seeks to illustrate briefly the current German, British, and French situations and attitudes on these problems.

• The FRG, at the center of the front line facing the Soviet/Warsaw Pact, is aware that it is the keystone to any concerted Western European defense, and, should the unthinkable occur and deterrence fail, it may well be the first devastated.[13] The surprise resignation of Chancellor Willy Brandt in May 1974 has left most European commentators wondering which of his policies will survive and with what emphasis. The new Chancellor, Helmut Schmidt, faces many challenging problems, but also has the opportunity to undertake new initiatives with regard to European integration, the Atlantic alliance, and the Soviet Union and Eastern Europe.

Chancellor Schmidt's coalition government remains one of the strongest in Europe, but will be challenged increasingly by growing leftist sentiment. Continued economic prosperity appears a prerequisite for political stability. Although FRG dependence on Arab oil is not as great as its neighbors', it still sufficiently threatens this prerequisite. With official reserves in excess of $30 billion, the FRG can absorb increased energy cost, at least for a time, and continue to survive an inflation sustained by policies favoring overemployment and labor scarcity.

In defense, the FRG has consistently espoused the strongest possible ties with the United States and NATO. So far the FRG has not pressed its allies heavily over the fact that it alone remains nonnuclear in the German-French-British triangle. It is also most sympathetic with the current US balance of payments problems resulting in part from US defense expenditures for NATO. At the same time, the government is facing increasing popular pressure to reduce its own defense expenditures from a wide range of popular opinion.

The FRG has supported and at times been the vital instrument in furthering Western European economic integration. At other times it has appeared curiously reluctant to assume leadership, preferring that either France or Britain take the responsibility. At the same time, FRG leaders argue persuasively that a gradually-integrating Western Europe is not inconsistent, in an era of gradual detente between the United States and the Soviet Union, with FRG efforts of its own to improve relations with Eastern Europe and the Soviet Union.[14] The Brandt government placed a considerable amount of its political prestige on the anticipated results of a policy of *Ostpolitik.* Under this policy, in exchange for increasing recognition of the status quo in Eastern Europe and the legitimacy of both Eastern European governments and Soviet presence there, the FRG hoped to improve the situation of West Berlin, establish formulas for greater trade and economic cooperation, and ultimately create an environment that would not foreclose on a chance for eventual reunification of the two Germanies.

To date, *Ostpolitik* has not produced anything very promising for the FRG and Chancellor Schmidt has announced that he intends to reduce emphasis on it. However, the Soviet Union might renew

171

encouragement of reunification, pressuring the FRG to proceed very slowly with Western European integration. Also, in the unlikely event of a period of US vacillation over European defense, the Soviet Union could conceivably induce the FRG to withdraw from NATO and Europe, and adopt a neutral position to preserve the possibility of eventual reunification.

The FRG government continues to affirm its commitment to NATO and looks to the United States for deterrence and defense. It favors continued cooperation in the integration of Western Europe including some form of political and economic union by 1980. Amelioration of relations in an atmosphere of detente with Eastern Europe and the Soviet Union may be given somewhat less emphasis, but the attraction of eventual reunification will remain powerful.

The FRG recognizes the vital US role in European defense and has kept expressions of national policy in other areas within the bounds dictated by its ties to the United States despite often strong popular anti-American sentiment. However, the FRG is wary of the progress of MBFR negotiations, for a unilateral US force reduction would be a severe blow to FRG defense. And a US-USSR detente concluded over the heads of the Western European states might also reduce the opportunities for FRG initiatives toward the Soviet Union and Eastern Europe in pursuit of its own interests.

Chancellor Schmidt's cordial relations with the newly elected French President may provide renewed opportunities for joint cooperation in defense and stimulate efforts toward Western European integration. FRG political and economic vitality continues to provide its government with a firm base upon which the EEC can be revitalized and political integration more firmly pursued.

• The election of Valéry Giscard d' Estaing as President of France makes possible improved relations with the rest of Western Europe and the Atlantic community. Policies of ultra nationalism and independence from strong military ties with the Atlantic community, known as Gaullism, may have a lesser importance in the new government. A potent political force in France for some time, it is unlikely that many of Gaullism's essential elements will be discarded by the successor government too readily.

French politics have produced governments of delicate balance of center and moderate right interests, with Western Europe's largest Communist Party in opposition. The most recent election followed this pattern. However, the Socialist candidate, François Mitterrand, with

Communist Party support, came within a fraction of a percent of winning. The new government must contend with a powerful opposition which is against defense ties to the United States and strong Western European integration.

Economically, France has a strong if sometimes inefficient agricultural base, well-diversified industry, and good labor force, which keep alive the expectation that someday France will exceed the FRG in industrial and financial strength. The Arab oil crisis has shaken this expectation and accounts in part for French preparedness, during this period, to risk Western European and US irritation by independent initiatives toward its oil suppliers.

Since World War II, French defense policy has focused on the FRG.[15] The French have feared, on the one hand, political and economic ties to a more powerful FRG within the framework of a European union. On the other hand, and at the opposite extreme, the French have feared that eventually the FRG will do what it must to achieve reunification, either by accepting neutralization or by forsaking Western Europe and reaching accommodation with the Soviet Union. Either course would leave France in the front line of potential conflict. Therefore, while supporting integration in the hope of anchoring the FRG more firmly in Western Europe, France has been unwilling to sacrifice much political or military sovereignty to European institutions for fear that if the anchoring process fails, it would have thereby lost ability to protect itself. And while calling for a continued firm US commitment to European defense and the presence of its forces in Germany, France fears that lack of US resolve and apparent willingness to pursue MBFR will weaken the Western hold on the FRG. And finally, while participating in some aspects of NATO, France has refused to relinquish control of any part of its military forces or its possession of an independent *force-de-frappe*. If the FRG should drift into neutrality, or reach an accommodation with the Soviet Union, France believes that it must possess enough nuclear threat to discourage further Soviet incursion.

With past attempts to retain its options in the event that efforts to keep the FRG in Western Europe fail, France may well have weakened the effectiveness of many of these efforts. French political commentators have recognized this and have increasingly perceived that the options so expensively retained may not be realistic. Nevertheless, worry over the future of the FRG and the continued US willingness to act as guarantor of Western European status quo are likely to remain paramount in French policymaking. With greater confidence in this regard, France could conceivably throw itself wholeheartedly into the construction of an integrated/unified Western Europe and stabilization of relations with Europe's eastern neighbors.

• In many ways Great Britain's recent policy and economic accomplishments have been a disappointment to both Western Europe and to itself. Only just slightly behind France in population and GNP, it has been plagued by weak governments unable to deal effectively with either its domestic or its Western European problems.

Prime Minister Wilson has headed a minority government since the March 1974 election. Prime Minister Heath, his predecessor, succeeded in bringing Great Britain into the European Community over the serious misgivings of perhaps a majority of Britons, but stumbled with his treatment of the domestic energy crisis. In internal politics, Wilson has no clear mandate from the electorate beyond the immediate requirement to get coal and oil moving again. Inflation, problems with labor productivity, trade balances in the face of dramatic increases in energy prices, a weakening currency, and persisting conflict in Northern Ireland, suggest that Britain may be in no position to pursue vigorously Western European integration.[16]

The Heath government was prepared to support the French position in Western Europe at length in return for admission to the Community, even allowing some deterioration in relations with the United States. Wilson's election was a severe blow to the policies of President Pompidou. The new governments of both countries will hopefully begin the process of fence-mending and establish a new set of understandings for further progress toward European integration.

Great Britain will also want to reestablish firmly the Atlantic connection with the United States, and work for policy changes within the EEC which would relieve some popular British doubts over membership. Britain will probably try to reduce the size of its contribution to the budget of the European Community and its Common Market, which looks burdensome to an already threatened economy, and seek a review of EEC agricultural policies which are increasing British food prices. Britain must also reexamine the impact of EEC membership on its trade with the Asian Commonwealth countries.

It may be a time before Great Britain can settle its severe domestic problems and find a new formula for participation in the European Community.[17] However, it is strengthening connections with the

United States and the Atlantic community, and is intent on constructing policy coordination mechanisms between the United States and Western Europe which tie the two more closely together.

AN ERA OF UNCERTAINTY

Events during the "Year of Europe" demonstrated no consensus in Western Europe as to the nature of integration, and the current integrated structures are still fragile. However, growing Western European economic interdependence and the extension of EEC efforts for economic agreements elsewhere in the world are providing strength and impetus to the institutions of integration.

Also during the "Year of Europe," relations between the United States and Western Europe deteriorated with the failure of consultation mechanisms during the Middle East War and the oil crisis, the absence of agreement for a renewed Atlantic charter, and the inability to agree upon a new set of economic and political relationships. Out of these events and this deterioration, however, have begun to emerge a new basis for Atlantic accord:

• The United States has become increasingly aware that a politically stable, economically healthy, militarily viable Western Europe, intent on maintaining and augmenting its orientation toward and association with the United States and the Atlantic community, is among its most vital of national security interests abroad.

• The oil crisis, by making the United States relatively stronger and Western Europe relatively weaker, has given the United States a renewed opportunity to revitalize relationships with Western Europe. At the same time, the new governments in the FRG, Great Britain, and France may be more receptive to a strengthening of the Atlantic community.

• Much editorial comment in the Western European press favors acting in concert with the United States. Most of this comment, however, views success in this direction as largely dependent on continued US commitment to the defense of Western Europe.

• To the extent that Western Europe perceives the United States as unable to establish its priorities and policies, to seek new solutions as problems arise, and to provide leadership and vitality in the pursuit of solutions—to that extent are Western European countries likely to vacillate and drift, be quarrelsome among themselves, irritable toward the United States, and fearful of and/or attracted to the Soviet Union.

The great danger faced by the United States in the coming period is progressive isolation from Western Europe and the rest of the world, not as a matter of conscious policy choice, but through alienation by policy and opportunity mismanagement, unwillingness to adapt to changing circumstances, and reluctance to continue a role of world leadership.

From a review of the Western European side of the Atlantic equation, some suggestions can be forwarded on avenues open to the United States for seeking improvement in Atlantic relations.

With respect to political relations between the United States and Western Europe, it may be wise for the United States to place primary emphasis on structuring efficient mechanisms of policy coordination where all sides are confident that their interests are receiving full consideration. In limited areas, the nine EEC member states are authorizing either one member state or an EEC body to act as spokesman and negotiator for all. Success in these areas will promote both necessary efficiency and the integration process itself.

The United States must also recognize and work within the Western European predilection for low-key diplomacy and the construction of institutions which are the embodiment of interests, as opposed to grand declarations of intent.

The United States might also desist from further accusations of European parochialism as compared to its own worldwide focus and interest. Such charges grate needlessly on European partners, and are inaccurate. A renewal of Western European initiatives toward Eastern Europe, Japan, the Middle East, Africa, and South Asia is taking place, and Western Europe remains the largest trading entity in the world. The problem for the near future is again producing the mechanisms of consultation and policy coordination which harmonize, to the extent possible, US and Western European initiatives elsewhere.

The military defense of Western Europe will require the serious attention of Europe and the United States for some time. As yet, Western Europe fails to discern the thrust of US policies with respect to defense burden sharing, SALT, and MBFR in the face of continued shifting of the military balance in favor of the Soviet Union. Many Western Europeans are also openly questioning the reliability of US strategic nuclear guarantees.

European sources have characterized recent US pressure on the FRG, for agreement to offset in part its defense expenditures to support forces in Europe, as approaching blackmail. In their opinion, if

Western Europe is a vital security interest to the United States, the current expenditure rate shouldn't be considered "burdensome" considering that US support of Vietnam, where almost everyone agrees no vital US interest is involved, continues in excess of $1 billion per year. Western Europeans also reject the US observation that their countries average somewhat more than half the percentage of GNP that the United States devotes to defense, so that Europe should take on a more equitable share of the "burden." Given the nature of the US economy, they argue that the level of defense expenditure is less "burdensome" to the United States than one-half that level is to Western Europe, and also point out the continued heavy burden of aid which several European nations devote to developing nations once their colonies. The recently agreed upon FRG offset payments have reduced Congressional pressure over the unequal burden issue, but it may prove to be increasingly unpopular in the FRG in the coming years.

In the longer term, Western European military planners may find greater degrees of defense freedom provided by the coming generation of military technology. To the extent these planners judge prudent, the conventional defense of Europe may come to rest more on effective forward defense provided by precision guided munitions, barrier defense, and detection devices, and less on attempts to match the Soviet Union force-for-force. The long-term advantage is that an increasingly integrated Western Europe would be able to look after its own conventional defenses while relying on the US strategic nuclear deterrent, through Atlantic defense agreements, to counter the Soviet nuclear threat. The US defense alliance with Western Europe would be more secure because conventional military challenges anywhere on the European continent would not automatically necessitate escalation to nuclear war.

The Soviet Union would oppose the development of an effective Western European defense system, but may be persuaded to accept it on two grounds. First, the Western European military capability would be purely defensive. Without mobile armies or armor, it could not take advantage of Soviet military preoccupation elsewhere to thrust into Eastern Europe. Second, such a purely defensive system might be effective without total reliance on an integral nuclear capability. By encouraging and participating in the development of such a Western European defense, the United States might forestall those pressures which encourage the arming of the FRG with nuclear technology. In the long run it might also contribute to a lessened sense of need in

France and Great Britain to support an expensive and perhaps ineffective nuclear capability.

While the events of the "Year of Europe" strained relations within the Atlantic community, they have also given rise to new opportunities for progress. The problems of integrating Europe remain, but new European governments have the opportunity to deal with them from fresh perspectives.

11

Precision Weaponry in the Defense of Europe

Stanley D. Fair

Military technological advances have changed the nature of war throughout history, but in several cases the impact of these developments was not fully appreciated.[1] One example is the machine gun, first used during the Russo-Japanese War of 1904-05. The increased potential in firepower volume was not properly evaluated because of the small number of machine guns involved. During World War I the wide availability of machine guns on both sides was the major cause of the high casualty rates and the stalemate of trench warfare. Another case is the tank, introduced during World War I. At the beginning of World War II, the French had tanks scattered among their forces as a supporting source of firepower. The Germans, on the other hand, used their tanks in mass and provided tactical air support in blitzkrieg tactics to achieve spectacular success. The latest instance might be precision weaponry, highly accurate bombs and missiles representing a quantum jump in firepower effectiveness.

Precision weaponry, an accurate firepower system, consists of several interrelated components which function with a high probability of hitting targets with single-round efficiency. One component of the system is the target acquisition capability necessary to detect and locate targets, a fundamental prerequisite to the effective use of any firepower resource. A second component, the command and control equipment and procedures, provides the essential link between finding targets and directing precision fires. The precision munition, the third component, is guided terminally or at mid-course by a variety of technologies and techniques enabling the munition to hit the acquired target, be it stationary or moving.[2] In addition, certain hostile environments may require the associated components of countermeasures, which protect these systems and friendly forces from enemy precision weaponry systems, and counter-countermeasures, which overcome enemy countermeasures.

In recent years, precision weaponry has been used in three combat zones. The US Air Force conducted strategic interdiction operations against North Vietnam during the spring of 1972, and a few aircraft, using terminally-guided bombs, accomplished what hundreds of earlier sorties had either failed to do, were incapable of doing without unacceptable collateral damage, or achieved at disproportionate cost in lost aircraft and crews. The US Seventh Air Force estimated that North Vietnam suffered more damage in the first two months of this bombing effort than it had during the four years of the previous air campaign.[3] Precision weaponry was used also by the US Army in South Vietnam in 1972, when the TOW (Tube-launched, Optically-tracked, Wire-guided) missile was used with considerable success against Soviet-made armor. The greatest precision weaponry employment in combat occurred during the Arab-Israeli conflict of October 1973. Both sides had precision antitank missiles; the Arabs used precision air defense missiles; the Israelis employed precision air defense suppression missiles; and "both Arab and Israeli forces lost a major part of their arsenals, particularly armor, aircraft, and antiaircraft systems."[4]

This combat experience represents both a warning and an opportunity for North Atlantic Treaty Organization (NATO) forces to adjust their concept for the European defense to the new precision weaponry era. The warning should be clear—the Egyptians were using Soviet military technology in their latest war with Israel. The Gainful air defense missile, which downed so many American-made fighter aircraft, and the Snapper antitank missile, which accounted for most of Israel's tank losses, were Soviet-built. These advances in Soviet military technology have not occurred overnight; in 1959 the Russians demonstrated their emerging capability with precision weaponry when they shot down an American U-2 flying at very high altitude. The opportunity should be equally clear—precision weaponry favors the defense because to advance, offensive forces must expose themselves to the highly accurate firepower. If available in sufficient quantity and correctly applied, precision weaponry could provide NATO the qualitative improvement in overall combat effectiveness of its conventional military forces needed to offset the Warsaw Pact quantitative advantage in numbers of tanks, artillery pieces, and aircraft.

ROLE OF PRECISION WEAPONRY

At present, NATO is generally considered incapable of successful defense against a large-scale conventional attack by Warsaw Pact forces. Precision weaponry could increase the conventional combat capability of NATO forces, contribute to the achievement of an effective direct defense option, and permit the strategy of flexible response to become a reality. This paper develops a concept for the use of precision weaponry in the defense of Europe and identifies military, political, and economic implications of the acquisition of these systems by NATO.

NATO relies on three interdependent components of military power for the defense of Europe: conventional forces, tactical nuclear weapons, and strategic nuclear forces. General Andrew J. Goodpaster, while Supreme Allied Commander Europe, described NATO's conventional military forces as having the capability "to deal with small-scale attacks, or with larger attacks for a limited period, or with still larger attacks that fail to do as well against us as might have been assumed."[5] Because these conventional forces are not sufficient to contain large-scale attacks indefinitely, NATO forces have been compelled to depend on the other two components of military power to deter or defend against aggression. General Goodpaster called a full conventional capability, one designed to defend successfully against large-scale attack, the "low-risk but high-cost option which goes well beyond what the nations have demonstrated they are prepared to provide."[6] Technology, in the form of precision weaponry, might be able to provide the desired full conventional capability at a price NATO nations can afford and would be willing to pay.

NATO strategy for the defense of Europe is based on the principle of flexible response, prepared to respond with weapons and forces appropriate to the situation. The political guidance given to NATO military authorities when the flexible response strategy was adopted was "to provide for the employment as appropriate of one or more [of the options] of direct defense, deliberate escalation, and general nuclear response."[7] Thus, the direct defense option implies meeting aggression in the form and level selected by the enemy to initiate his aggression; the deliberate escalation option suggests a change in the form or level of warfare selected by the enemy, as a means of increasing the costs or risks of aggression; and the general nuclear response option involves the use of strategic nuclear forces. Precision weaponry would have primary application in the execution of the direct defense option to counter a large-scale conventional attack by Warsaw Pact forces. However, this application would not preclude the use of conventional precision weaponry to attack some of those targets formerly considered to be nuclear targets, if the decision is made to combine the direct conventional defense with a conventional deliberate escalation option.

Warsaw Pact forces will also have a capability with precision weaponry systems, but it is expected that these systems will not have a major impact on the basic military doctrine of Warsaw Pact forces for offensive operations. Their emphasis on rapid, mobile, and massive operations with armored vehicles and aircraft for success in battle should continue because of their traditional preference for mass and their large investment in tanks, troops, and aircraft. Warsaw Pact forces would probably use their precision weaponry systems in the counterfire role against NATO's precision weaponry systems. They would make maximum use of cover, concealment, and deception, and mass where they consider the defense to be weakened or neutralized by their precision weaponry systems.

Warsaw Pact forces have the advantage of initiating aggression and of using their precision weaponry systems first. NATO should anticipate that these forces, if they should make an initial attack, would try to destroy fixed targets such as supply installations, ports, airbases, and communication centers, as well as NATO's precision weaponry systems. Ships could also be attacked by enemy precision weaponry systems, endangering US reinforcement and resupply of NATO by sea. A logical extension of current Warsaw Pact air power strategy would be their land forces' attempt to overwhelm the defense by saturating NATO's precision weaponry systems with targets, accepting the losses as necessary to continue the advance. Probably, attacks would be conducted frequently at night or during periods of reduced visibility to degrade NATO's target acquisition capability and to reduce the effectiveness of precision weaponry sensors.

NATO forces would have the usual advantage of the defense, but that advantage would be enhanced by the increased firepower effectiveness of precision weaponry. Their knowledge of the terrain could be exploited to organize the defense, centered on the use of precision weapons to destroy advancing enemy forces. To counter Warsaw Pact massing tactics, NATO forces should be equipped with missiles and rockets containing terminally-guided submunitions, each of which could home on individual tanks attempting to saturate the defense with targets. NATO forces would also need countermeasures to defend against enemy precision weaponry systems and counter-countermeasures to ensure their own precision weaponry systems function properly. Equipping NATO territorial forces with simple precision weaponry systems would also help to defeat the massing tactics of Warsaw Pact forces by providing depth to NATO defenses.

CONCEPT

The strategic interdiction operations conducted against North Vietnam in the spring of 1972 indicate that fixed targets are inherently vulnerable to attack by precision weaponry. The East European environment, with its comparatively large target complex and wide variety of well-defined fixed targets, means that NATO precision weaponry systems could be extremely effective in a strategic interdiction program. Such a program's purpose should be to impede movement of reinforcements and supplies, destroy support facilities, and disrupt operations in rear areas.

Because of range requirements, strategic interdiction operations would be conducted primarily with air delivered precision guided munitions, and both sides can be expected to protect their rear areas with concentrated air defense systems. For its interdiction program, NATO forces should make maximum use of electronic countermeasures for air defense suppression, penetration aids; decoys, remotely-piloted aircraft, and of the capability to use precision weaponry from a standoff delivery position. The standoff capability, in particular, would reduce the exposure of delivery aircraft to enemy air defenses. For defense against the Warsaw Pact interdiction program, NATO should rely less on fixed installations and recognize the need for multiple small installations, alternative key facilities, camouflaged and dummy positions, underground shelters, maximum dispersion consistent with control, and countermeasures against enemy precision weaponry systems. These countermeasures could be directed at any or all of the primary components of the enemy's precision weaponry systems and could include such activities as electronic jamming, obscuring targets with smoke, and using deceptive measures.

TOW missile use in South Vietnam and in some of the Middle East combat operations suggest that artillery and Army aviation precision weaponry systems could be very effective in complementing Air Force tactical interdiction operations in the area immediately beyond the engaged battle. The Army's precision weaponry systems would be especially useful when the Air Force may be concentrating on strategic interdiction operations and the battle for control of the air. NATO's tactical interdiction program should be directed primarily at neutralizing the Warsaw Pact second echelon forces, reducing their combat effectiveness to the degree that they will be unable to decisively influence the battle. NATO forces should expect the Warsaw Pact to use their precision weaponry systems similarly, attempting to destroy NATO's reserve forces. For this reason, these forces should consist of highly mobile and well-dispersed tank-mechanized and airmobile units that employ all available protection means and defensive measures.

The enormous destruction of major combat systems in the Arab-Israeli conflict of October 1973 indicates that the primary military objective for the use of precision weaponry in the land battle for European defense should be to impose the greatest possible loss of armored vehicles, artillery, and aircraft on the enemy while minimizing the loss of friendly forces and allied territory. Thus, the primary military objective would involve an attrition process that exploits the precision weaponry capability to destroy the enemy's advantage in military strength. In organizing for combat operations to achieve this objective, the battle area should be analyzed in detail: the main and secondary routes which the enemy must use to accommodate his armor formations identified; primary and alternate armor-killing positions selected; barriers, sensor fields, and fire plans prepared; maneuver forces, STANO (Surveillance, Target Acquisition, Night Observation) assets, and combat support elements deployed.

The battle area itself would be divided into attrition zones, assigned to covering forces, the main force, and reserve forces, with indigenous territorial forces deployed throughout the battle area.

As the enemy attack commences, covering forces, deployed generally along the international border, would identify the main thrust of the attack, confirm the enemy's major avenues of approach, and begin the attrition of enemy forces. Covering forces would be designed to defeat tanks, mechanized and other forces, using existing weaponry and skills, integrated with current and proposed precision weaponry systems. In addition to the conduct of reconnaissance and tank-killer operations, covering forces would acquire and designate targets for precision weapons of supporting artillery and aircraft, and canalize enemy forces into the attrition zone occupied by the main force.

In a precision weaponry environment, the main force would utilize the doctrine of delay on successive positions, with the zone occupied by the main force divided into corresponding attrition belts, providing defense in depth. Small, highly mobile tank-killer units would occupy terrain along likely avenues of approach which provide the best observation of the enemy and effective use of precision weapons. The enemy would be brought under fire at optimum ranges within the first attrition belt occupied by the main force. Before the enemy can close, defending elements would move to the next series of preselected tank-killing positions in the next attrition belt. During the attrition process, local reserves would take every opportunity to gain an advantage through offensive action. The enemy would be forced to move through successive attrition belts until reduced to manageable size, until major reinforcements significantly decrease enemy-to-friendly combat power ratios, or until insufficient depth remains in the combat zone for the attrition process to continue. At this point, decisive combat would be accepted and the reserve forces would be committed in offensive action or, alternatively, a mobile or area defense would be executed.

Highly mobile reserve forces, consisting primarily of tank-mechanized task forces and airmobile units, would be located in dispersed areas at the rear of the main force attrition zone. Once the enemy's main thrust(s) has been neutralized by precision weaponry and other conventional fires, reserve forces would exploit the effects of firepower and complete the destruction of enemy forces or eject them from friendly territory.

In central Europe many small territorial defense units can be mobilized, trained, equipped, and dispersed rapidly throughout the covering force, main force, and reserve areas. Territorial forces could provide greater depth and more adequate coverage of the wide frontage to be defended by NATO, contributing to its overall defense capability. These units should be further organized into teams, equipped primarily with small arms and short-range antitank and air defense precision weaponry systems, and provided with adequate communications equipment for coordination among themselves and with active forces.

Close Air Force support requires detailed coordination to preclude interference between supported land forces (i.e., field artillery, air defense, and Army aviation) and supporting aircraft. A standoff capability with precision weaponry should permit strike aircraft to deliver effective ordnance while remaining outside the air space immediately above the land battle. This capability should simplify air space control and reduce the size of the supporting infrastructure. Mobile air defense systems would be provided on an area basis for units operating in the main force and reserve areas. The perimeter of the air defense coverage would be large enough to permit movement of main force units to successive delaying positions without leaving the defensive umbrella. These systems would be supplemented by increased numbers of air defense weapons in direct support of divisions, to provide area and point defense to maneuver units.

IMPLICATIONS

Precision weaponry will increase the war-fighting capability of NATO forces, thereby enhancing their credibility as a deterrent to aggression. Because NATO forces have been considered inadequate to contain a large-scale conventional attack for a significant period of time, deterrence of aggression has relied on the threat of punishment from the nuclear capabilities of the United States, the United Kingdom, and France. Deterrence by denial, the defensive capability which induces the potential aggressor to calculate his expectations of military success will be denied by countervailing military force, has been impractical for NATO because of the superior conventional military power of the Warsaw Pact. With precision weaponry, NATO forces will have a more balanced military capability and can achieve deterrence through the prospect of denial as well as the threat of punishment.

Coupling is the relationship between the conventional military forces of NATO and nuclear forces that together provide the total deterrent. Some NATO leaders may view the improved combat capability provided their conventional forces by precision weaponry as reducing the likelihood that nuclear weapons will be used in the defense of Europe. The effect, in their opinion, would be a degree of decoupling and a reduced level of deterrence. However, the logic of coupling can be argued to the extreme that the weaker NATO's conventional forces the stronger its deterrent posture, a logic which lacks credibility under the conditions of strategic parity between the United States and the Soviet Union. As one author notes: "A substantial conventional option does not reduce the effectiveness of nuclear deterrence: insofar as it creates the only circumstances in which the decision to use nuclear weapons becomes at all probable it considerably enhances it."[8]

NATO leaders have been seeking alternatives to matching the Warsaw Pact with a large investment in mass and depending on US nuclear weapons for the defense of Europe. Precision weaponry systems provide such an alternative, one that should increase the morale and will to resist among NATO leaders. The firepower effectiveness of precision weaponry might improve NATO's defensive capability to the degree that a conventional large-scale Warsaw Pact attack could be stopped near the international border. If not, the concepts for the use of precision weaponry provide for defense in depth, including an important role for NATO territorial forces. These forces would not be merely supporting standing forces, some of whom are foreigners, but would be defending their homelands. The psychological effects of renewed confidence and independence could be extremely important as a counter to the fears of US unilateral force reductions and the uncertainties of strategic parity between the United States and the Soviet Union.

It might appear that the improvement in firepower effectiveness provided by precision weaponry, with the resulting increase in total force efficiency, would permit the unilateral reduction of US or other NATO forces in Europe. To the contrary, precision weapons would compensate for the current inadequacy in the conventional direct defense option for NATO, and the unilateral reduction of NATO forces in Europe would detract from that capability. As to the Mutual and Balanced Force Reduction (MBFR) talks, precision weaponry systems are not likely to be a major consideration during the first phase of the meetings. During later phases, the talks could be influenced by the improved defense possibilities of precision weaponry. Indeed, residual force levels may be decided by the availability of precision weaponry systems, concepts for their use, and structuring alternatives.

One study of US Army formations in Europe, in relation to their ability to withstand a Soviet blitzkrieg type of attack, concludes that "they are not properly designed for a purely central European role, that they do not sufficiently emphasize the defensive nature of their task or have enough initial combat power."[9] The availability of precision weaponry systems to the enemy and the concepts for their use by NATO forces presented above reinforce this conclusion. The current NATO logistics system is too complex, vulnerable, and dependent on fixed installations to survive and function in an environment of precision weaponry. The structure of forces for combat will change because of the shift in combat roles: infantry, Army aviation, and field artillery can assume the antitank role formerly held by armor, and armor can be released for missions that require offensive shock effect. More air defense units will be needed, especially for direct defense of maneuvering forces. NATO territorial forces should be integrated with standing forces. As one author noted: "the absence of any serious plans for popular participation in Western European defense is one of the most curious characteristics of NATO planning."[10]

Precision weaponry systems are not cheap, but the cost of destroying a target by this means is far less than the use of many times the number of unguided munitions from many more delivery systems. Precision weaponry offers the possibility of significant reductions in the vast tonnages of ammunition now expended by the artillery. This reduction should result in savings of manpower, physical space requirements, and equipment devoted to moving, storing, and securing ammunition. Interdiction targets could be destroyed with precision weapons at far less cost than with unguided weapons in terms of collateral damage and attrition of friendly aircraft. Manpower savings should be possible too, as a direct result of force restructuring. For example, antitank firepower delivered by a four-man tank crew could be replaced by one or two infantrymen with a shoulder-fired or jeep-mounted precision antitank weapon. The cost of precision weaponry systems for NATO, and of a capability for territorial forces, should include consideration of tradeoffs in logistic savings and manpower economy, as well as comparative costs of imprecise systems.

The use of conventional precision weaponry will create a tactical environment similar to that expected in nuclear warfare. Forces will be dispersed to reduce their vulnerability to enemy precision weapons and to degrade the enemy's target acquisition capability. They will be highly mobile to evade detection, to control the larger areas of responsibility imposed by increased dispersion, and to exploit the effects of precision weaponry fires. Therefore, the problem of transition from the congested formations of conventional conflict to the dispersed posture considered necessary for nuclear warfare would be alleviated, and NATO forces would be prepared for the use of nuclear weapons. Conventional precision weaponry could delay the need for NATO to use nuclear weapons, perhaps reducing the numbers and types of nuclear weapons deployed to Europe that have been justified by some early-use scenarios. Conventional precision weaponry could assume some of the interdiction and antitank target missions now designated for nuclear weapons, further reducing the European stockpile. Nuclear weapon storage sites vulnerability to destruction by precision weaponry indicates a need to reexamine the location and distribution plans within NATO. Those implications of precision weaponry for the numbers and types of nuclear weapons deployed to Europe require detailed study, including the impact on deterrence if nuclear weapons are removed.

SUMMARY

The objective for the use of precision weaponry systems is to provide NATO forces with the increased firepower effectiveness needed to offset the advantage of Warsaw Pact forces in tanks, artillery, and aircraft. This objective focuses on an attrition process that exploits the accuracy of precision weaponry to destroy the enemy's military advantage, including fixed targets that support his military forces. These systems would be used in strategic and tactical interdiction programs, in the land battle, and in control of air space. Defense would be conducted in depth and would include the utilization of NATO territorial forces equipped with simple precision weaponry systems.

Precision weaponry is expected to enhance the deterrent posture of NATO forces by improving their conventional war-fighting capability, yet not detract from the effectiveness of nuclear deterrence. Its deployment should also increase the morale and will to resist among Western European leaders and restore their confidence in NATO's ability to oppose political coercion and military aggression. The concept for the use of these systems by NATO has implications for the current force structure, its design, and the roles of combat and combat support units. The cost effectiveness of these systems should be studied in relation to other weapon systems, and the impact of conventional precision weaponry systems on nuclear warfare requires further investigation. At present, however, precision weaponry appears to provide a viable alternative for the defense of Europe.

FOUR

Focus on the Middle East and Asia

12

Soviet Prospects in the Middle East

Robert L. Day

In the post-World World War II era, the USSR has pursued several established goals and policies in the Middle East. However, its approach and achievements, like those of the other powers, have often been marked by fluctuations and inconsistencies. The degree of intensity with which Soviet interests have been pursued has varied depending on the attitudes of the Kremlin leaders, and their perceptions of Soviet interests and threats to Moscow's security.[1] It now appears that the Kremlin, in rearranging priorities, will relegate the Middle East to a lesser position than held recently. This new approach reflects a changed military-strategic environment; a growing and worrisome Chinese threat; domestic agricultural and industrial problems; and developments in the Middle East itself, where the Soviets have had only limited success in transforming their military power into political influence. In short, the Soviet leaders believe that during the next decade they have more to gain from detente with the West than does the United States. This does not mean that the USSR has changed its long-range objectives or will withdraw from participation in Middle East affairs but, rather, will attempt to achieve its goals by shaping the environs and avoiding risks of war and military confrontation.

OBJECTIVES IN THE MIDDLE EAST

The most obvious reason for Soviet interest in the Middle East is its location. The proximity of the Middle East and its relevance to USSR defense is a major factor in Soviet decisionmaking. The most compelling Soviet interest in the area, therefore, involves the scope and depth of the strategic threat posed by any US forces in the region. Apart from strategic considerations, the lines of communication traversing this area and its role in energy supply to the West underline its importance to Moscow. However, while the Middle East is one of the most important foreign areas to the USSR, it is *not* vital; its products will be of marginal significance to the USSR for the foreseeable future, its military forces pose a negligible threat, and even its political roles are of only intermittent importance.

From the Soviet viewpoint, international relations are first characterized by the unrelenting struggle with the West and especially the United States for predominance. The primary objective is to achieve a shift of global balance of forces in favor of the Soviet Union and the state of this balance at any time determines Moscow's strategy choices. Consequently, Soviet Middle Eastern objectives must be treated not in isolation, but only within the context of broader global aims. For the foreseeable future, primary Soviet emphasis will be to reduce Western presence and influence, particularly that of the United States, while seeking to halt and reverse trends unfavorable to itself. Related Soviet objectives in the Middle East include:[2]

• Strengthening Soviet security by altering the military balance in Moscow's favor.

• Increasing Soviet access to Arab oil, and, more importantly, enhancing Soviet capacity to influence the political actions of oil producing countries concerning Western oil allocation.

• Barring or neutralizing Chinese influence in the Middle East.

In sum, the Soviets will continue to play an active role in the Middle East. Soviet objectives will include increasing economic, military, and political influence to whatever extent possible, without permitting tensions to develop into a military confrontation with the United States.

USSR PRESENCE IN THE MIDDLE EAST

On the whole, the most important objectives of post-World War II Soviet Middle East policy—those determined by security requirements and the political needs inherent in great power status—have been met. Western influence in the Middle East has not become a threat to the USSR. The Central Treaty Organization (CENTO) is a defensive alliance and no threat to the Soviet Union; and, Iran and Turkey enjoy relatively good relations with their northern neighbor while tacitly adhering to traditional, implacable hatred and suspicion of all things Russian. Support for US global initiatives is scarce in Middle East countries, and US policies in support of Israel have received less support than formerly from other North Atlantic Treaty Organization (NATO) nations. Fewer ports welcome vessels of the Sixth Fleet, and certain other strategic forces considered hostile by the Soviet Union have diminished in size. Since the early 1950's when only a few states in the Middle East maintained diplomatic or other relations with the USSR, Soviet involvement has grown across the entire spectrum of political, military, social, and cultural relations.

However, Soviet attempts at political or military domination of individual nations have generally been unsuccessful. There are no Communist regimes in the area, nor permanent Soviet military facilities, and Soviet influence on regional matters is consistently subordinated by local governments to their perceived self-interest. A sizeable Soviet military presence exists only in the shape of the Soviet Mediterranean Squadron, in the unpredictable and unstable Ba'ath regimes of Syria and Iraq, and to a lesser extent in Algeria, Somalia, and South Yemen. A number of advisors remain in Egypt, but this protracted relationship has been both costly and politically embarrassing. In other areas, including the economically important oil producing states, the Soviet military and political presence has not grown significantly.

Thus, the rewards of Soviet participation in Middle East affairs have been mixed, and not without economic and political costs. Military and economic aid has been expensive—more costly by comparison than equivalent amounts are to Western economies. Even before the Arab-Israeli war of October 1973, there were indications that the Soviet economy was in trouble. Additionally, the replacement of Arab losses in the October War cost the Soviet Union between $7 and $10 billion in equipment, plus sizeable transportation costs.[3] While some of this huge amount may have been offset by Arab cash, on the whole it is likely that this added economic strain will impede the desired expansion in the Soviet economy. Although foreign aid will surely continue, it is becoming a less popular cause with many Soviet leaders during periods of economic slowdown and domestic shortages. The Kremlin cannot afford to ignore the risk of political fallout from overextension in Middle East aid and support, particularly when there appear to be diminishing returns.

Moscow has also incurred political costs from Middle East ventures. The allure of an unknown alternative for Western capitalism and colonialism has disappeared with greater USSR participation in the Middle East. The Soviets are now a known factor and must compete on common ground with other countries for influence in the area. They too now face the necessity of making choices. Almost any significant improvement in relations with one regime tends to alienate others. Because of the numerous intraregional conflicts it will be more difficult in the future for the Soviet Union, or any great power, to uniformly increase its influence over the area.

The Arab-Israeli dispute, which yielded the Russians their most dramatic gains in the Middle East, also created their most serious problem. In October 1973, the Arab countries, supplied with Soviet weapons and tactics, for the first time fought a competent modern war. Yet, when the conflict ended, the United States held the upper hand for negotiating purposes. The Arabs now recognize that the Soviets have little leverage in assisting the Arab countries to achieve their goals. Only Israel can satisfy Arab demands for the return of their land, and it is Washington, not Moscow, that may be able to persuade Jerusalem to move from its current stand. Although disengagement negotiations enhanced US political prestige, the Soviets cannot afford to block diplomatic progress in the Middle East. To do so would not only raise tensions with the United States, but also run counter to the desires of most Arab states for a negotiated settlement.

There are several points worthy of speculation in regard to the lowered Soviet profile in some parts of the Middle East in support of the Arab cause versus Israel. The 1973 conflict proved that there was little "control" in the state of "controlled tension" which the Soviets previously have desired—it almost involved them in a military confrontation with the United States. Soviet influence in the Middle East benefited in the late 1950's and early 1960's from the growth of a spirit of nonalignment and decolonization throughout the less-developed countries of the world. During the past decade the Kremlin's entree to the Arab World has been the Arab-Israeli conflict which cast the United States as the primary ally and arms supplier of Israel. The Soviets have thus reaped the easy benefits to be gained in the Middle East, but any further penetration will require greater involvement in regional affairs with its attendant risks.

DETENTE AND THE MIDDLE EAST

The degree to which Soviet Middle East objectives are pursued will be largely conditioned by domestic factors and international considerations external to the Middle East. Certainly the Middle East conflict indicated the top Soviet priority is a constructive bilateral relationship with the United States. Therefore, the Soviets did not, and do not now, want to take any great risk in the Middle East which could produce either a military showdown or the destruction of the US-USSR relationship.

The reasons for the Soviets' desire for detente are many, and their long-standing views concerning Strategic Arms Limitation Talks (SALT) and the consolidation of Eastern Europe are well known. However, more recent developments concerning China and the Soviet domestic economy deserve brief comment.

It is an old axiom that no power can afford a two-front confrontation, let alone a two-front war. The Soviet Union, with its small population density and enormous geographic area, is no exception; any strategy devised by the Kremlin is necessarily divided between the Eastern and Western fronts. As relations between the Soviet Union and China have deteriorated, it is not surprising that the Kremlin has been busy mending its fences with its Western neighbors, Japan, and the United States. Moreover, fear of a rapprochement between the United States and China has caused Soviet officials to seek better relations with the United States. A major aim of Soviet diplomacy will be to dissuade the United States and Japan from moving too close to Peking.[4]

The Sino-Soviet conflict is deep and bitter, and the major problems that plague their relationship are not easily resolved. The replacement of the Peoples Republic of China (PRC) and USSR leaderships—which is likely in the next few years—may facilitate negotiations, but will not in itself result in a major improvement in relations. While the original dispute may have been primarily based on differing interpretations of Marxist-Leninist ideology, it has developed over the years to cover many issues. As China continues to emerge from her "cultural revolutionary cocoon," polemics with the Soviet Union have increased and the racial, nationalistic, and territorial aspects of the conflict have become more obvious. There is increasing evidence that Kremlin leaders view China as potentially their most urgent problem in the early 1980's.

The Soviet Union's creative talents and selective allocation of critical resources have enabled it to launch spaceships and develop sophisticated weaponry, but in establishing its priorities it has fallen well behind the United States in general development. The Soviet Union is a largely underdeveloped country which has proven, in spite of Mr. Khrushchev's prophecy of "catching and surpassing America," that it cannot compete effectively with the United States in productivity or modern mass technology. The objective of economic self-sufficiency has long since been modified, and Soviet leadership is looking to the West and Japan for the money and expertise to shore-up a sagging economy.[5] For a variety of reasons ranging from low productivity and technological inadequacies to bureaucratic overcentralization and mismanagement, the USSR has suffered spectacular setbacks in some sectors of its economy during the past few years.

Agricultural productivity has been a priority item for Soviet planners for years, yet farm productivity has been almost stagnant for six decades. Thirty-one percent of Soviet Russia's labor force is engaged in agriculture, compared to four percent in the United States.[6] During periods of low productivity the claim of bad weather is heard, but it is increasingly apparent that the shortages are primarily the consequence of gross mismanagement and inefficient farming methods. A hint of the vast problems facing this sector of the Soviet economy is the fact that 35 billion rubles (about $45 billion) is scheduled to be spent in 1976-80 to develop marginal lands in Western Siberia.[7]

In the industrial sector, expansion has lagged behind anticipated levels to such an extent that, in terms of growth rates, the Soviet Union has been falling behind some of its Eastern European satellites. Compared to the United States, it is hardly competitive. Industrial output of a Soviet worker is less than half of his American counterpart.[8] The Soviets have serious deficiencies in mass production techniques and in the production and utilization of highly sophisticated equipment. More importantly, the recovery of their natural resources located in the far North requires an amount of technology and capital investment which the USSR does not possess. The transfer of this technology from the United States and other industrial countries is a critical factor in revitalized economic growth. US exports to the USSR and Eastern Europe have grown from $384 million in 1971 to $1.8 billion in 1973.[9] Economic considerations will thus provide a powerful stimulus to political accommodations in the years immediately ahead.

SOVIET RISK-TAKING PROPENSITY

Soviet leaders remain basically conservative, traditional, cautious, and legalistic in their behavior and their aims. The tendency of the present leaders to create, exploit, and manipulate risks of crisis has declined. In the Middle East, the USSR has not been willing to court a major risk in pursuit of its objectives. Rather, Soviet policy has been characterized by a great deal of self-restraint.[10] Although willing to support the Arabs and to a lesser extent the Palestinian resistance's short-term political aims, Moscow has never espoused elimination of Israel or use of terrorism. In the supply of weapons, qualitative self-limitation has been a consistent element. Even when the possibility that much Soviet investment in Egypt might be at stake—after the expulsion of Soviet advisors in 1972 and after the 1973 conflict—these conditions were largely maintained. The Soviets have, however, pushed the qualitative limitations upward when their interests warranted it. This was true in the case of Syria after relations between the Soviets and Egypt had cooled in early 1974.

How important is Communist ideology in Soviet Middle Eastern policy? Manifestly, communism is not the basis of good relations with the governments of the area. There have never been any Middle East Communist regimes, and yet Moscow has enjoyed very close relations with a number of countries—at the very time indigenous Communist parties were being brutally suppressed. Indeed, the Soviet Union has consistently found local Communist parties almost as much a burden as an asset. Considerable effort has been required to reinforce Moscow's role in Communist leadership, arbitrate between competing leaders and groups, and ensure that Soviet goals are not supplanted on the local level by conflicting nationalist goals. Local Communist parties appeal to radicals. The Soviet Union, however, particularly in the Middle East, is *not* pursuing radical ends. Therefore, Soviet policy and the aspirations of Arab Communists are often at odds. Moreover, where relations with Arab states have become particularly close, the Soviet Union does not want to see a small revolutionary group, Communist or otherwise, damage these relationships. Certainly, then, in accepting or rejecting risks in the Middle East, the Soviet leaders will continue to be motivated first and foremost by security considerations and classic great power politics. Further, Soviet leadership will support those parties and individuals, regardless of political affiliation, when they believe it will advance their interests. Soviet desires that countries with which it is allied follow the "progressive" path, however, were brought home by the obvious Soviet concern expressed over Sadat's internal policies following his rapprochement with the United States in mid-1974.

Another important consideration in Soviet risk taking is its ability to project forces to the Middle East. Primary emphasis, not unlike that of the United States, has been accorded to strategic nuclear forces. Second priority has been given to the general purpose forces on the USSR's two principal fronts on the Eurasian continent. Present trends do not indicate a change in these priorities. This being so, the USSR's ability to conduct military operations in distant areas, against significant opposition, will remain severely limited—far less so than US capability. These limitations include serious deficiencies in airlift and sealift, lack of basing and overflight rights, and a lack of air-to-air refueling capability which would seriously limit close air support. The general configuration of both the Soviet navy and air force is defensively, rather than offensively, oriented. For example, the Soviet navy lacks a strike carrier force; its naval infantry is a relatively small force of 15,000; the size and number of amphibious assault ships has been expanded only moderately; and the armament of its destroyers and cruisers consists primarily of ship-to-ship missiles rather than heavy guns for amphibious assault preparations. Finally, the construction of two helicopter carriers and a small carrier for vertical take-off landing (VTOL) aircraft does change Soviet offensive capabilities, but it does not change, to any great degree, the emphasis towards an offensive weapons concept.[11]

Because of its preoccupation with China, domestic economic troubles, and Eastern Europe, Moscow is not likely to indulge in high risk Middle East adventurism. Present Soviet priority for achieving its Middle East objectives is subordinate to the gains presumably offered by global detente with the West. As has been pointed out, the Soviets do not have *vital* interests in the Middle East; however, they have obligations to a number of Middle East countries, they seek to extend Soviet influence and limit US influence in the area, and, perhaps most important, they have their prestige on the line.

INDIVIDUAL COUNTRY PROSPECTS

The Soviet gains in the Middle East have been primarily dependent upon military and economic assistance. These programs in turn have opened the way for the development of military positions, but the maintenance of these positions requires an adequate political foundation. The questions are: How solid is the foundation on which Soviet gains rest? What is the outlook for Moscow in the future?

Iran and Turkey. The benign neutrality of the northern tier countries, Iran and Turkey, has been, and remains, basic to the Soviet position in the Middle East. Their size, location, military alliances and bilateral arrangements with the West make each more important than any single Arab state. Following its hostile and aggressive policies during and immediately after World War II, the Soviet Union has emphasized cooperation and normalization of relations since the mid-1960's. In determining policy and commitments toward the nearby Arab states, effects upon relations with Turkey and Iran are important considerations to the Soviet leadership.[12]

The Soviets have been eager to abet the continuing Turkish drift away from rigid alliance with US policies. As the United States has decreased military and economic aid, the USSR and Turkey have exchanged numerous high-level visits, and have concluded several economic agreements. Nevertheless, there is no Soviet military aid program or military cooperation with Turkey. Moscow has no influence over Turkish foreign policy, which continues its solidarity with NATO, nor can Turkey's internal problems be easily used to Soviet advantage. For the foreseeable future the Soviets will continue to support an independent Turkey, and use every opportunity to encourage its greater independence from NATO and Washington.[13]

USSR policy toward Iran has been similar to its Turkish policy. After an aggressive period in the aftermath of World War II, Moscow has shown a great deal of flexibility in dealing with the Shah and his emerging policy of supernationalism. Although Iran has concluded a variety of long-term economic agreements with the USSR, and has purchased limited amounts of military equipment, Iran's primary arms supplier remains the United States. Iran's increasingly independent stance, military strength, and financial position help to insulate it from outside pressures, including both the USSR and the United States. The Shah is convinced that Iran must be the protector in the Persian Gulf—not only against the great powers, but also against Arab states, especially those radical states like Iraq. Under present conditions, Moscow is not likely to jeopardize its relations with Tehran by attempting to establish a large military presence in the Arab states of the Persian Gulf area.

Egypt. The Soviet Union has invested more resources, and has become more involved in Egypt than in any other country of the Middle East. Despite recent events including the Soviet exodus in 1972 and the political changes evolving after the 1973 conflict, Egypt remains a major voice in Arab councils, the leader in Arab-Israeli negotiations or conflict, and occupies a strategic position vis-a-vis the Mediterranean, the Suez Canal, and the Red Sea. In addition, Egypt is a major USSR trading partner, sending almost 40 percent of her exports to the Soviet Union as repayment for previous military and economic assistance.[14] For these reasons the Soviets will want to prevent a further deterioration in the relationship. In the near term, Soviet leaders will likely pursue a policy of low visibility, "treading water" until the political interaction between Egypt and Israel, under US sponsorship, gives a clearer indication of possibilities.

The mid-range prognosis for the USSR, however, does not appear good. Egypt, once the mainstay of Soviet influence in the Middle East, is not only pursuing greater ties with the West in foreign policy, but is also gradually modifying the Socialist economy that Soviet aid was intended to promote. President Sadat has removed pro-Soviet cabinet members from his government, encouraged Western capital investments, welcomed American mediation for the disengagement of Egyptian and Israeli forces, and accepted Western help instead of Soviet offers to assist in clearing the Suez Canal and rebuilding cities along its western bank.[15]

A complete breakdown of Soviet-Egyptian relations is precluded by the fact that the Egyptian armed forces, with their relatively sophisticated weapons systems, are completely dependent on the USSR for supply of major spare parts. But it would appear that the Soviets overplayed their hand in Egypt, and have achieved widespread resentment, particularly within the Egyptian military leadership, by their personal conduct and interpersonal relationships. The Egyptians know, however, that they need them.

There is a possibility that Egypt intends to pursue a policy of political settlement with Israel regardless of the success of the Geneva conference which will include most, if not all, of the Arab combatants of the 1973 conflict with Israel. Egypt, of course, is also under constraint from the desires of the other Arab states. If there should be an Egypt-Israel settlement, and that is no doubt looking pretty far ahead, the end of Egyptian participation in the Arab-Israeli dispute would reduce Egypt's dependence upon the USSR for military and political backing. The United States should encourage—but not participate in, at least initially—Egyptian arms purchases from the West. Such purchases would lessen Egyptian reliance on continued Soviet support, and provide our European allies with a partial offset to spiraling oil import costs.

Syria. Soviet-Syrian relations have developed broadly over the period since President Assad took power. Since the withdrawal of Soviet military advisors from Egypt in 1972, Syria has gained importance as an anchor of Soviet influence and will likely continue, along with Iraq, to be a major recipient of arms from the Soviet Union. Although Soviet naval units continue to use the Egyptian ports of Alexandria and Port Said, the Syrian ports of Latakia and Tartus provide a hedge against a possible future loss of Egyptian facilities.

Although the Soviets have stressed cultural exchanges and achieved some success in societal penetration, the controlling Ba'ath party is wary of Soviet motives and remains basically staunchly anti-Communist. Since coming to power in 1970, President Assad has moved away from the Marxist dogma of his immediate predecessors and underlined Syrian independence of the Soviet Union by turning down a Soviet "friendship and cooperation" treaty in May 1972. Since the beginning of the current Arab-Israeli negotiations, indications that the Syrians will also be more receptive to new Western economic and diplomatic initiatives have increased, although Syria's total dependence on Soviet arms and military expertise remains a limiting factor.

The Soviets have been anxious to move the Arab-Israeli negotiations from direct American sponsorship under Dr. Kissinger to joint Soviet-American sponsorship in the context of the Geneva peace conference. Although displeased at being shut out of Dr. Kissinger's shuttle diplomacy, Moscow had little leverage in these negotiations, and made no serious attempt to force its way into the disengagement talks concerning the troublesome cease-fire line in the Golan Heights. Contrary to much public opinion, the disengagement of forces in the Golan Heights was welcomed by the Soviet leaders. The talks have now returned to Geneva where once again the Soviets can assume a position of leadership and better exert influence and control upon their client states.

Should the disengagement talks have failed and Mr. Assad have continued his "war of attrition," longer term Soviet support may have become costly and run greater risks in relation to possible gains. This may also be true if the talks at Geneva reach a stalemate, and Mr. Assad should once again attempt to force a solution, and will be particularly true if the Israelis should eventually adhere to their previous policy of retaliation in force. While Syria is anxious to receive the greatest possible military and economic assistance from the USSR, it is not willing to accept more than a minimal amount of Soviet control or influence, including military presence. The Syrians have pursued this policy toward Russian assistance and related influence throughout the 1960-70 era, and there is no indication that greater political penetration will result from continuing economic and military support. However, Moscow will probably be willing to pay the necessary costs and accept the higher risks of maintaining a preeminent position in Syria. That position tends to demonstrate to Sadat and the Egyptian military the value of Soviet friendship; it checks Israel; it keeps the Soviets associated with Arab nationalism; and, finally, it underscores Soviet determination to remain and participate in eastern Mediterranean affairs—with or without Egypt.[16]

Iraq. Soviet activities in Iraq have been wide ranging since 1967, and good economic and political relations between Baghdad and Moscow are the result of Iraqi agreement with current Soviet Middle Eastern policies. Iraq is the one Arab country with a strong Communist party and where a Communist regime is a possibility. Politically and economically, the possible rewards to the Soviet Union of a successful political penetration of Iraq are relatively high. Such an achievement would maintain Soviet entree to the Gulf area with its vast oil resources, provide the advantages of good relations with an important oil producing nation, and furnish a foothold for a greater role in the area.

However, there are a number of problems, in addition to the basic instability of the Iraqi regime, which suggest that good Soviet-Iraqi relations will be short-lived. First, indications are that Iraq will increasingly look to the West for assistance in its desire to take advantage of the sellers' oil market. Much of Iraq's present production is consigned to the USSR and Eastern Europe for barter payments. To accumulate the sizeable hard currency reserves essential for internal development, Iraq must expand its production facilities and increase its petroleum exploration activities. Only the West can provide this form of needed aid; contracts for the construction of two new facilities have been awarded to a French and an American firm. In addition, Western oil companies have been invited to bid on new oil exploration proposals. A second major issue is the Kurdish problem.[17] For many years the Soviet Union found it politically useful to encourage Kurdish nationalism, and later gave refuge to Mustafa Barzani, the tough Kurdish leader. However, in recent years the USSR's support of self-determination for the Kurds took second place to cooperation with Baghdad. Renewed fighting has confronted the Soviet Union with the type of intraregional problems it is trying to avoid. This particular problem is all the more difficult since Iran is the main arms supplier of Barzani's 70,000-man army. It is not surprising, therefore, that the Soviets have attempted to downplay the recent fighting. Lastly, it would be difficult for the Soviets to use Iraq as a conduit for the extension of Soviet influence in the area. An excessive military presence would threaten present Soviet-Iranian relations, which Moscow has labored hard to achieve, and would antagonize major Arab states as well as Iran.[18]

Moscow has found that customers do not always make clients, and that presence does not provide control in the complexities of Iraqi politics. The Soviet Union can be expected to maintain firm limits on its support of Iraqi policies except those concerning the Arab-Israeli issue. However, the Soviets clearly need to demonstrate their support for Iraq's anti-Kurdish measures, despite the problems this raises in possible damage to relations between the Soviet Union and Iran.

Other Arab States. The Soviet leaders have learned a number of lessons in the last 15 years concerning radical and conservative Arab regimes and the supposed laws of revolutionary change. Some of the conservative regimes have showed unexpected strength and a surprising ability to adapt to changing conditions. A number of the radical regimes have floundered and been unable to turn social revolution theories into successful modern practice.[19] National interests, and personal rivalries and ambitions have all interfered with the textbook pattern of social and political development. In some states there has been no correlation between the revolutionary fervor and cooperation with the Soviet Union. Libya, with the most radical revolutionaries, continues to be a fervent anti-Communist regime. Libya, however, bought Soviet tanks and surface-to-air missiles in 1974, but restricts the number of Soviets who come into the country to give training and technical support.

Both Iraq-Kurdish policy and Libyan policy demonstrate Soviet compulsion to keep its hand in Middle East events, despite US diplomatic successes and the setbacks in Soviet-Egyptian relations. The Soviets will not apply a general approach to the area as a whole, but will adopt separate policies towards the individual states. They will likely pursue their goals in these states through the established regimes, and avoid the vagaries and conflicting interests of radical groups or individuals vying for power.

Soviet Middle East policy has always been an exercise in the "art of the possible." It is true today, and will probably remain so in the future. However, it will be increasingly difficult for the Soviets to pursue their policies with consistency and logic. The more the Soviet Union becomes a global power, the more it is faced with the same kinds of inconsistencies and the need for the same kinds of pragmatic solution of critical problems as the United States. The more active the Soviet role in the Middle East, the more it will be caught in the cross current of regional disputes. The USSR will have the problem of squaring worldwide interests with varying parochial interests of these very diverse countries. In the past, the Soviet military *modus operandi* in the Third World has been heavy-handed and unperceptive. For these reasons, the Soviets will remain vulnerable to the kind of reverses they have suffered in Sudan and, more recently, in Egypt.

USSR AND THE INDIAN OCEAN

The presence of Soviet warships in the Indian Ocean has attracted an amount of attention which their number would not appear to justify.[20] The presence of a Soviet naval squadron is cited by some as an indication of Moscow's determination to assert its influence in that part of the world. Others see it as a means to interfere with the flow of Arab and Iranian oil to Japan and the industrial nations of the West.[21] This overreaction tends to give greater credit to Soviet naval activity than it deserves. The political effect of this limited naval deployment is at best only a "showing of the flag" exercise, and provides tangible evidence that the USSR will play to the full its role as one of the world's two global powers. However, these vessels do not thus far threaten US interests in the Indian Ocean or the Persian Gulf.

The presence of the Soviet Navy in the Indian Ocean is not currently large enough—approximately 20 vessels, shuttled in and out from the Northern and Pacific fleets, about half combatants—or sufficiently supported to achieve far-reaching naval objectives.[22] In addition to establishing a Soviet presence, these vessels, according to the Soviet claims about them, have a defensive mission oriented to an anti-Polaris and anticarrier role, with an additional political objective of securing denuclearization of the Indian Ocean.[23] The Soviets, as a regional power, claim to have a strategic denial interest in the Indian Ocean. The Soviets have had difficulty in substantiating these claims, and many countries bordering the Indian Ocean have expressed doubts as to their legitimacy. The Soviet Navy also supports Soviet diplomatic initiatives in the nations of the Indian Ocean littoral. The reopening of the Suez Canal is not likely to increase significantly either Soviet merchant or naval power in the Indian Ocean. Soviet merchant trade with the Third World is less than 12 percent of total Soviet overseas trade—most of which is destined for areas which would not require passage through the Suez Canal if reopened—and the current Russian 5-year plan does not envisage a growth in its relative importance.[24] The major growth in Soviet trade east of Suez is with Japan. This traffic, which consists primarily of raw materials, will, for the most part, continue to move from the Urals and Eastern Russia to the Pacific coast by rail.[25]

A reopened Canal would permit easier linkup of Soviet naval forces as a peacetime advantage only. In a crisis, the Canal could be quickly closed, leaving the Soviet Union essentially cut off from major support facilities and vulnerable to counterattack by more powerful US fleets which dominate other routes into the area. Present air and ship support facilities to which the Soviet Union has access in the area are neither permanent nor significant enough to support major actions—and these facilities are extremely vulnerable to attack. Soviet naval forces are likely to be substantially increased only (1) if American forces sent into the Indian Ocean are significantly larger than their own, are dispatched more frequently, are permanently based, or include nuclear missile submarines; (2) to counter Chinese inroads into the area; and (3) in the event of a serious threat to India.

Other factors will also inhibit a conspicuous growth of Soviet military presence in the Indian Ocean area. Any Soviet action which threatened US and Western access to oil could not be divorced from the likelihood of a larger USSR-US confrontation spreading beyond the Middle East. Short of that, threats to oil access might upset not only Europe and Japan, but the Arab oil producing nations as well.

A large-scale military presence would also carry a high price in regard to the regional powers. Iran will strongly object to a substantial great power presence—US or USSR—in the Persian Gulf or northern Indian Ocean. Likewise, India will be unwilling to concede a major military role in the Indian Ocean to outside powers. In furtherance of this policy, the Indian leaders have denied the Soviets naval base rights. This policy is not likely to change except to counter a significant presence of another major power; specifically, China or the United States.

USSR AND OIL

Soviet economic objectives in the Middle East have not played a major role in the development of Soviet policy toward the area, nor does it appear that they will be of more influence in the future. The single exception is oil, and its importance lies largely in the opportunity it presents to undermine the economic position and influence of the Western nations and Japan.

The USSR ranks second only to the United States in both production and consumption of oil. It is expected to pass the United States in production in 1974, although it consumes only about one-third as much as the United States.[26] In the absence of large-scale foreign assistance in the exploitation of remote Siberian fields, crude production is expected to peak about 1980, and present consumption patterns would indicate that the USSR will have an export surplus through the early 1980's. Last year the Soviets exported about one million barrels per day (bpd) to Communist countries and another one million bpd to Western Europe. Oil exports are the Soviet's largest single source of hard currency, although the precipitous increase in the world market price of gold offers the USSR a trading alternative. By the late 1970's, any export surplus will likely go to the West for hard currency. The Soviets have already advised Eastern Europe to seek more oil from other sources.[27] In recent years the Soviet Union itself has used Middle East oil to earn foreign exchange credits and to meet its commitments to Communist countries. This oil was primarily obtained from Egypt, Algeria, and Iraq on a barter basis, and the Soviets will undoubtedly continue to take advantage of such opportunities in the future.

Expanding Soviet political influence in the Middle East has not been accompanied by any significant Soviet role in oil matters. Compelling practical consideration will continue to limit such Soviet participation, including: the nationalistic attitudes of the oil producing states; the difficulty of marketing vast quantities of oil; inadequacies in Soviet technology; and a severely limited tanker fleet—its 185 small tankers represent only 2.5 percent of the world tonnage.[28] More importantly, the USSR cannot absorb nor pay for substantial quantities of Arab oil. Though Eastern European countries of the Soviet bloc will require increasing amounts of oil, the quantity involved is a small fraction of that supplied to Western Europe and Japan. The Arabs, therefore, see little economic advantage in substituting Soviet middlemen for Americans or Europeans.

A key factor through 1985 will be the significantly greater dependence of the United States, Western Europe, and Japan on oil imports as compared with the Soviet Union. It would be entirely inconsistent with past Soviet behavior not to attempt to exploit such a favorable situation. The question facing Soviet leaders is how best to take advantage of the growing confrontation concerning the control and price of oil between the Middle Eastern and Western states. The Soviets will proceed cautiously, as there are a number of factors which will constrain their policy alternatives. First, the major oil producing nations are outside the present Soviet sphere of influence; second, for reasons already discussed, the Soviet Union will not be able to offer itself as a principal broker for Arab oil sales; and, last, any new Soviet initiatives on this extremely sensitive issue would not be welcomed by either the Arab states or the West. To push an oil denial policy to extreme lengths would involve risks the Soviets are probably not willing to undertake. Therefore, for the time being, new initiatives are not likely, and the Soviets will follow the lead of the producer countries, while trying to influence critical politico-economic decisions in those countries through traditional means.

The main thrust of Soviet policy will be to encourage the producer countries to limit their production, use oil as a political weapon, and, more importantly, to gain complete independence in their oil resources by reducing or eliminating the role of Western oil companies. Unfortunately, this latter policy will find increasing support among the major oil consuming nations. In the wake of the oil embargo, Japan and the Western European nations have been assiduously negotiating bilateral arrangements with the producer countries for future oil supplies. These nations, dependent on US oil companies as their major source of supply, are attempting to divorce themselves from US policy which they consider pro-Israel; a policy they do not support, nor wish to suffer for. They fear that renewed hostilities, or a breakdown in Arab-Israeli negotiations, would result in a new embargo, either of a general nature or one directed solely at the United States. They worry that US oil companies, which produce 50 percent of Middle East oil, would divert oil to the United States at their expense. In addition, they can foresee substantial dollar savings—perhaps more imagined than real—by eliminating the US oil "middleman" through country-to-country negotiations. Elimination of the Western oil companies would also remove the symbol of capitalism and undermine US influence with the more conservative Arab oil producers in the area. Some observers contend that favorable relations with these states have been maintained over the years as much through the efforts of US oil companies as American diplomacy. Should nation-to-nation agreements become the norm, it will become much easier and involve less risk for the Soviets to isolate and pressure individual producer or consumer nations than to attempt such tactics against US oil companies.

The Soviet Union will also encourage the producer countries to maintain high crude oil prices. High prices benefit Soviet sales of oil to the West, which constitute 6 percent of Western Europe's needs. In addition, present price levels will seriously weaken the economies of the Western powers, giving rise to divisions and growing competition within the Western community. Already the prospects of serious balance of payments deficits are causing the British and other Europeans to consider reductions in their defense budgets.

The above Soviet interests are essentially compatible with the self-conceived policies of the oil producing countries themselves, and run little risk of drawing the Soviet Union into a military confrontation with the West. But if successful, these Soviet supported actions will have effectively neutralized predominant Western influence in Middle East oil matters—with minimum peril to Moscow of serious impairment of its structure of detente with Washington.

SUMMARY

Although the USSR has achieved superpower status because of nuclear parity with the United States, it is finding it difficult to translate military power into political influence. While Soviet political influence in the Middle East has increased, it is narrowly based, and rests more on conditions arising from the Arab-Israeli dispute than on any cultural or ideological affinity with the Arabs. The Soviets have generally supported regimes which have been unsuccessful in war and unstable in peace—they have been singularly unsuccessful in the political domination of a single Arab state. The volatility and unpredictability of their Arab clients portend additional difficulties for the USSR in the future.

The Middle East has, in relative terms, lost much of its importance to the Soviet Union. The Kremlin is increasingly concerned with its eastern neighbor, China—a country stronger now than anytime in the last three centuries. At home, the USSR has suffered setbacks in all sectors of its economy—the solutions to which require western, particularly American, capital and technology. In the Middle East the USSR has achieved certain limited objectives. Further gains can only be achieved if the Soviets are willing to take sides, alienating and prejudicing other regional interests and powers. The current Arab-Israeli negotiations, under US leadership, threaten to further erode Soviet influence in the area. For all these reasons, the Kremlin is not likely, in the near future, to resurrect its former "activist" policy in the Middle East; Mr. Brezhnev is not expected to jeopardize detente with Washington for the sake of nonvital Middle East objectives. This does not mean that the USSR will withdraw from participation in Middle East affairs, but rather she can be expected to play a more passive role—exploiting low-risk opportunities while avoiding high-risk endeavors. Today, Soviet influence in the Middle East represents but a minor threat to US and Western interests. To the extent US interests may be threatened, the danger is not likely to derive from Soviet policy and influence, bur rather from Arab reaction to US policy in the area.

13

A New Look at Suez

Kenneth E. Roberts

The Suez Canal has long preoccupied strategic planners, and now, after seven years of disuse, its role in world affairs must be reconsidered. Closed to world shipping since June 6, 1967, it appears likely that the Canal will soon be reopened. This development is the result of successful Egyptian-Israeli negotiations in which the United States played a major role. Egypt appears eager to bring unprecedented prosperity to the Canal and the deserted cities along its banks. After restoration, a multimillion dollar decision regarding widening and deepening the waterway must be made. These projects offer the United States an opportunity to participate in an important social and industrial revolution in the Third World and a chance to make Arab-Israeli peace more lasting.

Just as the Canal's closing affected nations differently, so will its reopening. This action itself will not suddenly alter superpower relationships and the Canal will probably·never completely regain the same global importance it once held. Long-term US interests may be affected in more subtle ways, however, and the reopening will certainly play a significant role in future US-Middle East relationships. These issues are important because US interests will continue to expand in the region during the next 25 years.

The purpose of this analysis is to examine the international economic, political, and strategic implications of a reopened and enlarged Suez Canal. Issues to be considered include a Soviet naval buildup in the Indian Ocean; future Arab-Israeli confrontations; altered international trade patterns; world petroleum requirements; the growth of Egypt as a moderate leader in the Arab world and as a key nation in US foreign policy; and, finally, the role of the Third World, particularly Africa and the Middle East, in future balances of power and as resource bases for the future. Analysis will be oriented toward the relationship of these factors to US security requirements.

THE PENDULUM OF HISTORY

The first of many navigable canals linking the Red Sea, the Nile, and the Mediterranean was constructed in Egypt more than 4,000 years ago. The strategic importance of these predecessors of the Suez, the Canal itself, and the region has varied as the attention of the world's great powers shifted alternately from a Mediterranean to an Atlantic focus. Trade routes between the Mediterranean and the Far East crossed in Egypt during the Age of Rome and throughout the Middle Ages. The Turkish capture of Constantinople in 1453 and the Portuguese discovery of a new route to India via the Cape of Good Hope in 1498, however, shifted the strategic balance away from the Mediterranean to the Atlantic.

Another shift occurred with the rise of industrialization when Western powers expanded their influence in search of resources and markets. As competition among them increased, a direct sea route linking Europe with the Far East became more appealing. Europe sought such a route to offset the advantage Britain enjoyed in her trade with the East via the Cape of Good Hope.

Ferdinand de Lesseps gained approval for the project from his friend, Mohammed Said, the Viceroy of Egypt, and in January 1856, a formal 99-year concession was granted to the Suez Canal Company under his direction. Serious construction of the current 101-mile, sea level canal was begun in 1866 following several years of British obstructionism. Twenty countries eventually financed the undertaking, although France contributed more than half and Egypt herself nearly a third of the cost. At a ceremonial opening of the Canal on November 16, 1869, all major nations of Europe were represented, many by reigning monarchs and heads of state. Once again Suez was regarded as the center of the world.

The "international status" of the Canal was guaranteed in 1888 by the Convention of Constantinople, and surprisingly the system functioned well until the First and Second World Wars when the waterway was denied to the enemies of Britain. Until that time it had remained in London's interest to keep Suez open. Britain's long, thin line of communications stretching from Gibraltar to India made Egypt the focus of her lifeline to the East.

Between the two world wars, Britain's position in the region was greatly enhanced by possession of Palestine, friendship with Jordan, influence throughout the Arabian peninsula and Iran, and bases in Iraq. Suez therefore became less important strategically. After the Second World War, however, Britain's favored position in Arabia was lost, and Suez was once again regarded vital. Andre Siegfried, writing in *Foreign Affairs* in July 1953, stated that:

> As an intercontinental crossroad Suez is so important that the great World Powers must, of necessity, either establish a foothold in it or at least make sure of its availability to them. If I know who was to be its master 10 or 25 years from now, then I should know who has mastery of the whole world as well.[1]

In more recent times the Atlantic-Cape route has regained some of its former favor because of development of supertankers; vulnerability of the Suez Canal to modern weapons; and because nationalization and subsequent closings of the Canal in 1956 and 1967 underscored its political vulnerability.

Suez handled one-sixth of the world's commerce and Egypt was increasingly coming under Soviet influence when the Canal was last closed. No peaceful solution to Arab-Israeli hostilities was apparent. The world environment has changed greatly since 1967, however. The Vietnam War has ended, minimizing one of Russia's primary excuses for seeking easier access through the Canal, and peace appears at least possible between the Arabs and Israelis. The international oil companies have successfully rerouted their tanker fleets around the Cape of Good Hope. Western dependence on Middle East oil has been recognized and British withdrawal east of Suez has been completed. US and Soviet interests in the Middle East-Indian Ocean area have increased, and US-Egyptian relations have improved dramatically. Egypt has announced that henceforth it will not rely on the USSR as the source for all its modern arms and has hinted that other nations might be granted naval facilities, previously reserved for the Soviet navy, in

Egyptian ports. President Nixon even made a symbolic trip to Cairo to dramatize this shift in policy.

The attention of US military strategists must therefore once again shift from the Atlantic to the Mediterranean. Will Egypt, if not the Canal itself, be the hinge upon which future global balances of power will rest? Who will benefit most from the Canal's reopening, and how? As A. T. Mahan noted in 1900, ". . . nothing, not the sanding up of the Canal itself, can change the natural conditions which make Egypt the strategic center of the chief highway between the East and the West. "2 If Africa and the Middle East become the world's resource base for the future, Egypt may regain much importance as a crossroads. The final answers require a thorough strategic analysis involving careful consideration of many different factors.

MILITARY IMPLICATIONS

The two most important US strategic considerations in the Middle East-Indian Ocean area are prevention of the region's dominance by the Soviet Union or any other single power and continued access to Persian Gulf oil for the United States, Western Europe, and Japan. The development of supertankers and alternate routes has reduced the vital strategic importance of Suez for the United States and especially for Western Europe. Because of its location, however, the Canal does allow rapid, easy access for both merchant and naval shipping between the Mediterranean and the Red Sea/Indian Ocean.

Despite the widely held belief, strategic benefits of a reopened Suez Canal do not necessarily favor the Soviet Union more than the United States. The Soviet Black Sea and Mediterranean fleets could, of course, more rapidly reinforce their Indian Ocean capabilities in times of crisis, but such deployments must be based on assurance that the Canal will not be blocked. Closure may be undertaken either officially by Egypt, or by any other nation using the waterway by scuttling a ship in mid-canal or by mining the channel. Soviet strategists would probably not gamble on deploying a substantial portion of their naval units at the wrong end of a blocked canal. The danger was perceived as early as 1890, when Sir Charles Dilke wrote:

> The Canal, considered as a means of communication in time of war, is as delicate as a thread of a spider's web. A ship or two sunk in it, two or three charges of dynamite exploded in the portion nearest to the Gulf of Suez, a few torpedoes laid down in the night—none of these difficult matters to

213

manage . . . would close the passage against ships for days or weeks, and
would prevent the transport by the Mediterranean of anything except
troops without baggage.[3]

The reopening of Suez will probably not precipitate a Soviet naval
escalation, although use of the Canal will increase Soviet flexibility. The
USSR developed a presence in the Indian Ocean after the Canal was
closed and while Egyptian-Soviet relations were still relatively cordial.
Closure has not inhibited Moscow from increasing its naval presence in
the Indian Ocean, although that presence has been maintained at
greater cost and inconvenience than using Suez would have required.

The Soviet Indian Ocean presence supports Moscow's desire to prove
its great power status. The force is primarily political and defensive—a
visible reminder that the Soviet Union can protect its interests in the
area. Increased Soviet naval capabilities would most likely not increase
Moscow's prestige and political influence in the littoral states, however.
During the 1971 Indo-Pakistani hostilities, the United States dispatched
a naval force off East Pakistan, but important Soviet gains resulted
from shrewd diplomatic maneuvering rather than use of any military
presence around the subcontinent.

A more convenient passageway from the Black Sea naval bases to the
Indian Ocean may even minimize Soviet naval expansion. Easier access
would reduce the need and may thus minimize the inclination for a
large permanent fleet. The distance from the Black Sea through the
Mediterranean to the Cape of Good Hope is about 11,000 miles,
compared to approximately 2,200 miles through the Suez Canal. At
present, the Soviet Indian Ocean presence is supported from the Pacific
fleet at Vladivostok.

The Suez Canal, at its prewar depth, can be used by US naval vessels
of cruiser size or smaller. If Egypt chooses to deepen the Canal to
handle 250,000 dead weight ton (dwt) oil tankers, even US aircraft
carriers would be able to use the waterway. This development of the
Canal would probably cost $1 billion, and could be achieved in 5 to 10
years. Many US vessels will enjoy greater mobility by being able to use
a reopened Canal even at its current depth, however.

The 1973 Middle East War proved that the Suez Canal is not the
important military barrier both Israel and Egypt had assumed. Egyptian
commando units crossed the Canal in a number of locations and
launched a surprise attack. After a cease-fire had been signed, units of
each force were awkwardly positioned on both sides of the Canal.

Thus, the Canal's vulnerability to modern weapons and political pressures underline its limited military importance and lessen its impact on strategic balances and capabilities. Since 1967, both superpowers have become accustomed to doing without it. Today, the Canal is no longer anyone's lifeline to anything, but merely a convenience for all who use it. Control of the geographic nexus at which Suez is located is strategically much more important than the operation of the Canal itself. From this continental hinge, military operations in North and East Africa, the Mediterranean, the Near East, and the Arabian Peninsula may be easily initiated or opposed.

POLITICAL IMPLICATIONS

The importance of a reopened Suez Canal for Middle East peace prospects will transcend whatever strategic gains the Soviets may achieve. Arab-Israeli accommodation would lessen both Arab requirements for Soviet military support and the danger of a great power confrontation in the Middle East.

Political factors have historically played a greater role than economic factors in determining the use of Suez by both the Arabs and Israelis. These tactics have failed for the Arabs since the Canal's primary users have adjusted to alternate routes; denial of oil has proven to be a much more effective foreign policy weapon. The Israeli military position on the Canal's east bank was a key bargaining point after the 1967 War. Israeli shipping had been restricted from Suez for 24 years, so little was to be gained by its reopening. Israel unsuccessfully sought Western support for her position on "secure borders" in exchange for progress toward reopening the waterway. With the Canal open, however, Israel will probably be subjected to less political pressure from Western nations. Although it is too early to tell, Israeli withdrawal may alleviate some of the criticism of Israel's intransigence as well as assure broader sympathy for other Israeli territorial claims.

The reopening will yield important political gains for Egypt also by increasing her position in Afro-Asian power considerations. Egyptian naval vessels will enjoy the same advantages as US and Soviet ships in exploiting the Mediterranean-Red Sea link for political purposes. A resurgent Egypt could send forces into the Indian Ocean to impress the smaller Arab emirates or the coastal states of East Africa. This may increase the danger of regional naval competition among Iran, Egypt, and, possibly, Saudi Arabia.

Egypt has received compensatory payments amounting to $235 million yearly since 1967 from Libya, Saudi Arabia, and Kuwait.

Although Libya has already ceased these payments for political reasons, conservative Saudi and Kuwaiti influence over Egyptian foreign policy will be lessened after the Canal is reopened and these payments stop. Egypt may thus be more inclined to expand her influence on the Arabian Peninsula and in the Gulf area. Substantial Saudi, Kuwaiti, and Iranian investment in redevelopment and other commercial projects in Egypt will mitigate this tendency, however.

President Sadat's political power will be greatly enhanced by a reopening of the Suez Canal. The return of one million Egyptians to the cities along its banks from which they were evacuated with the outbreak of the October War will help solve a serious political problem for Sadat and placate a potentially revolutionary force within the country. Especially if current development plans succeed, Egypt will gain substantial political prestige throughout the world. Her position as leader of the Arabs will gain credibility, and this time, under Sadat's leadership, that guidance is likely to encourage more moderate, pro-Western values than were espoused by Nasser.

If the Canal is reopened before a wider settlement to Arab-Israeli disputes is accomplished, however, independent of the wishes of other Arab states, Egypt may lose political prestige and would probably even be branded as a traitor by the more radical Middle East states such as Iraq, Syria, Libya, and Algeria. These developments would most likely force an even closer Egyptian identification with the West, but the resulting interregional rivalry and discord would not serve long-term US interests. Top Egyptian officials emphasize that the reopening and redevelopment of the Canal will not stop further conflicts if Israel refuses to withdraw from all Arab territory occupied in 1967, but such warnings are probably intended more for Arab than Israeli audiences.

Any Soviet political benefits will result from an increased presence attributable to the ease with which temporary deployments can be accomplished through the Suez Canal. Since most Arab states are suspicious of Soviet motives, real political gains are not likely to be significant. Moscow's attempts to persuade the Arab oil producers to continue their boycotts against the United States indicate that the Soviets also view denial of oil as a more powerful political weapon than use of the Canal.

An important aspect of Soviet strategy which would benefit, however, is the desire to isolate or "contain" Communist China. Soviet activity in Taiwan, Mongolia, Afghanistan, India, North

Vietnam, and North Korea indicates that Moscow is using the same politico-military tactics Dulles used against the Soviet Union in the early days of the Cold War.[4] Indications that the United States may be taking sides or showing a preference between the USSR and China is contrary to US policy.

The reopening of the Canal as a result of negotiations under US sponsorship will greatly enhance US prestige. Traditional US allies such as Jordan and Tunisia will cease to be isolated among their Arab neighbors since it will no longer be so fashionable to be anti-American. Reduced dependence on commercial ports in South Africa and on the South African Navy will increase US political flexibility in Africa.

European influence may be more easily extended into the region with the Canal open. This would serve US interests by: (1) enabling Arab leaders to reduce reliance on either the United States or the USSR, thus lessening the danger of great power confrontation, (2) forcing Soviet moderation as long as detente with Western Europe and Japan retains its current importance, (3) enabling the United States to concentrate more effectively on those areas of the Middle East in which American interests are strongest, (4) bolstering Atlantic unity by demonstrating the possibility of the coexistence of differing economic policies within a coordinated politico-military strategy, (5) restoring mutually beneficial European educational, economic, and cultural ties with Middle East nations, and (6) increasing European and Japanese economic and military security.

US support for reopening Suez will strengthen a traditional policy favoring freedom of the seas. Additional respect and credibility will be gained for US rights and positions in free passage disputes elsewhere. To act otherwise would display a significant inconsistency in US foreign policy.

ECONOMIC IMPLICATIONS

The Cape route has been far more expensive for world shipping than the short transit through Suez would have been. Two related questions emerge: (1) What has been the cost of rerouting and who has borne it, and (2) what are the country-by-country economic implications of a reopened Canal? Political and technological developments since 1967 make these questions very difficult to answer.

In 1966, during the last full year of operation, 242 million metric tons of cargo passed through the Canal in 21,250 vessels—more than double the traffic in 1955. Due to oil, which accounted for 75 percent of the Canal's traffic, there were great imbalances between northbound (83 percent) and southbound (17 percent) cargoes. Other important northbound cargoes, however, included bulk ores (e.g., iron and manganese from India), grain from Australia, and fiber crops. Southbound cargoes included fertilizers, cereals and foodstuffs, metals, and manufactured goods. Surprisingly, the trade of India, Pakistan, and Sri Lanka depended most on the Canal. Normally, 40 percent of their trade would transit the Canal, compared with 20 percent for Malaysia, Australia, and Great Britain.[5]

Though estimates vary, the total average cost of the Canal's closure can be put at roughly $1 billion per year since 1967. Four factors account for most of the costs:[6]

• Routes throughout the world underwent increases in tanker charter rates. Spot shortages of ships contributed to a scramble and consumers had to accept higher prices.

• For those tankers able to transit the Canal, either fully loaded or in ballast, the greater distance between Europe and the Persian Gulf via the Cape route has resulted in greater costs.

• The price of North African and Mediterranean crude increased because of its accessibility in relationship to Gulf oil.

• General cargo (non-oil) has been transported via the longer route by freighter between Europe and Asia or Australia. Only crude oil can be transported in quantities large enough to make the Cape route preferable.

Although Europe has borne the largest financial burden, the poorer nations of the developing world have probably suffered most from the Canal's disuse. India and Pakistan, for example, have paid an extra 17.5 percent surcharge on transport from Northern Europe or the United States. The surcharge for the Arabian/Persian Gulf was set at about 25 percent; for the Red Sea area between 45 and 50 percent; and for East Africa, 15 percent.[7]

When the Suez Canal is reopened, sailing distances and times will decrease sharply for many cargoes, surcharges will be abolished, freight costs will be lowered, and a ship surplus will be created. Only about one-fifth of the world's petroleum transport can be expected to be diverted back to Suez because of the shift to supertankers—a substantial decrease from 75 percent when the Canal closed. The amount of dry cargo passing through the Canal will probably increase significantly over 1966, however, making the overall drop in traffic less dramatic.

In 1966 the United States ranked fourth in total transiting commodities—after Italy, Great Britain, and France—and US usage was increasing at a rate of about 17 percent a year.[8] American consumers and exporters will benefit generally from the worldwide reduction in shipping rates, although American manufacturers may face greater competition from Japanese goods in European markets. Recently the American President Lines suspended its round-the-world cargo service because of "steadily increasing costs attributed to the Suez shutdown."[9] In general, commercial benefits will outweigh liabilities for the United States, though benefits will be marginal in the near term.

In the short term, Europe will gain most commercially from the Canal's reopening, though the country-to-country effects will vary. European consumers will generally benefit from cheaper raw materials and foodstuffs (e.g., ores, wheat, and cotton). Most of Europe's Persian Gulf oil will still be transported in supertankers via the Cape, but empty tankers returning through Suez will bring some rate benefits. The usage of Suez for general cargo will create changes in European shipping patterns. Mediterranean ports in Yugoslavia, Greece, Italy, France, and Spain will benefit at the expense of Atlantic ports in Portugal, France, and the Low Countries.

The economic impact of the closure on the Soviet Union and Eastern Europe, except for Yugoslavia, has not been significant. In 1966 the Soviet share of the Suez traffic was no more than four to five percent, and an even smaller amount of total tonnage.[10] Most of that trade was oil. Since then, exchange deals have been worked out with several international oil companies for swapping Soviet oil in the Black Sea for Gulf crude so that the USSR could meet the demands of her Asian customers. With the Canal open, eventual development of Soviet Siberian reserves will encourage the USSR to develop petroleum markets in North America and the Far East while utilizing more Middle East oil in her European industrial cities. This potential Soviet market would probably receive Middle East oil via pipelines rather than through Suez, however. A large percentage of the Soviet Union's other trade would not flow through Suez even with the Canal open.

The Soviet Union has legitimate strategic interests in the Indian Ocean area. As a result of Sino-Soviet differences, the USSR may rely increasingly on southern sea links to its Pacific provinces which would be greatly facilitated by a reopening of the Suez Canal. Because of the vulnerability of the Trans-Siberian Railway to Chinese military forces along the Sino-Soviet border, the Suez Canal-Indian Ocean route provides an important transit alternative in time of war.

Egypt's suffering as a result of closing Suez is difficult to establish because all direct losses have been offset by the Khartoum aid payments from Libya, Saudi Arabia, and Kuwait. There have been other important losses due to reduced earnings in foreign exchange, Egyptian merchant shipping, crude oil exports from the Gulf of Suez, and industries related to the transit trade. The big gains for Egypt will be long-term and may be substantial once the costs of reopening and redevelopment have been paid. Positive acts to encourage private investment in Egypt may launch that nation into a new era of development which will greatly increase her international power and prestige.

Israel has never had full access to the Suez Canal, so its closing had no adverse economic effects. Once the Canal is opened to Israeli shipping some commercial benefits will result, but these will be minimal since Israel can move her products for export to the Far East overland to the Gulf of Aqaba almost as easily as through Suez. The Filat-to-Ashod pipeline will not be greatly affected by a reopening until the Canal is substantially expanded, but Israel's withdrawal from Sinai will mean the loss of substantial revenues from the oil fields.

South Africa will lose some transit-related trade, but large oil tankers will continue to bunker and provision there. Several East African ports will regain traffic and the region's economy will be greatly stimulated. Transport costs for Ethiopian exports and imports, for example, were increased 35 to 50 percent subsequent to the Canal's closure. These costs resulted in reduced earnings on coffee, which accounts for 60 percent of total Ethiopian exports.[11]

India, Pakistan, Bangladesh, and Sri Lanka likewise will quickly notice significant trade benefits, even though none of these nations imports oil or other vital raw materials through Suez. Soviet economic and military aid to East Africa and South Asia will be facilitated by the reopening, but so will potential American and European assistance. Greater economic independence may lead to greater political independence among the nations of this region.

Japan will lose some shipping and shipbuilding income, but lower rates will probably create greater European markets for Japanese exports. European goods, however, will become more competitive with Japanese products in the Persian Gulf and South Asia. Chinese and Australian trade with Europe will also be facilitated.

In summary, world trade will get a significant boost from a reopening of the Suez Canal. Although trade patterns for oil will be affected little until Suez is enlarged, European and Japanese export markets will be expanded and the economies of the Third World will be stimulated. Only some shipbuilding companies stand to lose in the short-term, but increased trade may eventually minimize those deficits.

RECONSTRUCTION AND REDEVELOPMENT

We are working on the premise of peace with Israel, whether we get peace now or later.[12]

Osman Ahmed Osman,
Egyptian Minister of Redevelopment

Egypt is thinking big in planning its shift to a peacetime economy, whether peace with Israel comes now or later. The task will be enormous. Egypt is heavily in debt, particularly to the Soviet Union, for foreign loans and arms purchases. Eighty percent of the buildings in Suez City were damaged beyond repair or totally destroyed prior to or during the October 1973 War. In Ismailia and Port Said the destruction was even greater, and there was almost total destruction in Qantara.

The clearance and redevelopment will be coordinated by Mashour Ahmed Mashour, an ex-army officer and graduate engineer who has been chairman of the Suez Canal Authority since 1965. The real power, however, will be held by Minister for Reconstruction Osman Ahmed Osman, one of the principal builders of Egypt's Aswan High Dam and head of Egypt's largest building firm, Arab Contractors. Osman has the responsibility of rebuilding the devastated Canal Zone cities. If his plans are successful, Port Said and Suez City will become ultramodern free ports like Hong Kong or Singapore. Raw materials would enter the zones and finished products would leave with little or no taxation. Cheap labor and utilities and a good climate will make these areas extremely attractive if the political situation can be defused. According to Osman,

In each town we are going to set aside an area for each friendly nation to develop as it sees fit, with small industries, pilot agriculture, and tourist projects. Each area will carry that country's name. We have already had American offers to take part. You can be sure we will set aside a large zone for the United States.[13]

A 100-mile complex will be created with three major cities, five new or enlarged ports, two new international airports—all tied together by new superhighways, rail lines, and five tunnels under the Canal itself. Eventually 600,000 acres of land are to be made productive by bringing irrigation water from the Nile.

The Egyptians have invited offers from 18 nations to assist in clearing and reconstruction in the Canal Zone, but Soviet participation has not been encouraged.[14] Cost of the reopening and restoration of the Canal will probably range between $400-$500 million. When reopened, it will permit the passage of ships of 65,000 tons. Plans to deepen the Canal to accommodate ships up to 150,000 tons (250,000 tons in ballast) would take at least three more years. A third stage, allowing passage of ships of between 270,000 and 300,000 tons fully loaded, is also planned, but will require 7 to 8 years and cost more than $1 billion. Such deepening will be extremely difficult since the banks of the Canal are sand and substantial widening will be necessary. All these schemes will require large amounts of foreign financing.

Today, Egypt seems anxious for an economic miracle, and those able to accomplish it seem willing to accommodate. Sadat is determined to make Egypt a modern industrial state. The economic and political implications of that decision are very important, both for the West and the conservative Arab states who will be assisting Egypt in her new adventures. Nasser today is a bigger hero in Syria and Iraq than in Egypt, and, although he denies it, Sadat has made a significant shift away from the socialist policies of his predecessor.

THE FUTURE OF SUEZ

The world will experience no dramatic shifts in power or commerce in the year immediately after Suez is reopened. The future role of the Canal in international affairs will be determined by the interrelationships of: (1) decisions on enlarging the Canal, (2) maximum sizes of supertankers, (3) future Egyptian economic policies and her ability to attract development capital, (4) sources and markets for oil in the next twenty years, and (5) successes of alternate trade routes (e.g., shipping, pipelines, railroads).

Oil. The United States and Europe will be increasingly dependent on Middle East oil until at least 1980. Saudi Arabia, with the world's largest known reserves, will be the key nation for supply. Kuwait and Iran will also be important. Supertankers, present and currently planned pipelines, as well as the Suez Canal, will all be required to transport the large quantities of Persian Gulf oil which will be needed by the United States, Europe, and Japan in the coming decades if current import projections prove accurate.

The Supertankers. The trend toward supertankers has been accelerated by increasing awareness of the need for alternatives to the unreliable Suez route; possibilities of reducing costs by increasing size; and increased traffic from the Middle East to Japan and North America. Supertankers are those ships with a capacity for 150,000 dwt. Increases in size in world shipping have been accompanied by increases in speed.

SUMMARY OF TANKER SIZE[15]
(as of June 30, 1973)

Size Group dwt	Existing Fleet*	Vessels on Order
10,000- 49,999	2,116	237
50,000- 99,999	672	129
100,000-149,999	142	142
150,000-199,999	38	20
200,000-249,999	227	92
250,000-299,999	75	204
300,000-349,999	9	56
350,000-399,999	1	29
400,000 and over	1	22
TOTAL	3,281	931
Average size	59,400dwt	164,000dwt

*Oil companies and independent owners only. Of the vessels on order, as with the existing fleet, the ownership ratio is roughly two to one of independent shipowners to oil companies.

Despite the economies of scale, however, it would be inaccurate to predict that all the world's increased requirements for oil will be transported in ships that would use the Cape route even if the Suez were open. Few ports in either Europe or the United States have adequate loading, unloading, or storage facilities to safely handle the larger tankers. The dangers of accidents are greatly magnified, particularly in such narrow straits as Gibraltar, the English Channel, Malacca, and throughout the Mediterranean.

The spiraling costs of construction and increased insurance charges have greatly raised shipbuilding and shipping costs in recent years. The average carrier in the US oil trade is well within the current limits of the Suez Canal. Most ships of the world tanker fleet can currently utilize the Suez route, and these smaller ships will soon be supplemented by the Suez to Alexandria pipeline. Once the Canal is enlarged, if that decision is made, most tankers would be able to utilize it at full capacity, and most of the rest could transit it empty.

Another important consideration is that only crude products encourage such economies of size. Refined products can be transported economically in ships much smaller than supertanker size because less bulk is required to satisfy demands. With the shortage of refining facilities in the United States and increased Arab interest and investment in downstream petroleum operations, this factor may significantly affect future shipping patterns and requirements.

When vessels of 100,000 tons can use the Canal, they will lose their margin of advantage in using the Cape route.[16] Italy and Southern Europe will always be better served by small vessels using the Canal because of the lack of large port facilities, the dangers of supertankers in the Mediterranean, and lower transit costs. Likewise, most Soviet tankers will probably continue to be built to fit through the Canal even at its present size, primarily because of inadequate port facilities in the Baltic and Black Seas and relatively insignificant petroleum import requirements.

Pipelines, Railways, and Other Threats. Another important economic threat to Suez is oil pipelines. Although they may save thousands of sea miles in transit, pipelines have a number of disadvantages. They represent tremendously large investments which must be compensated by high charges, and they lack the flexibility of tankers. In addition, pipelines are even more vulnerable to closure and sabotage than surface transport using the Suez Canal. Frequently, as in the case of the Tapline, multinational approval is required for repairs and maintenance.[17]

Currently there are only two pipelines which compete directly with Suez—the Tapline and the Israeli pipeline. Kirkuk, the largest Middle East pipeline system, transports oil from Iraq to Syrian and Lebanese ports and is not competitive because the fields it serves have no link with the Gulf. The political problems of the Tapline have restrained its owners from further investment, and there have been threats to close it if the transit nations demand unreasonable fee increases. Arab oil will probably not flow through an Israeli pipeline for many years, and any future Iranian-Turkish pipeline is economically questionable.

The most discussed potential threat to the Canal is the Egyptian Suez to Mediterranean (Sumed) oil pipeline. The initial capacity in 1975 is expected to be 40 million tons per year, with a planned expansion to 110 million tons per year, or about the combined equivalent of all current Middle East pipelines.[18] The Sumed will be complementary to the Canal rather than competitive by handling the overrun when and if the maximum number of vessels able to transit the Canal is reached and when, after the Canal is expanded, the largest tankers over 250,000 dwt are utilized. Persian Gulf oil from these tankers could unload at Suez City at the southern end of the Canal and reload onto other tankers at Alexandria. This system would allow traffic which would not be available to Suez anyway to cut 14,500 miles, or approximately 23 days, from voyages to Europe, and the economy of Egypt would benefit. Certainly oil will never cease to flow through Suez as long as the Canal remains open, however. As it is enlarged, the Canal will play an increasingly important role as a highway for this vital resource.

Overland transport routes for dry cargo will offer some competition to a reopened Canal, but it will not be substantial. The CENTO railway between Istanbul, Teheran, and Karachi will yield some commercial advantages, as will transshipment by road and rail in Israel. Faster ships and containerization of freight will also affect the competitive advantage and revenues of the Suez Canal. Use of the Arctic route between Europe and Japan in summer may even become practical.

CONCLUSIONS

Projected US and European petroleum demands in the late seventies and early eighties are so great than an enlarged canal, oil pipelines, and a growing fleet of supertankers will all play complementary roles in supplying oil as efficiently as possible to the world's industrialized nations. If Canal dues are not substantially increased, the Suez will offer enough of a competitive advantage to dry cargo transport and to the smaller petroleum tankers, even at its old capacity, to make the reopening worthwhile. Expansion of the Canal will be costly, but if financing is made available, it would offer significant economic benefits for Egypt, Europe, and the world. The size of supertankers is unlikely to grow significantly due to reasons of safety, expense, and facilities. There has been talk of one million dwt ships, but tankers within the capacity of projected expansion plans of the Canal will probably remain typical. Thus, Suez will continue to be an important trade artery when it is reopened, although it will no longer be the vital lifeline it once was. The greatest danger today for Europe and the United States is not the closure of Suez or the disruption of Middle East pipelines, but rather a political decision to embargo Middle East oil or to raise prices to unaffordable rates.

Egypt will once again gain strategic importance, but in a somewhat different context than ever before. Europe has been the focus of international politics and international economics since World War II, when colonies became liabilities and the Cold War crystallized. Now the Third World has regained its independence and importance. These nations are undergoing what has been described as a revolution of rising expectations. Since 1967, the developed nations have recognized their own resource shortages, the wealth and potential power of the Third World, and the necessity of interdependence. In the future, Africa and the Middle East will become increasingly important as resource bases for oil and other vital raw materials. Today's East-West orientation will compete with an emerging North-South security framework. The result will be a growing realization of the political, economic, and military importance of Egypt and Suez as a crossroads.

When Suez is reopened, immediate US benefits will be largely political. Europe and Japan will primarily benefit commercially, and the Soviet Union will benefit militarily. Among the beneficiaries, the United States potentially has most to gain. US-Middle East relations are currently at a watershed, and important decisions must be made which will determine the course of those relations in the future. US interests in the region will continue to expand, as they have during the past two decades, and it will be in the US interest to remain a Middle East power.

Future US policies must avoid identification with outmoded ideas and institutions by exercising leadership in assisting inevitable social change and industrial revolutions. US policies and perceptions must cease to be governed by the current Arab-Israeli dispute and focus instead on gaining a stake in the development of the region's industry and resources. Innovative economic diplomacy will probably be the most successful instrument for furthering US interests in the Middle East. US products, markets, technical expertise, and managerial skills are respected in Egypt and throughout the region.

Egypt, along with Saudi Arabia and Iran, will be a key nation to the Middle East balance of power in future decades because of its position as political, intellectual, cultural, geographical, and industrial hub of the newly dynamic Arab world. It has the population and potential many of the oil-rich Arab states lack. The opportunity to implement an activist, enlightened US foreign policy is now present in Egypt, and current and future Suez redevelopment efforts may prove to be the key to its success. *Thus, the United States should view the reopening, expansion, and redevelopment of the Suez Canal as more of an opportunity than a threat.* Whatever military gains the Soviets make, and they appear to be few, would be minimized by a strong US-Egyptian partnership. US efforts in Egypt should not be viewed in the context of the Cold War or containment of Russia. They should be considered in terms of the more positive benefits—political, military, and economic—for Europe and the United States, for Egypt, and for the entire Middle East region, and as an important step toward achieving a lasting peace in the area. The result may be a recognition that the entire Middle East problem is not the simple zero-sum game both the United States and the USSR, as well as the Arabs and Israelis, have always thought.

14

The United States and the Indian Ocean Area

Barton M. Hayward

Every so often the economic trousers of the world are literally down to where its suspenders are at the breaking point. Most recently the suspenders were represented by Middle East oil, and much of the world quickly realized its economic trousers were in serious risk of falling. The humorous analogy is not so farfetched: the economic miracle of Japan has shown its Achilles' heel, Western Europe again was dealt a losing poker hand in a game they did not even want to play, and the citizens of the United States found little relief in gasoline sale restrictions and cooler building temperatures.

The examples cited are the result of a series of interwoven causes: the October 1973 Arab-Israeli War, with its resultant oil embargo; accelerating inflation throughout the world; as well as increased demands for energy, in particular in the developed countries. Historically, the Middle East has been the crossroads of continents and cultures. With the advent of increased oil moving by tanker from Persian Gulf ports across the Indian Ocean, particularly after the Suez Canal closing in 1967, it too has become an area of interest for many nations.

One interesting consequence of these and related events has been an increased focus on the Indian Ocean area's strategic importance. Two questions logically come to mind in this regard. What is the US role in the area, and what policies should be followed to insure the successful accomplishment of that role?

This discussion surveys the situation in the area and posits some suggested solutions. The problem posed by the above questions involves many issues. Insofar as is possible, the focus will be away from the Arab-Israeli issue, but cognizant of its impact. In this regard, the area under discussion includes the Indian Ocean and all the states washed by it and its adjoining gulfs, seas, and bays.

The interests of many nations converge in the Indian Ocean area because of the oil in the Persian Gulf states. Except for Indonesia, no other part of the Indian Ocean area has significant known oil reserves. While not vital to the United States directly at this time, assuming the validity of projected consumption trends and resource availability without alternative source development, it seems apparent that access to Middle East oil will become vital to the United States by the next decade. This same oil is currently, however, a vital interest of Western Europe and Japan. Access to it and the freedom of transit for oil is of critical importance to both. At the same time, it has been clearly demonstrated by the Organization of Oil Producing Countries' (OPEC) embargo and production slowdown that oil is the producing states' major weapon, and for many, their only resource.

SOVIET PRESENCE IN THE INDIAN OCEAN

While the availability of oil received the attention of the citizenry worldwide, military strategic planners have been concerned with the increased use of the Indian Ocean by Soviet naval forces, as well as the worldwide debate over the United States proposal to enlarge its facility at Diego Garcia. Soviet naval buildup in the area has been substantial. Current Soviet deployments have been estimated at about 20 ships, operating from time to time in Persian Gulf and Indian Ocean waters,[1] often in units of 4 or 5 vessels. While not operating any formal naval bases, Soviet vessels have access to port facilities in Berbera, Somalia; Umm Qasr, Iraq; and Aden, all of which can presumably be used by military as well as civilian vessels.[2] The port of Singapore is regularly used by all types of Soviet vessels for major repairs.

Soviet actions and pronouncements indicate some purposes for an Indian Ocean presence. First, Soviet planners have claimed to feel considerable anxiety over the suspected location of Polaris/Poseidon submarines in the Indian Ocean and particularly the Arabian Sea. Their reaction has been to develop an antisubmarine capability, including hunter-killer submarines and possibly land-based antisubmarine warfare (ASW) aircraft operating from Socotra, a large island belonging to the People's Democratic Republic of Yemen. Second, knowing the oil resources criticality to the West and Japan, the Soviets no doubt would like to be in a position to control or deny the flow of these resources. Actions of this drastic nature would probably occur only in the event of general war with the West. Third, is the peacetime defense of state interests. This ambiguous term would allow the Soviet fleet to engage in actions ranging from a goodwill visit to more positive contingencies, such as a show of force, coercion of a nation, or emphasis of the Soviet state's concern.

A fourth reason for the Soviet naval presence is the protection of shipping. The Soviet merchant marine has been a major factor in Soviet trade expansion with the non-Communist world. The countries on the Indian Ocean periphery account for a significant amount of Soviet foreign trade with developing countries.[3] Finally, the Soviets have demonstrated a willingness to use their naval vessels as it suits their political needs, such as the support of the Siad regime in Somalia. It can be expected that the Soviets will resort to intervention only when diplomacy has failed. Their Indian Ocean presence is a visible reminder that the USSR is capable of protecting its own interests and those of its friends.

NATIONAL INTERESTS

Soviet interests which may have prompted a naval force in the Indian Ocean area are suggested by the reasons listed above. Those interests, as well as the interests for other nations, are noted in Table 1, at the end of this chapter. Once the pervasive interest in Persian Gulf oil is understood, the other interests of nations in or concerned with the area are more easily enumerated. Neither the Soviet Union nor the United States have vital interests in the area, in the sense that a vital interest is defined as one which a nation will or should pursue or protect at all costs.

US interest in the Indian Ocean area is tied inexorably to the Soviet military presence and its capabilities. There is no evidence that the Soviets intend to deploy a permanent Indian Ocean fleet; however, the capability for such deployment and the perceived Soviet political need to increase influence by naval presence could bring that result. A gradual buildup over the next few years is most likely, with the opening of the Suez Canal facilitating such an increase. In its pre-1967 configuration, the canal is still limited by physical dimensions, capacity, and vulnerability to blockage or disruption. It does, however, significantly reduce sailing distances, measured in nautical miles (nm), from European and American ports. For example:

From - To	Via Suez Canal	Via Cape of Good Hope
New York to Basra, Iraq	8500 nm	12012 nm
Odessa to Basra	4520 nm	12455 nm
New York to Bombay, India	8178 nm	11382 nm
Odessa to Bombay	4198 nm	11825 nm

Soviet naval forces in the Indian Ocean provide support to Soviet policy in the Middle East to the extent that they may intimidate Saudi Arabia and the Persian Gulf states while reinforcing Soviet influence in Iraq. This potential is limited, however, by the obvious fact that the effectiveness and the very existence of the Soviet squadron depends on free access through the several strategic choke points leading into and out of the region. Such a vulnerability, inherent in the Soviet naval position, led to disaster the last time (1904-05) a Russian fleet sought to exert a significant strategic influence. The development of air power and of submarine and mine warfare in the decades since has made the passage of defiles even more hazardous. Even so, the extension of Soviet naval power into the Indian Ocean has the immediate effect of warning China that direct Soviet influence can be applied along China's southern flank, as well as along her northern border.

To what extent can the Soviet naval presence be translated into meaningful political influence? It has been argued that Britain exerted political power ashore during the days of its Indian empire by gaining control of the Indian Ocean.[4] Historical analogies, as Admiral Alfred T. Mahan warned, can be misleading. British sea power was meaningful because it made possible the projection of direct British commercial, military, and political power ashore, while effectively blocking any other power from projecting and maintaining comparable power ashore. In the context of the 1970's, Soviet naval power is neither essential to the projection of Soviet economic and political power, nor is it sufficiently strong to thwart its principal rivals' political and economic influence. Soviet influence in Iraq, Yemen, and India is a product of political and economic factors independent of the Soviet naval presence. To date, the Soviet merchant marine and the Soviet civil air fleet have been more potent factors than the navy in the extension of this influence. On the other hand, the introduction of Soviet warships in force may be counterproductive by dramatizing Soviet influence and the inherent dangers associated with it. A much greater Soviet naval presence in the Mediterranean was not able to prevent a drastic reduction of Soviet influence in Egypt.

In addition to oil and Soviet military presence in the area, several other factors weigh heavily in the current situation. The Arab-Israeli dispute, already mentioned, remains an unsolved problem, and until resolution, tensions will remain high. The antagonisms generated by this conflict have damaged intraregional relationships and to some extent US relations with its allies, and brought the world once again too close to a superpower confrontation. At the same time, regional antagonisms such as those between India and Pakistan, Ethiopia and Somalia, and Iraq and Iran offer additional dangers to the nations involved. None can afford open conflict, nor should any superpower be allowed to benefit from such antagonisms.

India, the world's second largest nation in terms of population, is confronted by enormous problems of poverty, public order, and maintaining a democratic form of government. Pakistan's normal difficulties have been compounded by the war over Bangladesh, while Indonesia's progress was disrupted by Sukarno's policies. East African states are likewise suffering the growing pains of modernization. The long-run welfare of the United States and of the world will not be served if the Indian Ocean states descend into deepening poverty, while the United States, Western Europe, and Japan continue their economic advance.

The position of India is especially important. Political disintegration in India could create conditions similar to those which Britain exploited to gain control. Even here, however, the analogy is inexact since in the 18th and 19th centuries there was no militant China prepared to move into South Asia to counter Western incursions. China today has not only the will, but substantial means to oppose Soviet incursions and will use every means available to prevent the Soviets from closing the ring. Criticism of overly friendly relations with the Soviets has arisen in the Indian Parliament. Whether or not it produced overt criticism, anything beyond a token Soviet naval presence would be counter to the expressed Indian desire that "we would like the Indian Ocean to be an area of peace and cooperation. Military bases of outside powers will create tension and great power rivalry."[5] This objective was indorsed by the Commonwealth Conference in Singapore in January 1971 and by the United Nations (UN) General Assembly in a resolution on the Indian Ocean as a zone of peace on December 16, 1971.

A vacuum of political power in the Indian Ocean area comparable to that found by the Portuguese, French, British, and Netherlands empire builders does not exist. As long as they maintain at least their present degree of political stability, Iran, India, Indonesia, and Australia will assert their independence against foreign encroachment from whatever source. The lesser states of the region derive some moral and political strength from the larger powers. The stability of the Indian Ocean area is likely to increase, therefore, in proportion to the progress of the regional powers and to decline as the fortunes of those states decline. US interests would appear to be best served by strengthening the independence and influence of these powers, and by avoiding actions that tend to lessen their influence. At the minimum, this involves giving credibility to US regional commitments and taking positive action to support the independence, economic development, and political stability of the littoral states. If the United States permits another state to develop hegemony in the Indian Ocean, this will, in time, have an adverse effect on the US global power position.

In attempting to deal with present and potential trouble spots in the Middle East-Indian Ocean area, the United States can expect little help from its friends. The 1956 Suez crisis and the 1967 and 1973 Middle East Wars established quite clearly that the North Atlantic Treaty Organization (NATO) will not always act as a unit in respect to crises external to the treaty area. In the Middle East Wars, US and Western European interests varied enough to rule out concerted action. The disparate dependence on Middle East oil, for example, is cause enough to preclude common crisis resolution policies. Members are not likely to regard crises in the Persian Gulf or in the Indian Ocean area as a NATO concern, even when two or more members—at least one of these being the United States—see their interests and the challenge precisely the same. There is no precedent for it, and little likelihood that action would be concerted.

The Indian Ocean area has significant mineral resources other than oil that, in the long run, will be important to the United States, Western Europe, and Japan. Zambian copper and Indian and South African manganese play an important contemporary role in the world economy. In assessing the future, the area's mineral potential has not been thoroughly surveyed.

US investments in the region are considerable. "The US oil industry has substantial capital investments in the Persian Gulf region, valued at approximately \$3.5 billion."[6] Until the present energy crisis, the profits have been substantial, a significant factor in offsetting the US balance of payments deficit. The continued growth and expansion of the American economy depends on access to the markets, raw materials, and investment opportunities, not only of the developed world, but of newly independent nations such as those bordering the Indian Ocean. As evidence of the importance attached to this interest, since 1956 the United States has negotiated investment guarantee agreements with Malagasy, Kenya, Tanzania, Somalia, Ethiopia, Iran, Pakistan, Indonesia, and Malaysia. However, the value to the United States of trade with the Indian Ocean littoral countries in commodities other than natural resources is small.

Worldwide inflation continues to worry world leaders and economists. The effect of higher oil prices is most devastating on those nations and economies least able to pay. For the producing nations, oil causes a serious imbalance in foreign exchange accumulation; for the importing nations, a problem of foreign exchange production. Although the industrialized nations are able at present to pay the higher prices for oil, these higher prices create a serious problem for the poorer nations. The latter require only a small percentage of the production, but their collective political pressure may not be fully understood by the oil producers. With oil production excepted, the countries of the Indian Ocean littoral continue to rely on an agricultural economy, in large measure at subsistence levels, with very low annual per capita incomes. India is industrializing, albeit precariously. Agricultural production in most areas is in danger of not keeping pace with population growth (2-3 percent in South Asia, 3 percent in East Africa) which will further exacerbate economic development and political stability.

STRATEGIC ALTERNATIVES

With these events in mind, the strategic alternatives open to the United States come more sharply into focus. In any scale of military strategy alternatives, an infinite number appear on the spectrum; however, for ease of presentation, only four, representing the major points on the scale, are discussed. In view of the facts discussed above, the obvious, and sometimes overlooked, choice of doing nothing has been discarded. The situation demands some action. The questions are: what is to be done, how will it be accomplished, and what are its implications?

The four options essentially address general purpose military forces. In all cases the deployment of strategic retaliatory forces is not questioned, nor is it recommended that present deployment plans be changed. It is important to note, however, that any alternative US military strategy adopted for general purpose forces has implications for the strategic retaliatory forces. For example, if US naval forces are increased, and the Soviets respond in kind, each increase would improve the Soviet's ability to locate US submarines.

• Alternative 1: Proxy Reliance Strategy. This option requires the withdrawal of all US combatant air and surface forces. A key feature of the alternative would be reliance upon proxies; that is, selected countries and allies to assist in promoting US interests. The primary means for projection of US influence would be political and economic. Supplementing the political and economic initiation would be the military security assistance to project a US military influence, and to reduce the need for direct US military intervention. To insure US preparedness to meet treaty commitments and support its regional interests, a Joint Operations Planning Staff located in the United States would be established. This staff would be responsible for conducting joint exercises and contingency planning for regional operations, to include land, air, and naval forces. Occasional US naval port calls would be scheduled by other fleet elements in accordance with policy established by the Department of State.

An advantage of this alternative is that it avoids any cause for an Indian Ocean arms race. It also promotes improved relations with the regional nations and supports their desires for a zone of peace in the Indian Ocean. In turn, this should provide maximum psychological advantage to the United States in pressing for a reduced Soviet presence. While improvements presently underway at Diego Garcia would be completed, no additional improvements would be required.

This course of action has disadvantages, however. First, there would only be a minimum capability for monitoring Soviet presence or reacting immediately to any Soviet intervention in the affairs of the region. Second, the use of proxies is risky in that, in time of greatest need, the proxy state might find that its interests have diverged from those of the United States. The United States may also find that the interests of two proxies differ to the point where the United States is drawn into conflict which develops between them.

In summary, this alternative provides maximum support to a national strategy that relies primarily on US economic and political initiatives and the military force of selected nations to maintain regional stability.

• Alternative 2: Low US Profile Strategy. This alternative provides for a minimum US naval presence consisting essentially of the three type ships (one command and two destroyer types) assigned to the Middle East Force (MIDEASTFOR) prior to October 1973. This force is sufficient to demonstrate US concern for its interests in the region, yet is not likely to provoke a superpower arms race. It puts the onus squarely on the USSR to limit an Indian Ocean arms race. To meet contingency requirements a Joint Operations Planning Staff would be established, responsible for the same mission as cited in alternative one.

Regional stability is enhanced through the use of improved security assistance programs with special emphasis on the navies of the regional nations. Diego Garcia improvements presently underway would be completed to provide refueling station facilities. No additional improvements at Diego Garcia would be required. Joint naval exercises would be accomplished employing existing resources. A limited intelligence capability would be maintained to observe the actions of those who might have hostile intentions and to monitor the size and activities of the Soviet presence. This option conforms to the pronouncements of the littoral nations calling for the Indian Ocean to be a zone of peace and fulfills the tenets of the Nixon Doctrine calling for nations to shoulder the burden of their own defense.

The disadvantages are obvious. The limited naval force is not capable of securing lines of communication (LOC) with the forces immediately available, nor can oil facilities ashore be secured if necessary; forces from outside the region would be required if either contingency arose.

In summary, this alternative is less costly, does not provoke the resident nations or provide the USSR with justification for a buildup, promotes regional stability, avoids an arms race, maximizes psychological advantage in favor of the United States, and supports the development of resident navies. It does not, however, secure the LOCs, or provide for the immediate projection of sea power into troubled areas.

• Alternative 3: Increased US Military Presence Strategy. A third possibility involves the deployment of additional US surface ships to the Indian Ocean. It is accomplished by the augmentation of the US forces stated for alternative two, supplemented by occasional visits by US naval forces of up to an attack carrier task force. As a minimum, such a carrier task force would be deployed to the area not less than twice per year, for periods of up to 30 days minimum. Additionally, to improve intelligence gathering capability, aerial surveillance would be initiated in the area on a continual basis and satellite reconnaissance efforts would be maintained. Of particular interest would be the improved ability to determine Soviet submarine positions and movement. To support the increased naval and air presence some improvements to Diego Garcia would be necessary to extend the runway and increase fuel storage capacity.

This option would improve the US ability to aid those countries requesting direct military assistance, primarily air and naval support during those periods when the carrier task group is present in the area. This alternative also provides a better capability to secure LOC and to project US power into the littoral states. It provides a better ability to deter or limit Soviet military aggression or intervention.

Several disadvantages to this alternative are apparent. It cannot be supported without shifting forces from other missions, or, assuming that is impossible, by some increases in naval forces. Improvements to Diego Garcia are necessary if this choice is adopted. The requirement for additional forces and for the construction at Diego Garcia will increase defense expenditures. An increase in US naval presence would also tend to promote an arms race in the area between the United States and USSR, particularly after the Suez Canal is reopened. As such, the option thus fails to support the UN resolution calling for the area to be free of such power races. Psychologically, the impact upon the Indian Ocean states would be largely negative, giving some states further reason for offering base rights to the Soviets. While the alternative provides increased naval presence, it does not provide the capability to seize oil production facilities if that became necessary.

In summary, this alternative would provide the United States with an improved capability to deal with events in the Indian Ocean area when the carrier task group is present. However, it would add fuel to the arms race, provoke the littoral states, reduce the US psychological advantage, and increase defense expenditures because of additional forces required and building costs on Diego Garcia. The Soviets would see our increased forces as helpful to the Chinese and while the United

States would have an improved capability to project power, this is more than offset by a decrease in image.

• Alternative 4: Full Range US Military Presence Strategy. To assert the United States as an Indian Ocean power, an Indian Ocean unified command would be established, complete with self-sufficient naval forces, and limited land (amphibious) and air forces. To provide support, large-scale improvements to Diego Garcia would be required. Other actions with friendly powers—naval presence, combined exercises, and security assistance—would be continued.

The additional air and surface units will dramatically improve the intelligence and reconnaissance capability, provided the use of additional airfields around the periphery of the area, especially in South Africa, in the Horn of Africa, as well as the Persian Gulf can be secured. It would permit the United States to project maximum power in the area. To the extent that LOC can be secured by direct military means—and that is very slim, at best—the forces deployed under this option provide a capability better to secure LOC than under any other alternative. Forces could be concentrated at given points which would enable the United States to respond if any nation in the area were to request direct military assistance. The larger force, with its greater capability best limits Soviet aggression or intervention and also has a greater deterrent value. Finally, choosing this alternative provides the United States with the capability of seizing and holding limited areas until augmented by other forces from the United States or other locations. As with securing the LOC, the ability to secure oil production facilities is a function of the force size a nation is able to employ, although the results are likely to be uncertain.

It is difficult to assess what effect the establishment of an Indian Ocean command would have on the nations in the area. While some would applaud US strength and presence, others would view the US action as destabilizing. While the United States would have a greater capability to deal with any eventuality, the whole resultant effect may cause more regional problems than it solves. There would be maximum stimulation of a US-USSR arms race in the area, especially in naval forces. Additional base rights in the area would be necessary for the United States. If the United States secured base rights, the Soviets would probably react with similar requests. India, now trying to avoid a US-USSR arms race in the area, would find it increasingly difficult to resist Soviet requests for basing rights. US naval forces would require major improvements at Diego Garcia to make it the primary US facility in the area. These improvements, the additional forces necessary, and other actions required for this option will be expensive; costs will be the greatest of the four alternatives considered. Regardless of how well-intentioned the United States might be, the increased forces will be viewed as tilting the Sino-Soviet balance in favor of the PRC. Favoring the Chinese, at a minimum, would require the Soviet Union to adopt client states to counter US presence and influence. India, Somalia, and Iraq are likely candidates for this status. Finally, these actions would not be supporting the intentions of the littoral states and the UN resolution to create a zone of peace.

The net impact would be a negative psychological effect. While a few nations would be pleased to see the increased US forces in the area, most would not indorse their presence. The Soviet Union would challenge the United States on any force buildup in the area thus gaining a great deal of propaganda advantage from it. This option, then, while providing the United States with the best military capability to deal with events in the Indian Ocean area, nevertheless has negative factors in cost and adverse political and psychological disadvantages.

RECOMMENDED STRATEGY

Having briefly reviewed the pros and cons of each alternative strategy, in my view alternative two has the best chance for success and should be adopted.

Adoption of alternative one is too risky because of reliance on proxy states, some of whom are unstable politically. This alternative does not allow the United States to influence the situation in a positive manner. The significant increase in US force presence and basing required by alternatives three and four could lead to a superpower arms race and confrontation in an area where our *vital* interests are not endangered. Further, increased US presence might be viewed as support to the Chinese since the Chinese view any Soviet increase in the Indian Ocean as a threat to their country's southern flank. Finally, the insertion of US forces would upset the existing regional balance of power and have an unsettling effect leading to increased arms presence.

Current political initiatives in the Middle East indicate there is a reasonable chance for a negotiated settlement of the Arab-Israeli conflict and continued oil supply to the Western nations. Such action would be significant in defusing the critical problems facing the Arabs and the Western World and would reduce the need for Arab countries to rely on the Soviets. Work already has begun on the reopening of the Suez Canal.

US public opinion will not support dramatic US force presence in foreign areas unless a clear threat is identified. Our experience in Viet Nam attests to this, as well as significant measures by Congress since then to enact legislation to reduce our oversea military presence. However, where our interests are threatened, US military action will be supported. It is questionable whether Congress or the people would support extended, increased presence against the existing threat in the area.

The Soviets have a right to a presence in the Indian Ocean deriving from the traditional freedom of the seas. Present Soviet forces are not considered unreasonable and they are consistent with the measured US presence in the area. When the Suez Canal reopens, the possibility exists that Soviet presence may dramatically increase, either as a positive action to extend their political influence or as a response to increased US presence and basing in the area, should this occur. It is essential that the Soviets not be given this latter reason as an excuse.

Political action to advise the USSR and all the nations of the area of our minimum force plans and basing in the region should coincide with the adoption of the military strategy suggested by alternative two. By so doing, the United States can obtain maximum political/psychological advantage among the countries of region, demonstrating the positive US effort to conform to their desires to avoid a regional imbalance or a superpower confrontation. At the same time, this political message should advise all concerned that ours is a prudent risk and one which will have to be reevaluated, should the United States note an increase in Soviet presence and/or provision for additional bases in countries of the region. By so doing, we are, in effect, providing the challenge to the Soviets, securing goodwill in the area, and accepting minimal risks to our interests. Then if the Soviets do greatly enlarge their naval activities in the Indian Ocean, the onus for provoking severe anxieties in the littoral countries will be on them. At that time, stepped-up US naval presence is more likely to be seen by local statesmen as a welcome American effort to balance the Soviet Union's newly threatening presence. If, on the contrary, the United States proceeds now to enlarge our facilities, it will be the United States which will be responsible for whatever superpower arms race ensues. If the United States is held responsible, the result will be to generate hostility to its future activities, severely limit their future effectiveness, and increase their future cost.

This study cautiously views Soviet presence in the Indian Ocean and does not indorse a major reinforcement of our force presence at this time. Such a course would be nonproductive in relation to political, psychological, and military gains and uneconomical in terms of US force utility. Rather, our present global naval strategic deployability provides the necessary continued force presence with a capability for reinforcement. Prudent action does indicate that a planning staff in the United States should be established to monitor this situation and to evaluate Soviet presence in the area now and after the Suez Canal reopens. Simultaneously, political action should be taken to inform all nations of our deliberate choice of minimum actions, with appropriate advice that we retain the right to reevaluate the situation as the factors change.

	VITAL[a]	MAJOR[b]
Arab States	External security Control of natural resources	Economic development
India	External security	Economic development Project influence as the dominant regional power Regional stability (no arms race or superpower confrontation)
Iran	External security Control of natural resources Access to oil Freedom of seas	Access to markets, trade, and raw materials
Japan		Economic development Access to markets, trade, and raw materials
PRC		Security of southern flank Extend regional influence
United States		Access to oil for the United States, Japan, and Western Europe Freedom of seas Settlement of Arab-Israeli dispute Access to markets and raw materials Limit USSR and PRC influence Regional stability (no arms race or superpower confrontation)
USSR		Manipulate Western nations by influencing the supply of oil Preservation of sea link to Soviet Far East from European Russia Defense against SLBM Extend regional influence Contain PRC
Western Europe	Access to oil Freedom of seas	

aVital interest is one that a nation will or should pursue or protect at all costs.
bMajor interest is one for which a nation will or should commit energy or resources.

TABLE 1. National Interests in Middle East-Indian Ocean Area

15

The United States in Northeast Asia

William V. Kennedy

To suggest at this time that the United States has a major role to play in Asia—specifically on the mainland of Asia—is akin to inviting the victim of a recent automobile accident out for a Sunday drive.

But if the victim of that accident depends on the automobile for a living, he must overcome his aversions to driving or accept a greatly reduced and constricted lifestyle.

In an essentially lawless international community, nations can accept a reduced role only at the peril of becoming victims rather than managers of the major forces and trends at work in the world.

US INTERESTS IN ASIA

One of the earliest articulations of US interests abroad was Thomas Jefferson's classic definition of US interests in Europe:

> We especially ought to pray that the powers of Europe may be so poised and counterpoised among themselves, that their own security may require the presence of all their forces at home, leaving the other quarters of the globe in undisturbed tranquility.[1]

The core of Jefferson's reasoning seems evident—once overwhelming power has been assembled, there is no effective restraint on its use. Survival, therefore, hinges on the ability to prevent the assemblage of power.

As the birthplace and long-time heartland of industrial power, Europe has been of foremost concern to the United States. In World Wars I and II, the United States acted to prevent Germany from establishing hegemony in Europe. Beginning with the Berlin Airlift in 1948, the United States has played an unprecedented peacetime role in Europe to prevent the Soviet Union from establishing hegemony.

Since 1945, a new industrial giant has arisen. In terms of plant, product, and mercantile ability, it exceeds any single European power and it rivals Western Europe as a whole. Together with the United States this giant is generating an entirely new economic community. The giant is, of course, Japan and the community is the Pacific Basin.

No one denies the facts of economic development in East Asia and the Pacific, but we are reluctant to accept the implications. Yet if the Jeffersonian assessment of our interests in Europe was and remains valid, that logic applies equally to the center of power that is arising in East Asia. Consider the elements of power in East Asia:

• The industrial plant, the skilled and disciplined population and the favorable trading position of Japan.

• The massive population of China with its amply demonstrated attributes of intelligence and energy.

• The industrial plant and natural resources of Eastern Siberia and the Soviet Maritime Provinces.

• The strategic depth and maritime position of continental East Asia and its outlying islands and archipelagoes.

Controlling only a fraction of this power, at a time when the Asian power potential was much less developed than it is now, Japan was able to strike a mighty blow at the United States and to contest control of the Western Pacific. When the nuclear factor is added to that experience, it seems reasonable to question whether the United States can continue to relegate East Asia and the Pacific to a secondary status in assessing the world power equation.

PAST US POLICY

However similar the forces at work, there are significant historical and strategic differences between Europe and East Asia. These must be considered in attempting to determine the part the United States should play.

For over half a century before 1945, Northeast Asia was a cockpit in which Japan and Russia struggled with a weak and disorganized China, and with each other for a position of dominance. The United States sought to play the role of a referee, protecting its own trade and seeking to prevent any of the main contenders from gaining a position of dominance or supremacy. As Dr. William H. Overholt of Hudson Institute pointed out, the United States "calculated with extreme care the costs of committing American funds and lives to the support of its [East Asian] policies. In 1941, our moral involvement in the region collided with our inadequate commitments of more mundane resources, and the multipolar competition which we had fostered with excessive zeal collapsed into war."

Whether the operative factor here was the size of our moral commitment or an inadequate understanding of our strategic interests is open to argument. Whatever the answer, the fact that our policies did collapse into war suggests the need for a clearer national understanding of our interests in East Asia than that which characterized our past policies. This need becomes acute as the Soviet Union, China, and Japan begin to reassume the uneasy relationship of the pre-World War II era, this time with nuclear weapons in the hands of two of the three powers.

VITAL INTERESTS

The word "interests" itself is a casualty of the Vietnam era, and the term "vital interests" is in particular disrepute. Yet nations do have interests and act on them. For the purpose of this discussion, two categories are identified— *vital* interests and *major* interests. The term *vital interest* is defined here as that which pertains to the continued existence of the United States and its institutions. A *major interest* is defined as one affecting the well-being of the United States to a significant degree and to which the United States is willing to commit substantial resources.

In the terms of this distinction the United States has but one vital interest in Asia—to prevent any single power or coalition of powers from marshaling the manpower, industry, and natural resources of Asia for aggression against the United States. At present, and probably for several decades to come, power of this magnitude cannot be marshaled in Asia except by control over the Japanese industrial base. In this sense, therefore, Japan is the only country in Asia that can be said to be of truly *vital* importance to the United States. It seems to follow that US relations with Japan are of parmount importance in Asia and fully equal in significance to our relations with Europe.

THE UNITED STATES AND JAPAN

The danger that Japan herself might seek to marshal Asia's power for aggressive war has been allayed for the past 29 years by her emergence as a viable parliamentary democracy, and by the very close relationship maintained with the United States. Up until the present at least, this relationship has relieved Japan of her old fears of possible domination by China, Russia, or a combination of the two.

The United States has agreed to use its nuclear deterrent on behalf of Japan if the latter is threatened. This agreement has relieved Japan of the necessity for maintaining a large military establishment. As a result, the United States has been able to assert a major influence on Japan's foreign and defense policies. In providing Japan with this shield, however, the role of the United States in Northeast Asia has changed from that of a relatively disinterested arbiter to that of a full participant in the traditional Asian power relationship.

The Soviet Union and the Peoples Republic of China (PRC)—each for separate and often opposite reasons—seek to loosen and ultimately dissolve Japan's ties with the United States. Those ties also are under considerable stress from Americans who fear injury from Japanese economic competition, or who see the mutual security arrangement as a dangerous and unnecessary military involvement.

If there is little or no likelihood that Japan could come under the domination of a power hostile to the United States, there is scant reason to continue to support the US-Japan security arrangement with substantial US forces. A consideration of Japan's strategic position, however, provides no such assurance.

THE DEFENSE OF JAPAN

No major nation is as vulnerable to modern nuclear and conventional weaponry as Japan. Her crowded population and industry can be wiped out in an instant by nuclear weapons. Her long sea-lanes are vulnerable to modern submarine warfare. Acquisition of nuclear weapons cannot change these vulnerabilities for they are inherent in the very geography of the Japanese islands. For this reason, Japanese strategic thinkers, as well as the Japanese press and public, are virtually unanimous in rejecting the nuclear option.

Of the three major strategic approaches to the Japanese home islands from continental Asia, one—that leading from Sakhalin and the Kuriles—is entirely in the hands of a mainland power. Powerful Soviet airborne forces can be marshaled along this route in a matter of hours. They can be supported by the amphibious assault capability of the Soviet Pacific Fleet, a capability that is likely to grow as overall Soviet naval power increases.

Considering Soviet power, Japan can do little unilaterally to assure herself a substantial degree of national security. This viewpoint, again the consensus of Japan's strategic thinkers, is the underlying theme of every document issued on the subject by the Japan Defense Agency.[2] It has led to the conviction that now and in the future Japan's security lies primarily in the field of international relations.

So far, the treaty relationship with the United States and the overall US presence in East Asia and the Western Pacific have provided the needed international supplement to the small Japanese "self-defense" forces. Many Japanese are not quite certain that the United States will risk all to honor its nuclear commitment to Japan, however.[3] Those doubts have been allayed up to now by a large American garrison in Korea—the principal land avenue of approach from continental Asia to Japan. The third major approach from mainland Asia to the Japanese home islands lies through the Ryukyu Islands.

A Japan Defense Agency "source," quoted in *Yomiuri* on November 23, 1972, stated that "the US forces around Japan do not lose effect as deterrent forces, as long as combat units of the US forces remain in such areas as the Republic of Korea and Okinawa." Reflecting the ambiguity of the overall Japanese government policy toward Taiwan, the same Defense Agency source opined that there seems to be little possibility of conflict in the Taiwan area, as long as the United States keeps its forces there under the US-Republic of China defense treaty. This direct involvement of the United States in the defense of Korea and Taiwan is the heart of the matter. The continued deployment of an American division in Korea places the United States just where a great many Americans want least to be involved—on the mainland of Asia. Further, the US troop presence in Korea places the United States at an historical juncture of Japanese, Chinese, and Russian interests.

The situation in which the United States finds itself in Taiwan is even more complex. From the time she assumed a role as a regional and world power, Japan has always regarded Formosa as only slightly less important than Korea to her national security. The current Japanese viewpoint toward Taiwan is obscured by a variety of political euphemisms. Formal diplomatic relations between Japan and the Republic of China were ended by Japan in the interests of a better relationship with mainland China, but a trade relationship with Taiwan is maintained by officials "retired" from the Japanese foreign service and then reinstated when their service in Taiwan is finished. A long and tortuous series of negotiations have taken place to resolve the problem of PRC objections to airline service between Taiwan and Japan.

In the three years since the reopening of mainland Chinese contacts with Japan and the United States, nothing in Japan's relationship with Taiwan has changed substantially. Business goes on as usual. All of this can be explained, perhaps, by the fact that Taiwan's economic importance to Japan continues to exceed that of all mainland China. Other factors, one of them probably Japan's dependence on seaborne commerce, also affect the relationship. The most significant concentration on this commerce is in the funnel formed by the island chains that extend southeast and southwest from the Japanese islands of Honshu and Kyushu.

Taiwan is the most important island in these chains. Under a government independent of mainland control, Taiwan presents no major danger to the security of Japan's ocean commerce. Linked to either of the major mainland powers, Taiwan could assume a menacing presence athwart and on the flank of Japan's most vital communications. Under control of mainland China, Taiwan could be a giant aircraft carrier, projecting Chinese air power into the Philippine Sea. Extending that arc to the northeast, possession of Taiwan would place mainland China in a position to dominate the southern Ryukyus.[4]

The status of Taiwan is further complicated by interests and potential interests of the Soviet Union. Naval and air base rights on Formosa would enable the Soviet Union to dominate the South China coast. It would effectively close the military and political chain that the Soviets have been forging around mainland China and, as a bonus, it would put Japan in a Soviet vise. While it is unlikely that the USSR would attempt to take Taiwan by force, it is not out of the question that the Republic of China might seek an alliance with the USSR if the Taipei government felt itself abandoned and isolated.

IMPLICATIONS FOR US POLICY

What does all this portend, then, for future US policy in East Asia? In the words of Masamichi Inoki, President of Japan's Defense College, "The Soviet Union has the armaments to invade Japan ... The Japan-US Security Treaty is absolutely necessary in the sense of supplementing Japan's defense power."[5] Loss of American protection—or loss of confidence in the American commitment—would certainly cause a reevaluation of Japanese foreign and security policies.

Vulnerable though she may be, it is unlikely that Japan would cast herself on the mercy of her neighbors by continuing to refrain from large-scale rearmament. In the absence of the American commitment, a possibility exists that Japan would seek to acquire nuclear weapons as a minimal bargaining position. Expansion of the Japanese Air and Maritime Self-Defense forces, to provide at least some measure of control over the most vital sea-lanes and airspace, also would be likely. All of this could be done in a relatively short period of time. Over a longer term, Japan has the skills and the industrial plant to build and deploy a nuclear ballistic missile submarine fleet sufficient to boost her into the status of a military superpower. A return to conscription would provide Japan with a formidable modern Army.

Even the modest level of rearmament undertaken by Japan to date has caused uneasiness in Peking and Moscow. Acquisition by Japan of an offensive capability would likely reawaken fears in Indonesia and the Philippines, as well as on the Asian mainland. Considering the reception accorded former Prime Minister Tanaka during his 1973 visit, such fears added to existing resentments could produce a severe reaction. The result could be a political realignment as inimical to the United States as it would be to Japan. Indications that Japan was about to develop a full-scale nuclear war machine could prompt the PRC and the USSR to resurrect their long-dormant alliance. Whether the USSR, mainland China, or both in concert would or could act to prevent Japan from developing a full-scale military capability is impossible to predict. Certainly, both would be tempted to do so.

An isolated Japan, exposed to the pressures that could be brought to bear by the Soviet Union acting alone or in concert with China, could be forced into an accommodation with the USSR, or into a defensive relationship with China. Either of those relationships—accommodation or a security agreement of some sort—would come dangerously close to establishing a link between Japanese and mainland power, a link that could someday confront the United States with an array of overwhelming power.

Whether compelled to accept accommodation, or a less humiliating defense agreement, Japan would be a junior and subordinate partner, forced to bargain for a residual national identity. The coin left to Japan in such a situation would be her skills, her capital, and her means of production—the very elements that the United States must keep out of the hands of an adversary power. The consequences of those choices are well understood within the Japanese government. "It is of the utmost importance, in the present fluid situation," Japan's Ambassador to Washington stated in 1972,[6] "that the United States continue to maintain an effective and credible deterrent in the Far East. We have no economic problems which would possibly justify diluting our political and security partnership." From such private and public expressions of Japanese governmental representatives, it is apparent that the existing US deterrent forces in the Western Pacific and East Asia are at the minimum level necessary to maintain Japan's confidence in the US commitment. An increased perception within the United States that this is the case and that any further reduction of forces would involve unacceptable risks would appear to be the foundation on which any workable future US role in Asia must be built. As with any other task, however, the foundation is but a start.

THE UNITED STATES AND CHINA

There is, first of all the problem of the relative priority the United States is to accord to its long-term relations with Japan and China. Dr. Overholt of Hudson Institute[7] and other American scholars[8] have warned that renewed American sentimentalism toward China is fraught with danger. These warnings have been underscored by Tadasu Aruga, professor of American history, Seikei University:[9]

> The Sino-US detente over the head of Japan hurt the Japanese people's pride and trust in the United States and led them to recall the history of US-Japan disputes over China. Was it not that the United States had always taken great interest in big China? Was it not that historically, China had been the center of America's Asian policy and that US-Japan relations had been no more than a mathematical function of Sino-US relations? Was it not that the United States had always been pro-China and that its hostile relations with China in the past 20 years had been only a reversal and a temporary reaction? Is it not possible to say that the history of US-Japan relations is a history of their relations surrounding China? These were what

they wondered in recollecting the history of the US policy toward China. They harbored a suspicion that the United States might be aiming at detente with China, regarding Japan as its competitor, and feared Japan's isolation by Sino-US collaboration and its economic effects.

Whether the test is political, economic, or military, the potential of US relations with Japan, good or ill, far exceeds the potential of US-China relations. The United States and Japan are twin, if not always complementary, economic furnaces fueling an unprecedented development of the entire Pacific Basin. Mainland China's role in this is less than Taiwan's, and is likely to remain so at least through the remainder of this century.

In the political and military sense, the United States survived 20 years of violent PRC hostility, 1949-69, with one relatively limited, and possibly avoidable, armed clash directly involving US and PRC forces. A much shorter period of comparable animosity between the United States and Japan in the 1930's resulted in a war that engulfed the entire Pacific. Deterioration of US-Japan relations to any level approaching that of the late 1930's would convulse the world once more. That would not be the case with US-PRC relations.

To say that US relations with Japan are of primary importance does not imply that US relations with mainland China are inconsequential. On the contrary, it is the current status of mainland China that gives to East Asian relations the fluidity cited by Ambassador Ushiba.

THE SINO-SOVIET CONFLICT

Neither Japan nor the United States can await with equanimity the final resolution of the struggle taking place between the Soviet Union and the Peoples Republic of China. The roots of that struggle go back nearly a thousand years; the ideological issues involved extend to the limits of man's future. The most basic human emotions—racial, nationalistic, economic, political, and ideological—are embroiled in the controversy. From the evidence available, it seems apparent that the most direct and the most immediate issue at stake is who shall dominate the East Asian mainland.

It was precisely this struggle—with Japan as the primary actor—that drew the United States ever deeper into Asian affairs in the period between 1900 and 1941. Now it is the Soviet Union that possesses the principal means to gain a position of dominance.[10] Whether attained by political or military means, success by the Soviet Union in reducing

China to impotency, and thereby asserting Soviet dominance on the mainland, would be of the gravest consequence to Japan. Such a success would almost certainly involve a return of Soviet sea and air power to the Liaotung Peninsula and beyond.

In a day when its fleets dominated the Asian seas and when its possessions in the Kuriles and Southern Sakhalin held Russian land power at arm's length, Japan would not have been immediately threatened by such an advance. In a day when there are Soviet garrisons within sight of Hokkaido, any major extension of Soviet power along the China coast would place Japan in grave danger of unmanageable Soviet influence. In particular, release of Soviet naval power from the geographic and climatological limitations of its present bases in the Maritime Provinces and Kamchatka would pose a major new threat to Japan's vital sea-lanes.

On a broader canvas, release of the Soviet Union from concern over China's emergence as a superpower would provide the Soviets with greater freedom of action in Europe, the Middle East, and wherever the USSR chose to deploy its growing naval power.

Attainment by the Soviets of the long-term goal set by General Alexei Kuropatkin in 1916[11]—a "border line from the Khan Tengri range . . . in a direct line to Vladivostok"—would effectively cripple China's development as a world power, by depriving her of most of Sinkiang and Manchuria, as well as Mongolia. Except for a brief period of altruism during the Russian Revolution and Civil War, when it was powerless to assert foreign claims, the Soviet government has moved as relentlessly toward this goal as did the empire builders of the Czar. The settling up of Mongolia as a vassal state in 1921 and the incorporation of Tanna Tuva into the Soviet Union in 1923 accomplished better than 50 percent of General Kuropatkin's goal. At various times during the 1930's and 1940's, there have been Russian garrisons in Sinkiang, Manchuria, and at Port Arthur-Dairen. Even during the era of close Sino-Soviet relations, in the early 1950's, there may have been a Soviet effort to produce a semi-independent Manchuria under the then Manchurian party chief, Kao Kang.[12] The Soviets never have ceased to exploit the minorities issue in Sinkiang, and if the present government in Peking is to be believed, the USSR has sought by every means to infiltrate and subvert the People's Liberation Army and the Chinese Communist Party. How far the United States can allow this process to go is perhaps the paramount unanswered—and to a considerable degree unstudied—question of current US foreign and security policy. Dr.

Thomas W. Robinson of RAND[13] has postulated a range of Sino-Soviet interaction and the implications for the United States. American interests, in Dr. Robinson's opinion, would be clearly involved if conflict between the USSR and the PRC reached a stage where major forces were involved and puppet governments were about to be established by the Soviet Union in China's border provinces. If the establishment of puppet regimes—and, thereby, the assertion of Soviet dominance in East Asia—is, in fact, the point where US interests are imperiled, the establishment of such regimes by political rather than military means would seem to be equally dangerous.

The Soviets must take into account the existing US military presence in East Asia in calculating their future policy toward China. Whether this presence is sufficient to restrain the Soviets from outright aggression against China, or exploitation of some internal crisis in the PRC, remains to be seen. That a further dimunition of the US role in Asia could serve only to encourage the Soviets seems to be obvious to some Chinese observers.

THE SHADOW OF THE FUTURE

The threat of Soviet dominance is an immediate and near-term thing. It is stimulated by more distant problems, perceived more clearly perhaps by the Soviet Union than by any of the other powers concerned.

China has staked out a claim to a large tract of Soviet territory. The seriousness of intent with which this claim has been advanced may be arguable, but the pressures moving China in the direction of Soviet East Asia are not. Whether China's population is within 100 million, plus or minus, of the current estimates, or whether it were to be reduced by one-half tomorrow, the certain march of the Chinese people toward industrialization and the inevitable appetites such a change will awaken, raise grave questions concerning the future of Russia's Far Eastern empire.

In theory, there is no reason why the resources of Siberia could not be developed by a happy combination of Soviet geography, Chinese labor and Japanese capital to the mutual benefit of all. In practical terms the Soviet Union looks upon that potential army of Chinese labor as just that—an army. At the same time, the Soviets are caught up in the dilemma aptly described by a former manager of the Chinese Eastern Railway, quoted to the effect that "Russia spent 1,800,000,000 rubles to settle on this railway 200,000 Russians and 15,000,000 Chinese."[14]

About that same ratio has pertained overall in the parallel development of the Soviet Far East and the northern Chinese provinces. As the railway manager observed, the Russians have created a great magnet, drawing millions of Chinese toward the borderlands. At the same time, neither the Czarist nor the Soviet government has been able to populate Eastern Siberia at a rate in any way commensurate. Indeed, there appears to be serious concern in Moscow that the caucasian population of the Soviet Far East has begun to decline in absolute as well as relative terms.[15]

Dr. Stefan T. Possony has provided a detailed analysis[16] of China's present and projected food requirement and of the importance of Mongolia and the Soviet Far East in meeting those requirements. Because of this and other economic attractions of the Soviet Far East, Dr. Possony concluded that, "The main population pressure in China is vectored toward Manchuria and points across the Amur."

The existing and enormous future potential of these demographic and economic pressures, the strategically tenuous nature of the overland and water communications between the European and Asian USSR, and the competing claims of the European and Asian regions of the USSR for capital investment suggests a long-term problem for the United States, as well as for the Soviet Union.

What if the Soviet Asian empire proves to be as transitory as the empires of France and Britain? The question is raised here not only in regard to the Far East and Eastern Siberia, but of Central Asia as well—in short, all of the Soviet Union east of the Urals and the Caspian Sea. If, in the short term, US policy in Asia must be preoccupied with Soviet power, it seems at least possible that in the long term we must address ourselves to Chinese power, for China is the heir apparent if the Soviet empire in Asia were to disintegrate as a result of a war or internal upheaval.

Domination of East Asia by a China operating at or near its full potential would confront the United States and Japan with problems at least as difficult as those that would arise from Soviet domination. The questions to be resolved here are vast.

• What is China's legitimate claim on the territories seized by Russia under the "unequal" treaties?

• How can the needs of China's burgeoning population and the rights of the resident Soviet population in East Asia be reconciled?

• What of Japan's present and potential claims in the Kuriles and Sakhalin?[17]

• Above all, how can China's just needs and claims be met without creating a political monster?

The United States cannot solve these problems by itself, and, alone, it may not be able to exercise a decisive influence on any of them. Its interests are deeply involved in all. None can be resolved by the United States attempting to shake the dust and the mud of mainland Asia from its boots. Whether the threat of an unacceptable imbalance of power in Asia be Japan, as in the past, the Soviet Union in the present, or China in the future, the United States will find itself pulled into the Asian equation as surely as it has been compelled to participate in the European equation. The result of any attempt to "opt out" is almost certain to result in a more severe penalty when it is recognized at last that participation is inescapable and inevitable.

THE FUTURE US ROLE

How long must the United States continue to play a major role in Asia? Possibly longer than it will be required to play a direct role in Europe. Europe, after all, is 3,000 miles from American shores. Asia is 60 miles away across the Bering Strait. Some hope of stability is emerging in Europe from the evolution, however tortuous and fitful, of the European Economic Community. Not a shred of such hope exists in Asia while two such giants as the USSR and China are contending for dominance. Hope would be even more remote if these two were to reconcile their differences in favor of joint action or separate action in mutually agreed upon spheres of influence.

How long the United States must continue to play a direct military role on the Asian mainland, specifically in Korea, probably depends upon some major rearrangement of the present political scheme. A unified Korea under a government supported by a majority of its people and able to sustain a substantial rate of economic development would be a major influence for peace in Northeast Asia. Such a Korea could marshal the internal military strength necessary to discourage open aggression, and thereby assure that the Korean Peninsula could not readily be used as an avenue of pressure or conquest, in either direction. That sort of Korea appears to be a long way off.

For some indefinite time in the future, therefore, it seems likely that the United States must maintain a convincing military presence in

Korea. From the Japanese Defense Agency statement cited earlier,[18] it seems plain that this means "combat units" in place and prepared for direct, immediate commitment. The retention of significant combat power in Korea can be meaningful only if three conditions are met.

• The government and people of the Republic of Korea continue to welcome the US presence.

• The United States is able to keep open the Pacific sea and air lanes.

• The United States is able to demonstrate a capability for rapid and continuous reinforcement of the forward American units.

ROLE OF JAPAN'S ARMED FORCES

Any suggestion of a continuing military role for the United States in Northeast Asia inevitably raises the question of what role the Japanese armed forces should play in keeping the peace. Substitution of Japanese combat units for American units in Korea is clearly unacceptable to everyone concerned—most notably the Koreans.

For reasons discussed earlier, deployment of a Japanese nuclear deterrent adequate to replace the present US commitments could drive the Soviet Union and China back into an active alliance. Even the development by Japan of an adequate air defense and tactical air support force is fraught with some political danger since the radius of action of all such forces would extend over the irredentist Japanese territory in Sakhalin and the Kuriles.

Considering the severe constraints imposed by foreign and domestic politics, and the manpower limitations of the present volunteer system, antisubmarine warfare would appear to be the most reasonable area for further Japanese military development.[19] In attempting to cope with her two great military vulnerabilities—to nuclear weapons and submarine warfare—antisubmarine warfare is the only direction in which Japan can move without encountering immediate and formidable political opposition. Even here, caution is required.

HOPE FOR THE FUTURE

Slim though the chances may seem, a recasting of traditional US policy in Asia may be the means to bring about the internal stabilization of mainland China in the period after Mao and the eventual stabilization of all Northeast Asia.

Unanswered and unanswerable at this stage is the question of whether the Soviet Union will permit China to develop internal cohesion, and to prosper. The prospects of just such development in South Vietnam in the years following the Geneva Conference of 1954 were considered sufficiently intolerable by the government in Hanoi to justify armed intervention. Soviet behavior in Hungary in 1956 and in Czechoslovakia in 1968 casts an ominous shadow, one that is pointed out by the government in Peking with urgency.

Ultimately, the slim hope for peace in Asia may be lost or maintained by the degree to which the United States allows itself to be governed by an emotional revulsion for "involvement on the mainland of Asia" or by equally mindless policies that would tend to erode the fundamental relationship with Japan. Either action could upset the delicate balance that now exists, with unknown and potentially catastrophic results.

It is no exaggeration, therefore, to conclude that only the visible, dependable presence of American power in all of its forms enables Asia, in particular Northeast Asia, to maintain cohesion, however shaky and uncertain. The costs of this role are by no means small and the ultimate value of the investment is uncertain. The risks of a further erosion of US power, moral as well as physical, are, however, sufficiently clear to warrant a halt to the retreat.

Endnotes

CHAPTER 1

1. Samuel P. Huntington, *The Soldier and the State*, Cambridge, Mass: Belknap Press of Harvard University Press, 1957, p. 346.
2. William Safire, "Each Other's Mail," *The New York Times*, May 9, 1974, p. 43. Also cited in *Harper's Magazine*, October 1973, p. 115.
3. Huntington, p. 144.
4. Daniel P. Moynihan, "Peace—Some Thoughts on the 1960's and 1970's," *The Public Interest*, Summer 1973, pp. 7-8.
5. Moynihan, p. 9.
6. General Marshall's exact words were "a democracy cannot fight a Seven Years' War." Interview, July 25, 1949. Quoted by Maurice Matloff, *Strategic Planning for Coalition Warfare: 1943-1944*. In series, United States Army in World War II, Office of Chief, Military History, Department of the Army, Washington: US Government Printing Office, 1959, p. 5.
7. Daniel Bell, *The Coming of Post-Industrial Society*, New York: Basic Books, 1973. See also Bell, "The End of Scarcity," *Saturday Review/Society*, May 1973, pp. 49-52.
8. "As We See It," *TV Guide*, October 13, 1973, p. 5.
9. Kenneth Kirk, *Conscience and Its Problems*, London: Longmans, Green and Co., Ltd., 1927, pp. 375-376.
10. Daniel P. Juda, "Voices of Doctors, Rabbis Join Outcry in Opposition to War," *Boston Globe*, May 19, 1970.
11. Amitai Etzioni, "The Search for Political Meaning," *Center Magazine*, March-April 1972, pp. 2-8.

12. Hasan Ozbekhan, "The Triumph of Technology: 'Can' Implies 'Ought'," System Development Corporation, Nr. SP-2830, June 1967.

13. David Riesman, *Individualism Reconsidered*, Garden City, New York: Doubleday (Anchor), 1954.

14. Jack D. Douglas, *Deviance and Respectability: The Social Construction of Moral Meanings*, New York: Basic Books, Inc., 1970.

15. Garrett Hardin, "The Tragedy of the Commons," *Science*, December 13, 1968, pp. 1243-1248.

16. *PS*, American Political Science Association Quarterly, Summer, 1973.

17. Max Lerner, "American Agonistes," *Foreign Affairs*, January 1974, p. 294.

18. John Stuart Mill, *The Subjection of Women*, London, 1965. Paperback edition, New York: Fawcett Publications, Inc., 1971, p. 27.

19. John Emerich Edward Dalberg-Acton, letter to Mandell Creighton, 1887, cited by Sydney E. Ahlstrom, "Lord Acton's Famous Remark," *The New York Times*, March 13, 1974, p. 37.

20. See, for example, Louis Harris, *The Anguish of Change*, New York: W. W. Norton and Co., 1973; and Anthony Lewis, "Winter of Discontent," *The New York Times*, April 15, 1974, p. 31.

21. "National Security Claim Hit," *The Washington Post*, November 13, 1973, p. 1.

22. "Shorter Campaigns Proposed by Nixon: Libel Changes," *The Washington Post*, March 9, 1974, p. 1.

23. C. L. Sulzberger, "The Kissinger Phenomenon," *The New York Times*, March 24, 1974, p. 17.

24. Ed Grossman, "Critic from Within," *Saturday Review/World*, September 25, 1973, p. 35.

25. Resolution 10.3f, *Report of the White House Conference on Youth*, Washington: US Government Printing Office, 1971, p. 242.

26. "Marshall SLAM's Media," *Absent Adage*, Student newspaper project, Defense Information School, Ft. Benjamin Harrison, Ind., August 29, 1972.

27. Arthur Hadley, "Goodbye to the Blind Slash Dead Kid's Hooch," *Playboy*, August 1971, p. 200.

28. W. E. H. Lecky, *History of the Rise and Influence of the Spirit of Rationalism in Europe*, London: Longmans, Green, and Co., 1866, Vol. I, p. vi.

29. Carl L. Becker, *The Heavenly City of the Eighteenth Century Philosophers*, New Haven: Yale University Press, 1933, p. 15.

30. Howard Tolley, Jr., "Children and War," *Intellect*, December 1972, pp. 187-194.

31. "U.S. Scholar Calls Soviet an 'Unreliable Partner'," *The New York Times*, September 23, 1973, p. 15.

32. Russell F. Weigley, *The American Way of War*, New York: Macmillan Publishing Co., Inc., 1973, pp. 142-143.

33. *Ibid.*, p. 128.

34. The lesson indicated involves relative scales and paces of gradualism. All rational application of military force is, or ought to be, gradual in some sense. Otherwise, we should expect all-out thermonuclear exchange in the first moments of any future war. Nevertheless, setting aside for the moment questions of coping with proliferating restraints in modern war, the Vietnam War illustrates

persuasively the futility of applying force in long-drawn-out escalatory steps which represent slight intensification. A resourceful enemy is thus provided with enough time to readjust and match each step, nullifying potential but unused strength, however preponderant it appears to be. The familiar "principle of war," mass, is relevant here: the massing of overwhelming (not merely slightly superior) strength at decisive points in time and space.

35. See, for example, "The Malaise of Democracies," *The Washington Post*, March 5, 1974, p. A22.

36. "Soldier's Return from 30 Years in Jungle Stirs Japan Deeply," *The New York Times*, March 13, 1974, p. l.

37. "Young Politicians in Japan Chafe at the Old Rigidities," *The New York Times*, March 12, 1974, p. 2.

38. *Notes on the State of Virginia*, cited by Bernard Brodie, *Politics and War*, New York: The Macmillan Publishing Co., 1973, p. 29.

39. Bruce Catton, *Grant Takes Command*, Boston: Little, Brown and Company, 1968, p. 143.

40. Louis J. Halle, "Does War Have a Future?" *Foreign Affairs*, October 1973, pp. 33-34.

41. Quoted by William L. Hauser, Lieutenant Colonel, US Army, *America's Army in Crisis*, Baltimore: The Johns Hopkins University Press, 1973, p. 1.

42. Morris Janowitz, "National Service: A Third Alternative?" *Columbia University Teachers College Record*, Vol. 73, No. l, September 1971, p. 31.

43. Robert Reinhold, "Problems of the 21st Century Confound a Parley of Thinkers," *The New York Times*, April 10, 1972.

CHAPTER 2

1. Robert E. Osgood, *Limited War: The Challenge to American Strategy*, Chicago: University of Chicago Press, 1957, pp. 280-281.

2. Melvin R. Laird, *Fiscal Year 1973 Defense Budget and Fiscal Years 1973-1977 Program*, Statement before the Senate Armed Services Committee, Washington: US Department of Defense, February 15, 1972, pp. 29-30.

3. *Ibid.*, p. 30.

4. *Ibid.*, p. 31.

5. Osgood, p. 279.

6. Jack Anderson, "The President's Feud With The Press," *The Washington Post*, March 3, 1974, p. B7.

7. Zechariah Chafee, Jr., *Government and Mass Communications*, Hamden, Connecticut: Archon Books, 1947, p. 13.

8. John Milton, "Areopagitica," reprinted in *The Tradition of Freedom*, Vol. 1, ed. by Milton Mayer, New York: Oceana Publications, 1957, p. 29.

9. Justice Oliver Wendell Holmes, dissenting opinion in "Abrams vs. U.S." *250 U.S. 616* (1919).

10. James B. Reston, *The Artillery of The Press*, New York: Harper and Row, 1966, p. 47.

11. Chafee, p. 710.

12. Max Lerner, *America As A Civilization*, New York: Simon and Schuster, 1957, p. 750.

13. Marvin Barrett, ed., *Survey of Broadcast Journalism 1970-1971*, New York: Grosset and Dunlap, 1971, pp. 32-49.

14. John Adams, as quoted by Vernon L. Parrington in *Main Currents in American Thought*, New York: Harcourt, Brace and Co., 1927, p. 316.

15. Ithiel de Sola Pool, "Newsmen and Statesmen: Adversaries or Cronies?" in *Aspen Notebook on Government and the Media*, ed. by William L. Rivers and Michael J. Nyhan, London: Praeger, 1973, p. 15.

16. *Ibid.*, p. 16.

17. (a) US Department of Defense, *Directive Number 5105.39: Director of Net Assessment*, December 6, 1971.

(b) US Department of Defense, *Secretary of Defense Memorandum Net Assessment*, October 13, 1973.

18. Hadley Cantril, *The Human Dimension: Experiences in Policy Research*, New Brunswick: Rutgers University Press, 1966, pp. 149-161.

19. *Ibid.*, pp. 190-191.

20. Stephen S. Rosenfeld, "Pluralism and Policy," *Foreign Affairs*, January 1974, p. 272.

21. *Ibid.*, pp. 265-266.

22. Reported in *Congressional Quarterly Weekly Reports*, (Washington), December 8, 1973, pp. 3214-3216.

23. Dumas Malone, "Jefferson's First Inaugural Address," in *An American Primer*, ed. by D. J. Boorstin, Chicago: University of Chicago Press, 1966, p. 217.

24. Ithiel del Sola Pool, pp. 151-153.

25. Judge Learned Hand, "U.S. v. Associated Press," *52 F. Supp. 362.*

CHAPTER 3

1. James R. Huntley, *Man's Environment and the Atlantic Alliance*, p. 12. Ecology is "the science of the relationships between organisms and their environment." The verb pollute means, "to dirty; contaminate;" and pollution, "the contamination of soil, water, or the atmosphere by the discharge of noxious substances." *The American Heritage Dictionary of the English Language*, ed. by William Morris, Boston: Houghton Mifflin Co., 1970, pp. 413 and 1015.

2. Expert opinion on the nature and cause of pollution varies as widely as do the problems and numbers of people involved. An example is the controversy which followed the publication of *The Limits of Growth*, by D. L. Meadows, Georgen Randers, and William W. Behrens, III. See the strong exceptions to *The Limits of Growth*, by Allen Kneese and Ronald Ridker, *The Washington Post*, March 2, 1972, p. B-1.

3. "World Population Growth," *The Population Dilemma*, ed. by Philip M. Hauser, 2d Edition, p. 33.

4. Livingston Hartley, "Changes to the Environment—Some International Implications," *Orbis*, Summer 1970, p. 491.

5. Hartley, p. 492.

6. Richard D. Lyons, "Chemical Debris Fouling Vast Areas of the Atlantic", *The New York Times*, February 13, 1973, p. 1.

7. Jules Arbose, "91 Nations Agree on Convention to Control Dumping in Oceans," *The New York Times*, November 14, 1972, p. 1.

8. Lawrence Krader, "Society and Its Physical Environment," *The Annals of the American Academy of Political and Social Science,* May 1970, pp. 12-13.

9. George A. Lincoln, "Winter Fuel Shortage: How Serious?," *US News and World Report,* December 11, 1972, p. 73. As long ago as 1954, the Senate Subcommittee on Minerals, Materials, and Fuels predicted the current energy shortages and recommended actions similar to many advanced by others today.

10. Huntley, pp. 23-25.

11. *The World Almanac and Book of Facts,* New York: Newspaper Enterprise Association, 1973, p. 953.

12. Walter Sullivan, "World Conference: The Need to Work in Concert Was Clear," *The New York Times,* June 18, 1972, p. E-7.

13. George F. Kennan, "To Prevent a World Wasteland—A Proposal," *Foreign Affairs,* April 1970, p. 401ff. See also Charles C. Humpstone, "Pollution: Precedent and Prospect," *Foreign Affairs,* January 1972, p. 336.

14. NATO has become increasingly involved in environmental programs in the past few years ranging from urban areas to the North Sea. See James R. Huntley, *Man's Environment and the Atlantic Alliance.*

15. The material in most of the remainder of this section follows Robert Leider, *From Choice to Determinant: The Environmental Issues in International Relations,* pp. 2-21.

16. Harold M. Schmeck, Jr., "Severe Shortage of Ores Is Feared," *The New York Times,* May 9, 1973, p. 1. Schmeck discusses a report by the US Geological Survey which is the first overall assessment of US mineral use and resources in 21 years.

17. Humpstone, p. 337.

18. "War on Pollution: How It's Faring," *US News and World Report,* August 21, 1972, p. 82.

19. Barry Commoner, "A Businessman's Primer on Ecology," *Business and Society Review,* Spring 1972, p. 53.

20. Chase Manhattan Bank, *Business in Brief,* No. 103, April 1972, p. 4.

21. Hedrick Smith, "70 States Reject Biological Arms," *The New York Times,* April 11, 1972, p.1.

22. *The 1972 Congressional Quarterly Almanac,* p. 150.

23. James A. Barber, Jr., "Ecological Impact of Military Activites," in *The Military and American Society,* ed. by James A. Barber, Jr. and Stephen E. Ambrose, p. 260. Much of the discussion in the remainder of this section follows Barber, pp. 259-270.

24. *Ibid.,* p. 271. One of the largest US underground nuclear tests in recent years was successfully completed at Amchitka Island in the Aleutians on November 6, 1971. Conservationists opposed the test because it occurred in a remote game refuge area, and others opposed it because it was a prototype of a military warhead. Opposition was carried to the Supreme Court which refused to order a delay. The governments of Canada and Japan also protested the test. E. W. Kenworthy, "Court of Appeals Refuses to Halt Amchitka A-Blast," *The New York Times,* October 29, 1971, p. 1; Fred P. Graham, "High Court, 4-3, Bars Delay in Amchitka Blast," November 7, 1971, p. 1.

25. Barber, p. 272.

26. *Ibid.,* p. 273.

27. Elizabeth B. Drew, "Dam Outrage: The Story of the Army Engineers," *The Atlantic Monthly,* April 1970, pp. 51-62.

28. Drew, p. 51.

29. Drew, p. 62.

30. Thomas S. C. Steinhauser, "Keep It Clean, Environmental Quality is 'IN' at the Pentagon," *Armed Forces Journal,* December 1972, p. 24.

31. Steinhauser.

32. J. L. Gregg, Major, Technical Division, Research Directorate, Office, Chief of Research and Development, Headquarters, Department of the Army, conversation with the author on May 28, 1973. The Army's current research program includes evaluation of " . . . the health effects of Army-unique pollutants and the development of environmental effects data . . . ; minimizing emissions from Army materiel . . . ; development of a special treatment process for munition production plant wastes . . . ; integration of installation utilities and waste disposal systems . . . ; and improving the efficiency and/or economy of present pollution control systems . . ." W. C. Gribble, Jr., Lieutenant General, Chief of Research and Development, Department of the Army, statement before the Committee on Armed Services, House of Representatives, 1st Session, 93d Congress, May 8, 1973, p. 15. As a matter of historical interest, in 1940 the entire annual budget for the Navy was $891 million, and for the Army it was $907 million. *The Statistical History of the United States from Colonial Times to the Present,* Stamford, Conn.: Fairfield Publishers, 1965, p. 718.

33. To illustrate the impact of inflation on defense costs, personnel costs have risen rapidly in recent years and they now amount to 56 percent of the annual defense budget. There are indications that such expenses will continue to be high; for example, in May 1973, the enlistment bonuses paid by the Army for combat arms volunteers rose from $1,500 to $2,500. "Ante Upped for Bonus Soldiers," *Army Times,* May 9, 1973, p. 4.

34. John Hamer, "Auto Emission Controls," *Editorial Research Reports,* April 18, 1973, pp. 306-307.

35. W. M. Oller, Rear Admiral, United States Navy, US Department of Defense, Defense Supply Agency, Defense Fuel Supply Center, Letter to the Armed Forces regarding revalidation of petroleum requirements, April 5, 1973.

36. Steinhauser, p. 26.

37. Barbara Ward and Rene Dubos, *Only One Earth: The Care and Maintenance of a Small Planet,* p. 140. An unofficial report commissioned by the Secretary-General of the United Nations Conference on the Human Environment, prepared with the assistance of a 152-member committee of corresponding consultants from 58 countries.

38. Hartley, pp. 491-492.

39. "Ecostrategy" is suggested in part by the word "ecotactics", which has been defined as "the science of arranging and maneuvering all available forces and actions against the enemies of the earth," in *Ecotactics: The Sierra Club Handbook for Environment Activities,* ed. by John G. Mitchell and Constance L. Stallings, New York: Pocket Books, 1970, p. 5.

40. Linda Charlton, "Senate Urges US to Seek End to All 'Environmental Warfare'," *The New York Times,* July 12, 1973, p. 2.

41. *Ibid.*

42. "Nature Is Fooled by Scientists," *Army Times,* September 12, 1973, p. 31.

43. US Congress, Senate, S. Res. 71, 93d Congress, 1st Session, Calendar No. 255, Report No. 93-270, p. 5.

44. Seymour M. Hersh, "US Admits Rainmaking from '67-'72 in Indochina," *The New York Times,* May 19, 1974, p. 1.

CHAPTER 4

1. Richard N. Cooper, "Economic Interdependence and Foreign Policy in the Seventies," *World Politics,* Vol. XXV, No. 2, January 1974, pp. 159-181. Cited hereafter as Cooper, "Policy."

2. "The International Transmission of Inflation," *O.E.C.D. Observer,* August 1973, p. 28.

3. Cooper, "Policy," and his book, *The Economics of Interdependence: Economic Policy in the Atlantic Community,* New York: McGraw-Hill, 1968. Cited hereafter as Cooper, *Economics.*

4. Cooper, *Economics,* p. 75.

5. Cooper, "Policy," p. 166.

6. *Ibid.,* p. 159.

7. Cooper, *Economics,* p. 78ff, notes these qualifications.

8. Cooper, "Policy," p. 180.

9. Cooper, *Economics,* p. 69.

10. Kenneth N. Waltz, "The Myth of National Interdependence," in *The International Corporation: A Symposium,* 1970, ed. by Charles P. Kindleberger, p. 216.

11. *Ibid.,* p. 219.

12. Raymond Vernon, "Multinational Business and National Economic Goals," *International Organization,* Vol. XXV, No. 3, Summer 1971, p. 697.

13. *Ibid.,* p. 698.

14. Joseph S. Nye, Jr. and Robert O. Keohane, "Transnational Relations and World Politics: An Introduction," *International Organization,* Vol. XXV, No. 3, Summer 1971, p. 341.

15. Lawrence Scheinman, "Security and a Transnational System: The Case of Nuclear Energy," *International Organization,* Vol. XXV, No. 3, Summer 1971, pp. 626-649.

16. Vernon, p. 697.

17. *Ibid.,* p. 695.

18. Peter B. Evans, "National Autonomy and Economic Development: Critical Perspectives on Multinational Corporations in Poor Countries," *International Organization,* Vol. XXV, No. 3, Summer 1971, p. 685.

19. Waltz, p. 207.

20. Vernon, p. 705.

21. Oran R. Young, "Interdependencies in World Politics," *International Journal,* Vol. XXIV, No. 4, Autumn 1969, p. 747ff.

22. The idea is from Young.

23. Karl Kaiser, "Transnational Relations as a Threat to the Democratic Process," *International Organization,* Vol. XXV, No. 3, Summer 1971, pp. 706-720.

24. Herbert E. Kelman, as cited by Donald P. Warwick, in "Transnational Participation and International Peace," *International Organization,* Vol. XXV, No. 3, Summer 1971, p. 667.

25. William J. Diebold, "U.S. Trade Policy: The New Political Dimensions," *Foreign Affairs,* Vol. 52, April 1974, pp. 472-496.

26. *Ibid.*

27. For example, Edward L. Morse, "The Transformation of Foreign Policies: Modernization, Interdependence, and Externalization," *World Politics,* Vol. XXII, April 1970, pp. 371-392; and "Crisis Diplomacy, Interdependence, and the Politics of International Economic Relations," *World Politics,* Vol. XXIV, Supplement (Spring 1972), pp. 123-150.

28. As cited by Nye and Keohane, "Transnational Relations and World Politics: A Conclusion," *International Organization,* Vol. XXV, No. 3, Summer 1971, p. 743.

CHAPTER 5

1. This chain of events is detailed in Herbert Feis, *The Road to Pearl Harbor,* 1950.

2. US Congress, Joint Committee on the Investigation of the Pearl Harbor Attack, *Pearl Harbor Attack,* 79th Congress, 2d Session, 1946, Part 14, p. 1407.

3. Roberta Wohlstetter, *Pearl Harbor, Warning and Decision,* 1962, pp. 382-386. Also see Roberta Wohlstetter, "Cuba and Pearl Harbor: Hindsight and Foresight," *Foreign Affairs,* July 1965, pp. 691-707.

4. Details regarding these and many other warnings are available in US Congress, Joint Committee on the Investigation of the Pearl Harbor Attack, *Investigation of the Pearl Harbor Attack,* 1946, and in the Wohlstetter book and article, note 3.

5. See US Congress, Senate, Committee on Armed Services, Preparedness Investigating Subcommittee, *Investigations of the Preparedness Program, Interim Report on Cuban Military Buildup,* 1963.

6. Several books contain interesting detailed accounts of the Cuban Missile Crisis decisionmaking process. Among these are Elie Abel, *The Cuban Missile Crisis,* 1966; Robert F. Kennedy, *Thirteen Days: A Memoir of the Cuban Missile Crisis,* 1969; and Walter Wells Layson, *The Political and Strategic Aspects of the 1962 Cuban Crisis,* 1971.

7. Ole R. Holsti, "Cognitive Dynamics and Images of the Enemy: Dulles and Russia" in *Enemies in Politics,* 1967, ed. by Daniel J. Finley, p. 30.

8. Klaus Knorr, "Failures in National Intelligence Estimates: The Case of the Cuban Missiles," *World Politics,* April 1964, pp. 462-463.

9. Roberta Wohlstetter, *Pearl Harbor—Warning and Decision,* 1962, p. 251.

10. US Congress, Senate, Committee on Armed Services, Preparedness Investigating Subcommittee, *Investigation of the Preparedness Program, Interim Report on Cuban Military Buildup,* 1961, p. 3.

CHAPTER 6

1. Carroll Kilpatrick, "Crisis in Minerals is Feared," *The Washington Post,* January 14, 1974, p. A-1.

2. *The Mineral Position of the United States, 1975-2000,* ed. by E. N. Cameron.

3. Yuan-li Wu, *Raw Material Supply in a Multipolar World.*

4. "Material Needs and the Environment Today and Tomorrow," *Final Report of the National Commission on Materials Policy,* June 1973.

5. *The Mineral Position of the United States, 1975-2000,* p. 53.

6. "First Annual Report of the Secretary of the Interior Under the Mining and Materials Policy Act of 1970," Washington: US Government Printing Office, 1972.

7. "Towards a National Materials Policy—An Interim Report," pp. 3-4.

8. US Congress, House, *Strategic and Critical Materials Stockpiling Act,* Pub. L. 520, 79th Congress, Washington: US Government Printing Office, 1946.

9. US Congress, House, *Defense Production Act,* Pub. L. 774, 81st Congress, Washington: US Government Printing Office, 1950.

10. *The Mineral Position of the United States, 1975-2000,* p. 16.

11. "Towards a National Materials Policy—An Interim Report," pp. 14-35.

12. Nazli Choucri, M. Laird, and D. L. Meadows, *Resource Security and Foreign Policy: A Simulation Model of International Conflict,* Report No. C/72-9, Massachusetts: Center for International Studies, Massachusetts Institute of Technology, March 1972.

13. *"Strategic and Critical Materials: Descriptive Data,"* Office of Preparedness, GSA, December 1973; and "Commodity Data Summaries—1974," Bureau of Mines, US Dept of Interior.

14. "Material Needs and the Environment Today and Tomorrow," pp. 9-26.

15. D. L. Gordon and R. Dangerfield, *The Hidden Weapon: The Story of Economic Warfare,* New York: Harper & Bros., pp. 6-12.

16. "Competitive Aspects of Foreign Aid," *SRI Journal,* 4th Quarter, California: Stanford Research Institute, 1959, pp. 177-178.

17. US Dept of the Interior, "United States Petroleum Through 1970," Washington: US Government Printing Office, 1968, p. 65.

CHAPTER 7

1. US Council on International Economic Policy, *International Economic Report of the President for 1974,* p. 44.

2. *Ibid.*

3. John G. McLean, "The United States Energy Outlook and Its Implications for National Policy," *The Annals,* November 1973, p. 101.

4. "Energy, Oil and Man," *Standard Oil Company of California Bulletin,* Summer 1970, Vol. XLVII, No. 3, p. 2.

5. Allan I. Demaree, "Arab Wealth, As Seen Through Arab Eyes," *Fortune,* April 1974, p. 109.

6. William A. Johnson, *Energy Crisis,* p. 3. Published remarks before Brookings Institution, July 17, 1973.

7. Supertankers of 300,000 deadweight tons (DWT) are coming into common use, but the largest tanker that can be accommodated along the eastern seaboard is 70,000 DWT.

8. S. David Freeman, "Is There An Energy Crisis? An Overview," *The Annals,* November 1973, pp. 2-3.

9. US National Commission on Materials Policy, *Material Needs and the Environment Today and Tomorrow,* June 1973, pp. 5-18.

10. McLean, p. 101.

11. Albert J. Meyer, *The Middle East and World Energy,* p. 12. Published speech before Senate Committee on Foreign Relations, May 31, 1973.

12. This is author's estimate. Primary data came from National Petroleum Council and Federal Energy Office publications, and were modified by author to reflect somewhat lower growth rates.

13. In 1972 the United States relied on oil for about 45 percent of its energy needs, Western Europe for over 60 percent, and Japan for about 75 percent.

14. US Council on International Economic Policy, p. 48.

15. The OPEC members are: Saudi Arabia, Iran, Kuwait, Iraq, United Arab Emirates, Qatar, Indonesia, Venezuela, Nigeria, Algeria, Libya, Ecuador, and Gabon, an associate member. Trinidad-Tobago is seeking membership.

16. Author's estimate. Base data provided by a number of sources.

17. Ronald Kovan and David Ottaway, "US Oil Nightmare: Worldwide Shortage," *The Washington Post,* June 17, 1973, p. A14.

18. So called because it has a high specific gravity and is too viscous to be produced or handled by normal methods.

19. Kovan and Ottaway, p. A14.

20. Today the United States is the leading producer at 9.5 million bpd with Russia and Saudi Arabia close behind. Russia soon is expected to nose ahead of the United States with Saudi Arabia passing both.

21. Kovan and Ottaway, p. A15.

22. In addition, it should be noted that the United States does not have the leverage in Iran that we have in Saudi Arabia—only 40 percent of Iranian oil is produced by American firms. Further, only a small fraction of US produced oil comes to the United States, as most of this oil is destined to foreign US subsidiaries.

23. US Council on International Economic Policy, pp. 49, 110 and 111.

24. Author's estimate based on expected imports as shown in Table 1 at a landed cost of approximately $9.00 a barrel.

25. US Council on International Economic Policy, p. 45.

26. *Ibid.,* p. 51.

27. *Ibid.,* p. 50.

28. *Ibid.,* p. 53.

29. *Ibid.,* p. 49, and author's extrapolation to 1980 based on oil income to producing country of $8.00 a barrel.

30. James E. Akins, "International Cooperative Efforts in Energy Supply, *The Annals,* November 1973, p. 78.

31. Demaree, pp. 115-116.

32. Demaree, p. 109.

33. Of the total private foreign investment in the United States, portfolio holdings account for about 64 percent, direct investments account for about 24 percent, and loans and credits the remaining 12 percent. Although foreign portfolio investment has essentially the same effects on the US economy as foreign direct investment, it seldom generates the real and imagined problems associated with foreign direct investment, especially the fear of foreign control.

The distinction between portfolio and direct investment is highly arbitrary, based only on the degree of ownership of stock. (If a foreign investor controls less than 25 percent of the stock of a US company, the investment is defined as a portfolio investment.)

34. US Council on International Economic Policy, p. 62.

35. *The Profit Situation, A Special Petroleum Report,* The Chase Manhattan Bank, April 1974.

36. *Ibid.*

37. *Ibid.*

38. *Ibid.*

39. US Department of the Interior, *Final Statement for the Prototype Oil Shale Leasing Program,* Vol. II, 1973, p. II-167.

40. Thomas C. Barger, *The Reality and Dimensions of the Oil Crisis,* Handout notes for presentation at School of Advanced International Studies, The Johns Hopkins University, September 18, 1973.

41. Dr. Dixy Lee Ray, *The Nation's Energy Future,* December 1, 1973, WASH-1281, p. 10.

42. "The Nuclear Debate," *Time,* Vol. 103, No. 15, April 15, 1974, p. 34.

43. Ray, p. 10.

44. John P. Henry, Jr., and Richard A. Schmidt, "Coal: Still Old Reliable?," *The Annals,* November 1973, p. 38.

45. Ray, p. 10.

46. Robert E. Hunter, *The Energy Crisis and US Foreign Policy,* p. 17.

47. *Ibid.,* p. 9.

48. Ray, p. 10.

CHAPTER 8

1. OPEC was formed in 1960 to counter threatened reductions in the posted price for oil. Its members now are Algeria, Ecuador, Indonesia, Iran, Iraq, Kuwait, Libya, Nigeria, Qatar, Saudi Arabia, the United Arab Emirates, and Venezuela. An interlinked satellite organization is OAPEC—Organization of *Arab* Petroleum Exporting Countries. That membership consists of those Arab countries who are members of OPEC plus Bahrain, Egypt and Syria.

2. Statistical Summary, *World Oil,* 1971.

3. National Materials Advisory Board, *Trends in the Usage of Tungsten,* NMAB-309, National Academy of Sciences-National Academy of Engineering, Washington, D.C., July 1973, pp. 15-44.

4. But the multiplier effect "cuts both ways." An increased rate of economic growth and modernization raises the demand for more resources.

5. Andries Van de Ree, "Geological Oceanography," *Science and the Sea,* Vol. II, US Naval Oceanographic Office, 1969, p. 5.

6. Arvid Pardo, "Sovereignty Under the Sea," *Round Table,* Vol. 58, October 1968, pp. 344-345.

7. Robert E. Vansant, Lieutenant Colonel, *Ocean Hard Mineral Resources and National Security Planning,* Monograph, Carlisle Barracks, Pa: US Army War College, October 22, 1973, p. 10.

8. William J. Cromie, "Who Will Own the Ocean's Wealth?" *United States Naval Institute Proceedings,* Vol. 91, No. 1/743, January 1965, p. 60.

9. Pardo, p. 345.

10. Gerard J. Mangone, The United Nations, *International Law and the Bed of the Seas,* Newark: College of Marine Studies, University of Delaware, 1972, p. 21.

11. Willard J. Pierson "Ocean Waves," *Science and the Sea,* Vol. II, US Naval Oceanographic Office, 1969, p.15.

12. Leigh S. Ratiner, "United States Oceans Policy: An Analysis," *Journal of Maritime Law and Commerce,* Vol. 2, January 1971, p. 229.

13. Frank Fedele, Colonel, "Overflight by Military Aircraft in Time of Peace," *USAF Judge Advocate General Law Review,* Vol. IX, No. 5, September-October 1967, p. 8.

14. Seymour W. Wurfel, *et. al.,* "A Brief Historical Survey of Freedom of the Seas," *The Surge of Sea Law,* University of North Carolina Sea Grant Publication, March 1973, p. 14.

15. Fedele, p. 8.

16. Harry S. Truman, "Policy of the United States With Respect to the Natural Resources of the Subsoil and Seabed of the Continental Shelf," *Proclamation No. 2667,* September 28, 1945.

17. Ratiner, p. 228.

18. *Ibid.,* p. 229.

19. John R. Stevenson, "Who Is to Control the Oceans: US Policy and the 1973 Law of the Sea Conference," *The International Lawyer,* Vol. 6, No. 3, July 1972, p. 467.

20. William R. Palmer, Commander, "Territorial Sea Agreement—Key to Progress in the Law of the Sea," *JAG Journal,* December 1970—January 1971, p. 6.

21. *Ibid.*

22. Stevenson, p. 472.

23. Stevenson, *Address Before the American Society of International Law,* Annual Meeting, April 29, 1971, p. 1; Stevenson, *The International Lawyer,* July 1972, p. 406.

24. An undated map prepared by Office of the Geographer, Department of State, entitled "World Straits Affected by a 12-Mile Territorial Sea" shows 124.

25. *Ibid.*

26. Fedele, p. 8.

27. Lester Gelb, "U.S. Jets for Israel Took Route Around Allies," *The New York Times,* October 25, 1973, p. 1.

28. In territorial waters "submarines are required to navigate on the surface, and to show their flag," *Article 14,* Territorial Sea Convention, 1958.

29. Frederic G. DeRocher, "Freedom of Passage Through International Straits: Community Interest Amid Present Controversy," *University of Miami Sea Grant Technical Bulletin No. 23,* 1972, p. 33.

30. *Ibid.,* p. 98.

31. *Ibid.,* p. 95, Note 193.

32. Stevenson, *The International Lawyer,* p. 469.

33. *Ibid.*

34. John R. Stevenson and Bernard H. Oxman, "The Preparations for the Law

of the Sea Conference," *American Journal of International Law,* Vol. 68, No. 1, January 1974, p. 10.

35. Nathaniel C. Kenyon, Colonel, "International Law and the Law of War, Introduction," (unpublished notes), 1973, p. 2.

36. Television interview with Abba Eban, on Edward Murrow's *Person to Person,* September 20, 1957.

37. Stevenson, *Statement to the Committee on the Peaceful Uses of the Seabed and the Ocean Floor Beyond the Limits of National Jurisdiction,* Department of State Press Release No. 169, Geneva, August 3, 1971, p. 3.

38. Stevenson and Oxman, p. 12, and Lewis M. Alexander, ed. "The Law of the Sea, Needs and Interests of Developing Countries," *Proceedings of the Seventh Annual Conference of the Law of the Sea Institute,* June 26-29, 1972, pp. 166-182.

39. Alexander, p. 170.

40. *Ibid.,* pp. 161-165.

41. US Department of the Navy, "An Assessment of the Contribution to Coastal Pollution by Transiting Ships in Selected International Straits," OCNAV/N5-72-1, July 1972.

42. De Rocher, pp. 30-31.

43. Richard M. Nixon, "Statement by the President on U.S. Oceans Policy," May 23, 1970, p. 1.

44. *Ibid.*

45. US Senate Resolution 82, July 16, 1973, Par. (1).

46. *Ibid.,* Par. (4).

47. Nixon, p. 1.

48. *Ibid.*

49. Choon-Ho Park, "Oil Under Troubled Waters: The Northeast Asia Seabed Controversy," *Harvard International Law Journal,* Vol. 14, 1973. (A somewhat ludicrous note is added by the fact that an American citizen possesses an Imperial Edict from the Dowager Empress of China, dated 1893, which gives him possession of the critically important Senkaku Islands.)

50. John Franklin Campbell, *The Red Sea and Suez,* Paper presented to the Conference on the Indian Ocean Area at the Center for Strategic and International Studies, Georgetown University, March 18-19, 1971, pp. 16-17.

51. "Energy From the Sea: The Possibilities Are Out of Sight," *The New York Times,* March 27, 1974, p. 63.

52. Edward Cowan, "Report on Atlantic Drilling Would Put It 30 Miles Out," *The New York Times,* March 23, 1974, p. 1.

53. Anthony Astrachan, "Who Owns Seabed Riches?" *The Washington Post,* December 2, 1973, p. 22.

54. "Manganese Nodules (II): Prospects for Deep Sea Mining," *Science Magazine,* Vol. 183, No. 4125, American Association for the Advancement of Science, Washington, D.C., February 15, 1974, pp. 644-646.

55. Barry Newman, "Mysterious 'Nodules' At Bottom of Oceans May Yield a Treasure," *Wall Street Journal,* September 21, 1973, p. 1.

56. We first heard the term "pinpoint sovereignty" in another context in a conversation with Colonel Erwin R. Brigham, a colleague also assigned to the Strategic Studies Institute. We can understand the difficulties such a term would pose to the international lawyer—especially where ownership rests with a

multinational corporation complicated by a joint-venture arrangement. Nevertheless, we still believe it is useful as a descriptive term of the politico-military dilemma these "points" might create.

57. Norman V. Beckner, *et. al., The Navy and the Common Sea,* Washington: Center for Naval Analysis, 1972, p. 36.

58. *Ibid.,* p. 79.

59. *Ibid.,* p. 89.

60. *Ibid.,* p. 64.

CHAPTER 9

1. Creighton W. Abrams, General, "The Will to Fight," *Vital Speeches of the Day,* Vol. XXXX, No. 4, December 1, 1973, pp. 122-123.

2. Richard M. Nixon, "State of the Union Message," *The New York Times,* January 31, 1974, p. 20.

3. Henry Kissinger, "Secretary Kissinger's News Conference of December 27," *The Department of State Bulletin,* Volume LXX, January 21, 1974, p. 46.

4. Donald M. Shapiro, "Testing Detente by Arms Curbs," *The New York Times,* February 28, 1974, p. 37.

5. Dwight D. Eisenhower, Dedication Address, Carlisle Barracks, US Army War College, August 31, 1966.

6. Leonid Brezhnev, "On the Policy of the Soviet Union and the International Situation," *Novosti Press Agency,* 1973, pp. 110-111.

7. *Ibid.,* pp. 227-228.

8. *Ibid.,* p. 229.

9. Victor Zorza, "Kremlin Policy Struggle," *The Washington Post,* February 26, 1974, p. A22.

10. Malcolm Mackintosh, "Influence on Foreign Policy," *Problems of Communism,* September-October 1973, p. 3.

11. Joseph Alsop, "SALT II: Agreement Unlikely," *The Washington Post,* March 8, 1974, p. A27.

12. Nikita Khrushchev, *Khrushchev Remembers,* Boston: Little, Brown and Company, 1970, p. 520.

13. "DOD Summary of Principal Impacts of the Strategic Arms Limitation Agreements," *Commander's Digest,* June 22, 1972, p. 7.

14. T. H. Rigby, "The Soviet Politburo: A Comparative Profile 1951-71," *Soviet Studies,* July 1972, p. 11.

15. Yu. Kostko, "Ravnovesiye Strakha ili Obespecheniye Podlinnoi Bezopasnosti," *Mirovaya Ekonomika i Mezhdunarodniye Otnosheniya,* June 1972, p. 88.

16. A. Yepishev, "Soviet Army's Historic Mission," *Soviet Military Review,* February 1974, p. 5.

17. Chou En-Lai as quoted in *Adelphi Paper No. 99,* London: International Institute for Strategic Studies, July 1973, p. 29.

18. H. D. S. Greenway, "Chou Maintains Line on US-China Detente," *The Washington Post,* February 23, 1974, p. All.

19. Pyotr Neporozhny, "Soviet-American Cooperation in Power Engineering," *Soviet Life,* January 1974, pp. 58-59.

20. "Is Short Term Gain an Illusion?" *Armed Forces Journal,* January 1974, p. 30.

21. George Murzin, "Long Term Cooperation," *Soviet Life,* February 1974, pp. 26-28.

22. Christoph Bertram, "Detente," *1974 Britannica Book of the Year,* Chicago: Encyclopedia Britannica, Inc., 1974, p. 25.

23. *Ibid.*

CHAPTER 10

1. For example, George Ball, "Parochialism in Europe; 'Creeping Gaullism' in America," *The Atlantic Community Quarterly,* Vol. II, No. 2, Summer 1973, p. 161; Walter Laquer, "The Idea of Europe Runs Out of Gas," *The New York Times Magazine,* January 20, 1974, p. 12; R. W. Komer, "Treating NATO's Self-Inflicted Wound," *Foreign Policy,* No. 13, Winter 1973, p. 34; George F. Kennan, "Europe's Problems, Europe's Choices," *Foreign Policy,* No. 14, Spring 1974, p. 3.

2. "Key Indicators," *The Economist,* March 16, 1974, p. 63.

3. "Key Indicators," *The Economist,* January 12, 1974, p. 54.

4. Pierre Uri, "Dialogue Not Dispute, GATT Talks Focus US-EC Relations," *European Community,* No. 169, October 1973, p. 17.

5. See Philippe Heymann, "The Grand Play, US-EC Relations as a Card Game," *European Community,* No. 171, December 1973, pp. 17-19, for brief comparison of the economic strengths and weaknesses of the United States and the EEC.

6. See Alastair Buchan, ed., *Europe's Futures Europe's Choices,* New York: Columbia University Press, 1969, pp. 149-167 for an appraisal of alternative futures of Western Europe; and Theodore Geiger, *The Fortunes of the West,* Bloomington: Indiana University Press, 1973, pp. 155-169; and Gerhard Mally, *The European Community in Perspective: The New Europe, The United States and the World,* Lexington, Mass.: Lexington Books, 1973.

7. Henry A. Kissinger, "A New Atlantic Charter," *The Atlantic Community Quarterly,* Vol. II, No. 2, Summer 1973, p. 151.

8. Kissinger, pp. 153-154.

9. François Duchêne, "The Strategic Consequences of the Enlarged European Community," *The Atlantic Community Quarterly,* Vol. II, No. 2, Summer 1973, pp. 211-212.

10. See Alain Jacob, "Kremlin's Foreign Policy Goals," *The Guardian,* March 9, 1974, p. 15, for an analysis of Soviet policies and intentions in Western Europe.

11. Karl Kaiser, *Europe and the United States,* Washington: Columbia Books, 1973, p. 90. Also recommended as an overall survey of Atlantic relations.

12. Christoph Bertram, "Mutual Force Reduction in Europe: The Political Aspects," *Adelphi Paper No. 84,* London: International Institute for Strategic Studies, 1972, pp. 9-12; "Prospects for SALT II and MBFR," *Survival,* Vol. XV, No. 4, July/August 1973, p. 195; "Mutual Force Reductions in Europe," *Survival,* Vol. XV, No. 6, November/December 1973, p. 275.

13. See "A Survey of West Germany," *The Economist,* December 1, 1973, pp. 1-54 for detailed appraisal of FRG domestic scene.

14. "German *Ostpolitik* and Super-Power Relations," *Survival,* Vol. XV, No. 6, November/December 1973, pp. 296-300.

15. Marc Ullmann, "Security Aspects in French Foreign Policy," *Survival,* Vol. XV, No. 6, November/December 1973, p. 262.

16. "And Don't Forget the World," *The Economist,* March 9, 1974, p. 18.

17. "The Way Europe Is," *The Economist,* March 23, 1974, p. 12; and "With Such Friends, Who Needs Enemies?" *The Economist,* March 16, 1974, p. 43.

CHAPTER 11

1. Historical Evaluation and Research Organization, *Historical Trends Related to Weapon Lethality,* 1964, p. 6.

2. Current examples of precision munitions are the Tube-launched, Optically-tracked, Wire-guided (TOW), Shillelagh, Redeye, and Chaparral missiles. Future possibilities are the Cannon Launched Guided Projectile (CLGP), HELLFIRE (Helicopter Launched Fire and Target Antitank Guided Missile), and the Stinger air defense missile.

3. Richard D. Hilton, "What Every Ground Commander Should Know About Guided Bombs," *Army,* June 1973, p. 29.

4. John T. Burke, "Precision Weaponry: The Changing Nature of Modern Warfare," *Army,* March 1974, p. 13.

5. A. J. Goodpaster, General, "Remarks," *NATO's Fifteen Nations,* December 1973 - January 1974, p. 24.

6. *Ibid.*

7. Harlan Cleveland, *NATO: The Transatlantic Bargain,* p. 81.

8. Michael Howard, "NATO and the Year of Europe," *Survival,* January/February 1974, p. 27. Michael Howard is a Fellow in Higher Defense Studies, All Souls College, Oxford.

9. Dr. Steven L. Canby, RAND Corporation, quoted by Kenneth Hunt, "The Alliance and Europe: Part II: Defense with Fewer Men," *Adelphi Paper No. 98,* Summer 1973, p. 27.

10. Howard, p. 27.

CHAPTER 12

1. Oles M. Smolansky, "Soviet Policy in the Middle East," *Current History,* Vol. 65, October 1973, p. 155.

2. Center for Advanced International Studies, *On Soviet Objectives and Strategy in the Middle East,* 1974, p. 24. Draft article to be published.

3. "How 'The Good Life' Eludes the Russians," *U.S. News & World Report,* November 19, 1973, p. 70.

4. Joseph Framm, "Russia vs China in Big War," *U.S. News & World Report,* August 27, 1973, p. 32.

5. Smolansky, p. 156.

6. "How 'The Good Life' Eludes the Russians," p. 71.

7. Hedrick Smith, "Brezhnev Unveils a Vast Effort to Farm Steppes of Northern Russia," *The New York Times,* March 16, 1974, p. 6.

8. Marshall I. Goldman, "The Soviet Economy: New Era or the Old Error?" *Current History,* Vol. 65, October 1973, p. 169.

9. Annual Report of the Council on International Economic Policy, *International Economic Report of the President,* February 1974, Table 31, p. 101.

10. George Lenczowski, "Egypt and the Soviet Exodus," *Current History,* Vol. 64, January 1973, p. 15.

11. Hannes Adomeit, "Soviet Risk-Taking and Crisis Behavior: Confrontation to Coexistence?" *Adelphi Paper No. 101,* Fall 1973, p. 27.

12. John C. Campbell, "Moscow's Purposes," *Problems of Communism,* September-October 1972, p. 40.

13. Campbell, p. 44.

14. United Nations, *Yearbook of International Trade Statistics 1970-1971,* 1973, p. 190.

15. John Leech, "US Seen Set to Aid Suez Canal Clearing," *The Washington Post,* March 16, 1974, p. A14.

16. Campbell, p. 47.

17. Campbell.

18. Campbell.

19. Campbell, p. 48.

20. Geoffrey Jukes, "The Indian Ocean in Soviet Naval Policy," *Adelphi Paper No. 87,* May 1972, p. 1.

21. Smolansky, p. 155.

22. "Soviet Steps Up Criticism of U.S. Base," *The New York Times,* February 28, 1974, p. 4.

24. Jukes, p. 22.

24. Jukes.

25. Jukes.

26. "Statistics," *Oil and Gas Journal,* January 28, 1974, p. 191.

27. Robert E. Hunter, *The Energy Crisis and U.S. Foreign Policy,* p. 37.

28. "Capacity of the World Tanker Fleet," *World Petroleum Report 1972,* Table 3, p. 10.

CHAPTER 13

1. Andre Siegfried, "The Suez: International Roadway," *Foreign Affairs,* July 1953, p. 605.

2. A. T. Mahan, *The Problem of Asia and Its Effect Upon International Policies,* London, 1900, p. 79, quoted in Charles W. Hallberg, *The Suez Canal, Its History and Diplomatic Language,* p. 317.

3. Sir Charles Dilke, *Problems of Greater Britain,* London, 1890, pp. 657-658, quoted in Charles W. Hallberg, *The Suez Canal, Its History and Diplomatic Language,* p. 316.

4. "Consequences Politiques et Economiques de la Reouverture du Canal de Suez," *Chronique de Politique Etrangere,* May 1973, p. 348.

5. Alan B. Mountjoy, "New Life for the Suez Canal," *Contemporary Review,* November 1971, p. 264.

6. Thomas R. Stauffer, "Who Needs the Suez Canal?" *MidEast,* October 1970, p. 31.

7. United Nations, Conference on Trade and Development, *The Economic Effects of the Closure of the Suez Canal,* p. 21. In cases where the specific "Suez surcharge has been reduced, this has been affected by increased freight rates."

8. United Arab Republic, Suez Canal Authority, *Suez Canal Report,* 1966, p. 113.

9. "Why Russia Wants Suez Canal Opened," *U.S. News and World Report,* Vol. 75, November 26, 1973, p. 36.

10. *Ibid.*

11 US Department of the Army, *DA Pam 550-28,* pp. IX, 427.

12. John K. Cooley, "Egypt Plans for Peace, Reconstruction and Suez Reopening," *The Christian Science Monitor,* December 13, 1973, p. 8.

13. *Ibid.*

14. John Leech, "US Seen Set to Aid Suez Canal Clearing," *The Washington Post,* March 16, 1974, p. A14.

15. *Petroleum Press Service,* September 1973, p. 333, quoted in Ragaei El Mallakh, *The United States and the Suez Canal: A Study in Economic Mutuality of Interests,* p. 5.

16. Mountjoy, p. 267.

17. Gunnar Alexandersson and Goran Norstrom, *World Shipping,* Upsala, Sweden: Almquist & Wikull, 1963, p. 70.

18. Ragaei El Mallakh, p. 17.

CHAPTER 14

1. "Soviet Steps Up Criticism of US Base," *The New York Times,* February 28, 1974, p. 4.

2. Elmo R. Zumwalt, Jr., Admiral, "Strategic Importance of Indian Ocean," *Armed Forces Journal,* April 1974, p. 29.

3. Geoffrey Jukes, "The Indian Ocean in Soviet Naval Policy," *Adelphi Paper No. 87,* p. 12.

4. R. M. Burrell and Alvin J. Cottrell, *Iran, The Arabian Peninsula and the Indian Ocean,* p. 39.

5. Prime Minister Indira Gandhi, speech delivered at the Third Conference of Heads of State and Government of the Non-Aligned Nations, Lusaka, Zambia, 1970, cited in *Neither East Nor West,* ed. by Henry M. Christman, p. 177.

6. Seymour Weiss, "U.S. Interests and Activities in the Indian Ocean Area," *The Department of State Bulletin,* April 8, 1974, p. 373.

CHAPTER 15

1. Thomas Jefferson, letter to Thomas Leiper, August 21, 1807, quoted by Hans J. Morgenthau, *A New Foreign Policy for the United States,* New York: Praeger, 1969, p. 160.

2. For example "The Defense of Japan," Japan Defense Agency, White Paper, October 1970.

3. Osamu Miyoshi, writing in *Shokun,* June 1972, summarizes the doubts expressed by many other writers and political leaders.

4. In 1960 the Peking government reissued *A Brief History of Modern*

China, by Lin Pei-hua in which the Ryukyus are shown among territories considered as former Chinese vassals.

5. *Kanagawa Shimbun,* January 18, 1973.

6. Ambassador Nobuhiko Ushiba, "Japan and America in the 1970's," *Freedom at Issue,* No. 14, July-August 1972, pp. 5-7.

7. William H. Overholt, "President Nixon's Trip to China and its Consequences," *Asian Survey,* July 1973, pp. 707-721.

8. Donald Brandon, "Dr. Kissinger's 'Grand Design'," *America,* Vol. 130, No. 9, March 9, 1974, pp. 166-170.

9. *Chuo Koron,* December 1972.

10. On February 12, 1973 *Shukan Gendai* quoted Chou En-lai on this subject as follows: "In the Sino-US Joint Communique, it is said that 'China and the US will not seek hegemony in the Asian-Pacific area, and that China and the US will not permit any other nation(s) to establish hegemony.' Frankly speaking, this was proposed by President Nixon... There is a nation which intends to seek hegemony at any cost."

11. Confidential report to the Czar, later published by the Soviet government, quoted by Prince Lobanov-Rostovsky, *Russia and Asia,* pp. 255-256.

12. Franz Shurmann, *Ideology and Organization in Communist China,* Berkeley: University of California Press, 1968, pp. 263-296; see also Edgar Snow, *The Other Side of the River,* New York: Random House, 1962, pp. 148 and 333.

13. Thomas W. Robinson, *The Border Negotiations and the Future of Sino-Soviet American Relations,* RAND Corporation P-4661, 1971.

14. Lobanov-Rostovsky, pp. 240-241.

15. W. Craig Wilde, "Issues in the Development of Siberia and the Far East," Proceedings, Washington, D.C. Chapter, American Association for the Advancement of Slavic Study, Chapter 19, May 20, 1972.

16. Stefan Possony, "Peking and Moscow: The Permanence of Conflict," *Modern Age,* Spring 1972, pp. 130-145.

17. A public opinion survey by Tokyo *Shimbun* of 3,000 eligible voters "throughout the country," published on November 24, 1972, showed that 32.9 percent of those questioned thought that reversion of the entire Kurile chain should be sought and that in addition reversion of Sakhalin should also be sought. Except for the "Northern Territories" question involving the four southernmost islands of the Kuriles, there has been no official or other public campaign aimed at recovery. The substantial public interest revealed by the poll is, therefore, of considerable significance.

18. *Yomiuri,* November 23, 1972.

19. For an excellent description of this overall problem see "Japan and Her Maritime Defense," by Hideo Sakino, Commander, Imperial Japanese Navy (Ret.), *Naval Review, 1971,* pp. 110-121.

Bibliography

CHAPTER 1

Apter, David E. *Political Change: Collected Essays.* London: Frank Cass and Company Limited, 1973.

Berger, Morroe; Abel, Theodore; and Page, Charles H. *Freedom and Control in Modern Society.* New York: D. Van Nostrand Company, 1954.

Berkley, George E. *The Administrative Revolution: Notes on the Passing of Organization Man.* Englewood Cliffs, N.J.: Prentice-Hall, Inc. (Spectrum), 1971.

Busha, Charles H. *Freedom Versus Suppression and Censorship.* Littleton, Colorado: Libraries Unlimited, Inc., 1972.

Cantril, Hadley. *The Pattern of Human Concerns.* New Brunswick, N.J.: Rutgers University Press, 1965.

Epstein, Edward Jay. *News From Nowhere: Television and the News.* New York: Random House, 1973.

Franck, Thomas M., and Weisband, Edward, eds. *Secrecy and Foreign Policy.* New York: Oxford University Press, 1974.

Gross, Bertram M., ed. *A Great Society?* New York: Basic Books, Inc., 1966.

Hargreaves, Robert. *Superpower: A Portrait of America in the 70's.* New York: St. Martin's Press, Inc., 1973.

Hornstein, Harvey A.; Bunker, Barbara Benedict; Burke, W. Warner; Gindes, Marion; and Lewicki, Roy J., eds. *Social Intervention: A Behavioral Science Approach.* New York: The Free Press, 1971.

Janowitz, Morris, ed. *The New Military: Changing Patterns of Organizations.* New York: Russell Sage Foundation, 1964.

McFarland, Andrew S. *Power and Leadership in Pluralist Systems.* Stanford: Stanford University Press, 1969.

Moskos, Charles C., Jr., ed. *Public Opinion and the Military Establishment.* Beverly Hills: Sage Publications, 1971.

Perloff, Harvey S., ed. *The Future of the U.S. Government: Toward the Year 2000.* Englewood Cliffs, N.J.: Prentice-Hall, Inc., 1971.

Pruit, Dean G., and Snyder, Richard C. *Theory and Research on the Causes of War.* Englewood Cliffs, N.J.: Prentice-Hall, Inc., 1969.

Rustow, Dankwart A. *A World of Nations: Problems of Political Modernization.* Washington: The Brookings Institution, 1967.

Sorokin, Pitirim, and Lunden, Walter A. *Power and Morality: Who Shall Guard the Guardians?* Boston: Porter Sargent Publisher, 1959.

Toffler, Alvin. *Future Shock.* New York: Random House, 1970.

Trager, Frank N., and Kronenberg, Philip S., eds. *National Security and American Society: Theory, Process, and Policy.* Manhattan, Kan.: The University Press of Kansas, 1973.

Wallia, C. S., ed. *Toward Century 21: Technology, Society, and Human Values.* New York: Basic Books, Inc., 1970.

Winter, J. Alan; Rabow, Jerome; and Chester, Mark, eds. *Vital Problems for American Society: Meanings and Means.* New York: Random House, 1968.

Wise, David. *The Politics of Lying: Government Deception, Secrecy, and Power.* New York: Random House, 1973.

CHAPTER 2

Cantril, Hadley. *The Human Dimension: Experiences in Policy Research.* New Brunswick: Rutgers University Press, 1967.

Emerson, Thomas I. *Toward a General Theory of the First Amendment.* New York: Random House, 1966.

Free, Lloyd A. and Cantril, Hadley. *The Political Beliefs of Americans.* New Brunswick, New Jersey: Rutgers University Press, 1967.

Hohenberg, John. *Free Press-Free People, the Best Cause.* New York: Columbia University Press, 1971.

Kristol, Irving. *On the Democratic Idea in America.* New York: Harper and Row, 1972.

Lippman, Walter. *Public Opinion.* Toronto: Collier-Macmillan Canada, Ltd., 1922.

Lowell, Abbott Lawrence. *Public Opinion in War and Peace.* Cambridge: Harvard University Press, 1926.

Mayer, Martin. *About Television.* New York: Harper and Row, 1972.

CHAPTER 3

Barber, James A. and Ambrose, Stephen E., ed. "Ecological Impact of Military Activities." *The Military and American Society.* New York: The Free Press, 1972.

Chase Manhattan Bank. *Business in Brief,* No. 103, April 1972.

Commoner, Barry. "A Businessman's Primer on Ecology." *Business and Society Review,* Spring 1972, p. 53.

Congressional Quarterly Almanac. Washington: Congressional Quarterly, Inc., 1971.

Hammer, John. "Auto Emission Controls." *Editorial Research Reports.* Washington: Congressional Quarterly, Inc., Vol. I, No. 15, April 18, 1973, pp. 306-307.

Hartley, Livingston. "Changes to the Environment—Some International Implications." *Orbis,* Summer 1970, p. 491.

Hauser, Philip M., ed. "World Population Growth." *The Population Dilemma.* New York: American Assembly, 2d Edition, Prentice Hall, 1969.

Humpstone, Charles C. "Pollution: Precedent and Prospect." *Foreign Affairs,* January 1972, p. 336.

Huntley, James R. *Man's Environment and the Atlantic Alliance.* Brussels: NATO Information Service, June 1971, p. 12.

Kennan, George F. "To Prevent A World Wasteland—A Proposal." *Foreign Affairs,* April 1970, Vol. 48, No. 3, p. 401ff.

Kneese, Allen and Ridker, Ronald. "The Limits of Growth." *The Washington Post,* March 2, 1972, p. B-1.

Krader, Lawrence. "Society and Its Physical Environment." *The Annals of the American Academy of Political and Social Science,* May 1970, pp. 12-13.

Leider, Robert F., Colonel, US Army. "A Different World," *United States Naval Institute Proceedings,* Vol. 99, No. 4/842, April 1973, p. 9.

Leider, Robert F., Colonel, US Army. *From Choice to Determinant: The Environmental Issues in International Relations.* Washington: The National War College, Strategic Research Group, February 15, 1972.

Lincoln, George A. "Winter Fuel Shortage: How Serious?" *US News and World Report,* December 11, 1972, p. 73.

Meadows, D. L.; Randers, Georgen; and Behrens, William W. *The Limits of Growth.* New York: Universal Books, 1972.

Steinhauser, Thomas S. C. "Keep It Clean, Environmental Quality Is 'IN' at the Pentagon." *Armed Forces Journal,* December 1972, p. 24.

US Congress. Senate. Resolution 71, 93d Congress, 1st Session, Calendar No. 255, Report No. 93-270.

"War on Pollution: How It's Faring." *US News and World Report,* August 21, 1972, p. 82.

Ward, Barbara and Dubos, Rene. *Only One Earth: The Care and Maintenance of a Small Planet.* New York: W. W. Norton & Co., 1972.

CHAPTER 4

Brown, Lester R. *World Without Borders.* New York: Random House, 1972.

Cooper, Richard N. *The Economics of Interdependence: Economic Policy In the Atlantic Community.* Council on Foreign Relations, The Atlantic Policy Studies. New York: McGraw-Hill, 1968.

Gilpin, Robert. "The Politics of Transnational Economic Relations." *International Organization,* Vol. XXV, No. 3, Summer 1971, pp. 398-419.

Kindleberger, Charles P. *Power and Money: The Economics of International Politics and the Politics of International Economics.* New York: Basic Books, 1970.

Kindleberger, Charles P., ed. *The International Corporation: A Symposium.* Cambridge: The MIT Press, 1970. Pp. 205-223: "The Myth of National Interdependence," by Kenneth N. Waltz.

Nye, Joseph S. Jr., and Keohane, Robert O. "Transnational Relations and World Politics: An Introduction," and "Transnational Relations and World Politics: A Conclusion." *International Organization,* Vol. XXV, No. 3, Summer 1971, pp. 329-349 and pp. 721-748.

CHAPTER 5

Abel, Elie. *The Missile Crisis.* Philadelphia: J. B. Lippincott Co., 1966.

Cleveland, Harlan. "Crisis Diplomacy." *Foreign Affairs,* Vol. 41, July 1963, pp. 638-650.

Feis, Herbert. *The Road to Pearl Harbor.* Princeton: Princeton University Press, 1950.

Feis, Herbert. "War Came at Pearl Harbor: Suspicions Considered." *The Yale Review,* Vol. 45, March 1956, pp. 378-390.

Finley, Daniel J., ed. *Enemies in Politics.* Chicago: Rand McNally, 1967. P. 30: "Cognitive Dynamics and Images of the Enemy: Dulles and Russia," by Ole R. Holsti.

Hilsman, Roger. *Strategic Intelligence and National Decisions.* Glencoe, Ill.: The Free Press, 1956.

Holsti, Ole R. *Crisis, Escalation, War.* Montreal and London: McGill-Queen's University Press, 1972.

Jervis, Robert. "Hypotheses on Misperception." *World Politics,* Vol. 20, April 1968, pp. 454-479.

Kennedy, Robert F. *Thirteen Days: A Memoir of the Cuban Missile Crisis.* New York: W. W. Norton and Co., 1969.

Knorr, Klaus. "Failures in National Intelligence Estimates: The Case of the Cuban Missiles." *World Politics,* Vol. 16, April 1964, pp. 455-467.

Layson, Walter Wells. *The Political and Strategic Aspects of the 1962 Cuban Crisis.* Ann Arbor: University Microfilms, 1971.

Schlesinger, Arthur M. *A Thousand Days.* New York: Houghton Mifflin Co., 1965.

Skillern, William Gustaf. *An Analysis of the Decision-Making Process in the Cuban Missile Crisis.* Ann Arbor: University Microfilms, 1972.

Sorensen, Theodore C. *Kennedy.* New York: Harper & Row, 1965.

Trotter, Richard Gordon. *The Cuban Missile Crisis: An Analysis of Policy Formulation in Terms of Current Decision Making Theory.* Ann Arbor: University Microfilms, 1971.

US Congress. Joint Committee on the Investigation of the Pearl Harbor Attack. *Investigation of the Pearl Harbor Attack.* 39 vols. Washington: US Government Printing Office, 1946.

US Congress. Senate. Committee on Armed Services, Preparedness Investigating Subcommittee. *Investigations of the Preparedness Program, Interim Report on*

Cuban Military Buildup. 88th Congress, 1st Session, 1963. Washington: US Government Printing Office, 1963.

US War Department. *Report of the Army Pearl Harbor Board.* Washington, 1944.

Wohlstetter, Roberta. "Cuba and Pearl Harbor: Hindsight and Foresight." *Foreign Affairs,* Vol. 43, July 1965, pp. 691-707.

Wohlstetter, Roberta. *Pearl Harbor, Warning and Decision.* Stanford, Calif.: Stanford University Press, 1962.

CHAPTER 6

Cameron, E. N., ed. *The Mineral Position of the United States, 1975-2000.* Madison: The University of Wisconsin Press, 1973.

Cottam, Richard W. *Competitive Interference and 20th Century Diplomacy.* Pittsburgh: University of Pittsburgh Press, 1967.

Driskill, John G., Lieutenant Colonel. *The US Stockpile Program: Asset or Anachronism?* Thesis. Carlisle Barracks: US Army War College, February 1970.

Holsti, K. J. *International Politics: A Framework for Analysis.* New York: Prentice-Hall, Inc., 1967.

"Material Needs and the Environment Today and Tomorrow." *Final Report of the National Commission on Materials Policy.* National Commission on Materials Policy. Washington: US Government Printing Office, June 1973.

Meadows, Donella H., *et. al. The Limits to Growth.* Washington: Potomac Associates, 1972.

Statistical Supplement. *Stockpile Report to the Congress, January-June 1973.* Washington: General Services Administration (GSA).

Stockpile Report to the Congress, January-June 1973. Washington: Office of Preparedness, GSA, October 26, 1973, p. 1.

Strategic and Critical Materials Descriptive Data. Washington: Office of Emergency Preparedness (OEP), Executive Office of the President, March 31, 1963.

"Towards a National Materials Policy—An Interim Report." National Commission on Materials Policy. Washington: US Government Printing Office, April 1972, pp. 3-4.

US Department of the Interior. "Mineral Facts and Problems," *Bureau of Mines Bulletin No. 650,* 1970, pp. 243-825.

US Department of the Interior. *USGS Professional Paper No. 820.* Washington: US Mineral Resources, 1973.

Yuan-li, Wu. *Raw Material Supply in a Multipolar World.* National Strategy Information Center, Inc. New York: Crane, Russak & Company, 1973.

CHAPTER 7

Akins, James E. "The Oil Crisis: This Time the Wolf Is Here." *Foreign Affairs,* Vol. 51, April 1973, pp. 461-490.

Berry, John A. "Oil and Soviet Policy in the Middle East." *Middle East Journal,* Vol. 26, No. 2, Spring 1972, pp. 149-160.

Chase Manhattan Bank. *The Profit Situation, A Special Petroleum Report.* New York: April 1974.

"The Energy Crisis: Reality or Myth." *The Annals of the American Academy of Political and Social Science,* Vol. 410, November 1973.

Fortune. Vol. LXXXIX, No. 4, April 1974, pp. 98-119. A series of energy related articles.

Hunter, Robert E. "Can the Arabs Really Blackmail Us?" *The New York Times Magazine,* September 23, 1973, p. 25.

Hunter, Robert E. *The Energy Crisis and US Foreign Policy.* Foreign Policy Association, Headline Series No. 216. Washington: June 1973.

Issawi, Charles. *Oil, the Middle East and the World.* Georgetown University, Center for Strategic and International Studies. New York: Library Press, 1972.

Landsberg, H. H. and Schurr, S. H. *Energy in the United States.* New York: Random House, 1968.

National Petroleum Council. Committee on Energy Outlook. *Guide to National Petroleum Council Report on US Energy Outlook.* Report for US Department of Interior. Washington: 1972.

Office of Emergency Preparedness. *The Potential for Energy Conservation.* Washington: US Government Printing Office, 1972.

Searl, Milton F. *Energy Modeling.* Working Papers for Energy Modeling Seminar, January 25-26, 1973, Washington, D. C. Washington: Resources for the Future, Inc., March 1973.

US Congress. House. National Commission on Materials Policy. *Material Needs and the Environment Today and Tomorrow.* Final Report. Washington: US Government Printing Office, June 1973.

US Congress. Senate. Committee on Commerce. *Council on Energy Policy.* Serial No. 93-6. Washington: US Government Printing Office, 1973.

US Council on International Economic Policy. *International Economic Report of the President for 1974.* Washington: US Government Printing Office, February 1974.

Williams, J. A. *Middle East Oil and Its Implications for the United States, 1975-1985.* Washington: US National War College (Individual Research Paper), March 1972.

Winger, John G. *Outlook for Energy in the United States to 1985.* New York: Chase Manhattan Bank, 1972.

CHAPTER 8

Alexander, Lewis M. "Geography and the Law of the Sea." *Annals of the Association of American Geographers,* Vol. 58, March 1968, pp. 177-197.

Anderson, William R. "Let's Send SABMIS to Sea Now." *Reader's Digest,* Vol. 96, No. 574, February 1970, pp. 102-106.

Beckner, Norman V., *et al. The Navy and the Common Sea.* Washington: Center for Naval Analysis, 1972.

Cheever, Daniel S. "The Role of International Organization in Ocean Development." *International Organization,* Vol. XXII, Summer 1968, pp. 629-648.

Columbos, C. J. *The International Law of the Sea.* (6th Revised Edition), New York: McKay Company, 1967.

Commission on Marine Science, Engineering and Resources. *Our Nation and the Sea—A Plan for National Action.* Washington: US Government Printing Office, January 1969.

Commission on Marine Science, Engineering and Resources. *Panel Report on Industry and Technology,* Vol. 2. Washington: US Government Printing Office, February 1969.

Commission on Marine Science, Engineering and Resources. *Panel Report on Marine Resources and Legal—Political Arrangements for Their Development,* Vol. 3. Washington: US Government Printing Office, February 1969.

Commission on Marine Science, Engineering and Resources. *Panel Report on Science and Environment,* Vol. 1. Washington: US Government Printing Office, February 1969.

Cromie, William J. "Who Will Own the Ocean's Wealth?" *United States Naval Institute Proceedings,* Vol. 91, No. 1/743, January 1965, pp. 52-61.

Emery, K. O.; Fye, Paul M.; and Cadwalader, George. "The Sea Bed." *Annals of the New York Academy of Sciences,* Vol. 216, March 1973, pp. 51-55.

"Manganese Nodules (II): Prospects for Deep Sea Mining." *Science Magazine,* Vol. 183, No. 4125, February 15, 1974, pp. 644-646.

Mangone, Gerald J. *The United Nations, International Law, and the Bed of the Seas.* Newark: University of Delaware, 1972.

Marine Resources and Engineering Development Act of 1966. U.S. Code, P. L. 89-454, 80 Stat. 203.

National Security Industrial Association. *After the Stratton Commission Report—What?* Proceeding of the Annual Meeting of the Ocean Science and Technology Advisory Committee. Washington, April 1969.

Panel on Oceanography, President's Science Advisory Committee. *Effective Use of the Sea.* Washington: US Government Printing Office, June 1966.

Pardo, Arvid. "Sovereignty Under the Sea." *Round Table,* Vol. 58, October 1968, pp. 341-355.

Presidential Announcement. "National Oceanic and Atmospheric Administration." *Reorganization Plan No. 4 of 1970.* The White House, July 9, 1970.

Ratiner, Leigh S. "United States Oceans Policy." *Journal of Maritime Law and Commerce,* Vol. 2, No. 2. Silver Spring, Maryland: Jefferson Law Book Company, January 1971.

Smith, Emory Clark. *The Regulation of Scientific Research in the Oceans.* Commentary presented to the XVIII Conference of the Inter-American Bar Association in Rio de Janeiro, Brazil, August 21, 1973.

Stanley, C. Maxwell. "Who Will Control Ocean Space?" *War and Peace Report,* March-April 1973, pp. 8-11.

Stevenson, John R. *Panel on Conflicting Approaches to the Control and Exploitation of the Oceans.* Address before the annual meeting of the American Society of International Law. Washington, April 29, 1971.

"The Law of the Sea: The Final Act and Annexes of the United Nations Conference on the Law of the Sea." *The International and Comparative Law Quarterly,* (A special supplement), London: 1958.

The National Council on Marine Resources and Engineering Development. *International Decade of Ocean Exploration.* Washington: US Government Printing Office, May 1968.

UN General Assembly. Resolution 2467A, B, C, D (XXIII), *Official Records: Twenty-Third Session,* No. 18, 1968.

US Department of State. Bureau of Intelligence and Research. *Sovereignty and the Sea.* Geographic Bulletin No. 3, Publication No. 7849. Washington, December 1969.

US Department of State. "Law of the Sea." *GIST,* No. 26. Washington: November 1973.

Young, Richard. "The Legal Regime of the Deep-Sea Floor." *American Journal of International Law,* Vol. 62, July 1968, pp. 641-653.

CHAPTER 9

Arbatov, G. A. "American Foreign Policy on the Threshold of the 1970's." *The Soviet Review,* Winter 1970-71, p. 307.

Buckley, James L. "On SALT II." *National Review,* March 15, 1974, pp. 312-317.

"Communique Of Conference on Political Consultative Committee of Warsaw Pact States." *Pravda,* March 18, 1969, p. 1.

"Declaration on Strengthening Peace and Security in Europe." *Pravda,* July 9, 1966, p. 1.

Kintner, William R. *SALT: Implications for Arms Control in the 1970's.* Pittsburgh: University of Pittsburgh Press, 1973.

Kraft, Joseph. "Mission to Moscow." *The Washington Post,* March 24, 1974, p. C7.

"Moving Toward European Security Talks." *Current Digest of the Soviet Press,* Volume XXIV, No. 50, 1973.

Murphy, Charles J. V. "What We Gave Away in the Moscow Arms Agreements." *Fortune,* September 1972, pp. 110-115, 203-208.

Newhouse, John. *Cold Dawn.* New York: Holt, Rinehart and Winston, 1973.

Nixon, Richard M. *US Foreign Policy for the 1970's.* A Report to the Congress by the President of the United States. "Building for Peace," February 25, 1971; "The Emerging Structure of Peace," February 9, 1972; "Shaping a Durable Peace," May 3, 1973. Washington: US Government Printing Office.

"Principles of Cooperation Between the Union of Soviet Socialist Republics and France." *Pravda,* October 31, 1971. Quoted in *The Current Digest of the Soviet Press,* Volume XXIII, No. 44, 1971.

Rhinelander, John B. "What We Gained from SALT." *Fortune,* October 1972, p. 64.

Rosenfeld, Stephen S. "Pluralism and Policy." *Foreign Affairs,* January 1974.

Sorensen, Theodore C. "Most Favored-Nation and Less Favorite Nations." *Foreign Affairs,* January 1974.

"Statement on Questions of the Strengthening of Security and the Development of Peaceful Cooperation in Europe," *Pravda,* December 4, 1970. Quoted in *The Current Digest of the Soviet Press,* Volume XXII, No. 49, 1970.

Trofimenko, G. A. "Sovetsko-Amerikanskiye Saglasheniye ob Ogranichenii Strategicheskix Vooruzhenii." *S Sh A,* No. 9, 1972.

Vernon, Raymond. "US-Soviet Economic Relations." *Foreign Affairs,* January 1974.

Wren, Christopher S. "Soviet Stresses US-Allied Split." *The New York Times,* March 20, 1974, p. 4.

CHAPTER 10

Burrows, Sir Bernard, and Irwin, Christopher. *The Security of Western Europe.* London: Charles Knight & Co., 1972.

"European Security." (Final Recommendations of the Helsinki Consultations, June 8, 1973.) *Survival,* Vol. XV, No. 5, September/October 1973, pp. 236-240.

Goodpaster, Andrew J., General. "NATO and U.S. Forces: Challenges and Prospects." *Strategic Review,* Winter, 1974, pp. 6-17.

Hallstein, Walter. *Europe in the Making.* New York: W. W. Norton and Co., 1972.

Harned, Joseph W., et. al. "Conference on Security and Cooperation in Europe and Negotiations on Mutual and Balanced Force Reductions." *The Atlantic Community Quarterly,* Vol. II, No. 1, Spring 1973, pp. 7-54.

Howard, Michael. "NATO and the Year of Europe." *Survival,* Vol. XVI, No. 1, January/February 1974, pp. 21-27.

Hunter, Robert E. *Security in Europe.* Bloomington, Ind.: Indiana University Press, 1969.

Ionescu, Ghita. *The New Politics of European Integration.* London: MacMillan, 1972.

Kintner, William R., and Foster, Richard B., eds. *National Strategy in a Decade of Change.* Lexington, Mass: D.C. Heath and Co., 1973.

Korbel, Josef. *Detente in Europe, Real or Imaginary.* Princeton: Princeton University Press, 1972.

Laloy, Jean. "Does Europe Have a Future?" *Foreign Affairs,* Vol. 51, No. 1, October 1972, pp. 154-166.

Laquer, Walter. *Neo-Isolationism and the World of the Seventies.* The Washington Papers No. 5. Washington: Center for Strategic and International Studies, 1972.

Longworth, Richard C. "NATO: Trouble at Twenty-Five." *Saturday Review World,* April 6, 1974, pp. 12-15.

Milton, T. R., General. "NATO and the Aging Process." *Strategic Review,* Winter 1974, pp. 39-43.

Morgan, Roger. "West-East Relations in Europe: Political Perspectives." *International Affairs,* Vol. 49, No. 2, April 1973, pp. 177-189.

NATO Handbook. NATO Information Service. February 1973.

Nixon, Richard M. *U.S. Foreign Policy for the 1970's.* A Report to the Congress by the President of the United States, February 9, 1972. Washington: US Government Printing Office, 1972.

Roach, James R., ed. *The United States and the Atlantic Community, Issues and Prospects.* Austin: University of Texas Press, 1966.

Rostow, Eugene V. *Peace In the Balance.* New York: Simon and Schuster, 1972.

Schaetzel, J. Robert. "Some European Questions for Dr. Kissinger." *Foreign Policy,* No. 12, Fall 1973, pp. 66-74.

Silberschmidt, Max. *The United States and Europe.* London: Harcourt, Brace and Co., 1972.

Von Riekhoff, Harold. *NATO: Issues and Prospects.* Toronto: The Canadian Institute of International Affairs, 1967.

CHAPTER 11

Burke, John T. "Precision Weaponry: The Changing Nature of Modern Warfare." *Army,* Vol. 24, No. 3, March 1974, pp. 12-16.

Burke, John T. "'Smart' Weapons: A Coming Revolution in Tactics." *Army,* Vol. 23, No. 2, February 1973, pp. 14-20.

Cleveland, Harlan. *NATO: The Transatlantic Bargain.* New York: Harper and Rowe, 1970.

Goodpaster, A. J., General. "Remarks." *NATO's Fifteen Nations,* Vol. 18, No. 6, December 1973 - January 1974, pp. 24-29.

Hilton, Richard D. "What Every Ground Commander Should Know About Guided Bombs." *Army,* Vol. 23, No. 6, June 1973, pp. 28-33.

Historical Trends Related to Weapon Lethality. Washington: Historical Evaluation and Research Organization. October 15, 1964.

Howard, Michael. "NATO and the Year of Europe." *Survival,* Vol. 16, No. 1, January/February 1974, pp. 21-27.

Hunt, Kenneth. "The Alliance and Europe: Part II: Defense with Fewer Men." *Adelphi Paper No. 98,* London: International Institute for Strategic Studies, Summer 1973.

CHAPTER 12

Adomeit, Hannes. "Soviet Risk-Taking and Crisis Behavior." *Adelphi Paper No. 101.* London: International Institute for Strategic Studies, Fall 1973.

Becker, Abraham S. *Oil and the Persian Gulf in Soviet Policy in the 1970's.* Santa Monica: Rand Corporation, 1971.

Campbell, John C. "Moscow's Purposes." *Problems of Communism,* Vol. XXI, September-October 1972, pp. 40-54.

"Capacity of the World Tanker Fleet." *World Petroleum Report 1972,* Vol. XVIII, p. 10.

Center for Advanced International Studies. *On Soviet Objectives and Strategy in the Middle East.* Miami: University of Miami. 1974, pp. 1-34. Draft article.

Chase, Alan C. *Soviet Military Goals in the Middle East.* Montgomery, Alabama: Air University, Report No. 0555-72, 1972.

Cook, Don. "The European Security Conference." *Atlantic,* Vol. 232, October 1973, pp. 6, 8, 10, 12.

Framm, Joseph. "Russia vs China in Big War." *U.S. News and World Report,* August 23, 1973, p. 32.

Habsburg, Otto Von. "USSR: Superpower or Paper Tiger?" *Saturday Evening Post,* Vol. 245, No. 4, July-August 1973, pp. 10-11.

Hunter, Robert E. *The Energy Crisis and U.S. Foreign Policy.* Headline Series No. 216. Washington: Foreign Policy Association, June 1973.

Jukes, Geoffrey. "The Indian Ocean in Soviet Naval Policy." *Adelphi Paper No. 87.* London: International Institute for Strategic Studies, May 1972.

Laqueur, Walter Z. "On the Soviet Departure from Egypt." *Commentary,* Vol. 54, No. 6, December 1972, pp. 61-68.

Malone, Joseph J. *Dynamics of Military Balance: Middle East/Mediterranean Final Report.* April 1, 1972.

"Middle East, 1973." *Current History,* Vol. 64, January 1973, entire issue.

Peabody, James B. "Escalation or Detente in the Middle East." *Military Review,* Vol. 52, No. 4, April 1972, pp. 35-49.

"Soviet Union, 1973." *Current History,* Vol. 65, October 1973, entire issue.

Thomas, John R. "The Dilemmas of Soviet Policy in the Middle East." *Parameters: The Journal of the Army War College.* Vol. 1, No. 2, Fall 1971, pp. 34-42.

US Council on International Economic Policy. *International Economic Report of the President.* Washington: Annual Report, 1974.

CHAPTER 13

Badeau, John S. "The Significance of the Suez Canal in Current International Affairs." *Vital Speeches,* Vol. 20, January 15, 1954, pp. 200-205.

"Consequences Politiques et Economiques de la Reouverture du Canal de Suez." *Chronique de Politique Etrangere,* Vol. 26, May 1973, pp. 345-349.

Cooley, John K. "Egypt Plans for Peace, Reconstruction, and Suez Reopening." *The Christian Science Monitor,* December 13, 1973, p. 8.

Fisher, John. "How Strategic is Suez?" *To The Point,* Vol. 3, March 1974, p. 16.

Hallberg, Charles W. *The Suez Canal, Its History and Diplomatic Language.* New York: Columbia University Press, 1931.

Hoagland, Jim. "Egypt Turning New Page–Canal Rebirth Seen." *The Washington Post,* February 4, 1974, pp. A1, A7.

"An Inside Look at Egypt's New Capitalism." *Business Week,.* February 5, 1974, p. A16.

Leech, John. "Suez Development Outlined by Egypt." *The Washington Post,* February 5, 1974, p. A16.

Loeffler, William H. *The Strategic Implications of the Reopening of the Suez Canal.* Individual Research Report. Carlisle Barracks: US Army War College, March 3, 1972.

Mountjoy, Alan B. "New Life for the Suez Canal?" *Contemporary Review,* Vol. 219, November 1971, pp. 263-268.

"Price of Peace." *The Economist,* Vol. 250, March 9, 1974, pp. 51-52.

Ragaei, El Mallakh. *The United States and the Suez Canal: A Study in Economic Mutuality of Interests.* New York: The League of Arab States, 1974.

Siegfried, Andre. "The Suez: International Roadway." *Foreign Affairs,* Vol. 31, July 1953, pp. 605-618.

Stauffer, Thomas R. "Who Needs the Suez Canal?" *MidEast,* Vol. 10, October 1970, pp. 18-20, 31-33.

"The Suez Canal Statistics." *The Middle East and North Africa.* 15th ed. London: Europa Publications Ltd., 1968, pp. 64-66.

"Suez Canal–Who Gains What If It Opens?" *The Economist,* Vol. 239, June 5, 1971, pp. 28, 31.

United Arab Republic. Suez Canal Authority. *Suez Canal Report.* Ismailia: 1966.
United Nations. Conference on Trade and Development, Trade and Development Board, Committee on Shipping, Sixth Session. *The Economic Effects of the Closure of the Suez Canal.* New York: January 26, 1973.
US Department of the Army. *DA Pam 550-28.* Area Handbook for Ethiopia. Washington: US Government Printing Office, 1971.
Yuan-Li Wu. *Raw Material Supply in a Multipolar World.* New York: National Strategy Information Center, 1973.

CHAPTER 14

Brezhnev, Leonid. *On the Policy of the Soviet Union and the International Situation.* Garden City: Doubleday, 1973.
Burrell, R.M. *The Persian Gulf.* New York: The Library Press, 1972.
Burrell, R.M. and Cottrell, A.J. *Iran, the Arabian Peninsula and the Indian Ocean.* New York: National Strategy Information Center, Inc., 1972.
Christman, Henry M., ed. *Neither East Nor West.* New York: Sheed and Ward, 1973.
Cleveland, Ray L. *The Middle East and South Asia.* Washington: Stryker-Post Publications, 1973.
Finney, John W. "Role of Indian Ocean Base is Discussed." *The New York Times,* March 13, 1974, p. 3.
Getler, Michael. "Indian Ocean Base Seen Unaffected." *The Washington Post,* March 7, 1974, p. A2.
Gilbert, Stephen P., *et al. U.S. Security Interests in the Persian Gulf Area.* Menlo Park, California: Stanford Research Institute, 1973.
Gorshkov, S. G., Admiral of the Fleet, Soviet Navy. "Navies in War and Peace." *United States Naval Institute Proceedings,* January 1974, pp. 18-26.
Hessman, James D. "New Realities and the Soviet Sea Strategy." *Sea Power,* Vol. 16, December 1973–January 1974, pp. 21-26.
Jukes, Geoffrey. "The Indian Ocean in Soviet Naval Policy." *Adelphi Paper No. 87.* London: The International Institute for Strategic Studies, 1972.
Levine, Richard J. "The Debate Over Diego Garcia." *The Wall Street Journal,* April 4, 1974, p. 18.
Nuechterlein, Donald E. *United States National Interests in a Changing World.* Lexington, Kentucky: The University Press of Kentucky, 1973.
Rand Corporation. *Worldwide Soviet Military Strategy and Policy.* Santa Monica, California: April, 1973.
Weiss, Seymour. "U.S. Interests and Activities in the Indian Ocean Area." *Department of State Bulletin,* Vol. 70, April 8, 1974, pp. 371-375.
Wren, Christopher S. "Soviet Affirms Right to Send Ships to Indian Ocean." *The New York Times,* May 9, 1974, p. 3.
Wriggins, W. Howard. "US Military Interest in the Indian Ocean." *The Washington Post,* February 26, 1974, p. A23.
Wu, Yuan-li. *Raw Material Supply in a Multipolar World.* New York: National Strategy Information Center, Inc., 1973.
Zumwalt, Elmo R., Jr., Admiral. "Strategic Importance of Indian Ocean." *Armed Forces Journal,* Vol. 111, April 1974, pp. 28-29.

CHAPTER 15

Dallin, David J. *The Rise of Russia in Asia.* New Haven: Yale University Press, 1949.

Japan Defense Agency. *The Defense of Japan.* (White Paper), Tokyo, October 1970.

Lobanov-Rostovsky, A. *Russia and Asia.* Ann Arbor, Michigan: Wahr, 1951.

Overholt, William H. "President Nixon's Trip to China and its Consequences." *Asian Survey,* Vol. XIII, No. 7, July 1973, pp. 707-721.

Palmer, Dave, Lieutenant Colonel. "The Eighth Road to Moscow." *Armor,* November-December 1969, pp. 50-55.

Possony, Stefan. "Peking and Moscow: The Permanence of Conflict." *Modern Age.* Spring 1972, pp. 130-145.

Robinson, Thomas W. *The Border Negotiations and the Future of Sino-Soviet-American Relations.* Santa Monica: RAND Corporation, P-4661, 1971.

Robinson, Thomas W. "The Sino-Soviet Border Dispute: Background, Development, and the March 1969 Clashes." *American Political Science Review,* Vol. 66, December 1972, pp. 1175-1202.

Sakino, Hideo, Commander. "Japan and Her Maritime Defense." *Naval Review, 1971.* US Naval Institute, pp. 110-121.

Salisbury, Harrison E. "Marco Polo Would Recognize Mao's Sinkiang." *The New York Times Magazine,* November 23, 1969, p. 14.

Salisbury, Harrison E. *War Between Russia and China.* New York: W. W. Norton and Co., Inc., 1969.

Summers, H. G., Jr., Major. "Power: The Crucible of Conflict in the Sino-Soviet Dispute." *Military Review,* March 1971, pp. 56-66.

US Department of State. US Embassy, Tokyo. *Daily Summary of the Japanese Press.*

US Department of State. US Embassy, Tokyo. *Summaries of Selected Japanese Magazines.*

Biographical Notes on Authors

COLONEL ERWIN R. BRIGHAM has been assigned to the US Army War College since January 1971 and in January 1973 joined the Strategic Studies Institute. He has held numerous command and staff positions in Europe, and the Far East. He received his masters degree in foreign affairs from the University of Virginia, after which he was instructor and associate professor at the US Military Academy for four years. Colonel Brigham is a graduate of the Pakistan Army Staff College as well as the US Army War College. He is a member of the American Political Science Association and has written numerous professional articles for periodicals and magazines.

MR. JOHN R. CAMERON is presently Assistant to the Director of the Strategic Studies Institute. Mr. Cameron has served as a research analyst for the Institute since 1964. He did his undergraduate and graduate work in political science at Temple University. He is primarily interested in national security policy and forecasting, and has written numerous articles on the subjects. In addition, he has chaired several Joint and professional symposium meetings on politico-military forecasting. Mr. Cameron is a member of the American Political Science Association, the International Studies Association, and the Association of Research Administrators.

COLONEL ROBERT L. DAY served four years in key offices with the UN Truce Supervisory Organization in the Middle East. In this capacity he traveled throughout the area and had frequent contact with senior officials of Syria, United Arab Republic, Lebanon, Jordan, and Israel. He holds business and economics degrees from Washington State College and the University of Washington. His US Army assignments have included command in South Vietnam and duty in the Office of the Deputy Chief of Staff for Military Operations, Department of the Army. Colonel Day was a member of the Strategic Studies Institute from June 1973 to July 1974 and is now assigned to Korea.

COLONEL STANLEY D. FAIR is a graduate of the US Military Academy and has a masters degree in radiobiology from the University of California. This is his second assignment with the Strategic Studies Institute having served before from 1968-71. In 1971-72, Colonel Fair was Commandant of the US Army Chemical School at Fort McClellan, Alabama. He has authored numerous articles for periodicals in the United States, Canada, Australia, and Europe.

COLONEL RICHARD O. GILLICK is a US Marine Corps officer currently assigned to the faculty of the US Army War College with the Department of Military Planning and Strategy. He is a graduate of the School of Journalism, University of Wisconsin, and received his masters degree from Shippensburg State College. He has held a variety of assignments in the Marine Corps, including service in Korea, Vietnam, and the Philippines. Colonel Gillick was an instructor at the USMC Command and Staff College from 1966-69.

COLONEL BARTON M. HAYWARD has been assigned to the Strategic Studies Institute since his graduation from the US Army War College in June 1973. Colonel Hayward graduated from Cornell University in 1952 and has his masters degree in geography from the University of North Dakota. He has been assigned to various command and staff positions in Korea, West Germany, and South Vietnam. For two and a half years he was an instructor at the US Army Command and General Staff College.

MR. WILLIAM V. KENNEDY has been a research analyst for the Strategic Studies Institute since 1967. Since graduation from Marquette University in 1951 he has specialized in the reporting and analysis of military affairs. Mr. Kennedy is a Lieutenant Colonel in the US Army Reserve and has served on active duty in Japan and China; as an intelligence officer, Strategic Air Command; and in the National Guard Bureau, Department of the Army. His publications include professional journals in Britain, Ireland, and France as well as the United States.

DR. ALWYN H. KING joined the Strategic Studies Institute in 1973. He received his masters degree in physical metallurgy from Columbia University and in economics from Babson College. In 1960 he received his D. Sc. in physical science from the Stuttgart Institute of Technology in West Germany. Dr. King was an industrial research and management consultant for A. D. Little, Inc., and a group leader in the Brunswick Corporation Research and Development Laboratories. Dr. King is also a Colonel in the Army Reserve.

LIEUTENANT COLONEL DONALD M. O'SHEI is a West Point graduate with a masters degree in civil engineering from Princeton University and a law degree from Georgetown University. He is a member of the Bar in Washington, D. C. Lieutenant Colonel O'Shei has taught at Brooklyn Polytechnic Institute and

New Dynamics in National Strategy

George Washington University. His military assignments overseas include Korea, Turkey, and two tours in South Vietnam. Lieutenant Colonel O'Shei has been a member of the Strategic Studies Institute since his graduation from the US Army War College in June 1973.

COLONEL JOHN G. PAPPAGEORGE graduated from the US Army War College in 1973 and subsequently joined the Strategic Studies Institute. He has a masters degree in government and politics from the University of Maryland. He has served in a wide range of command and staff positions including several tours in South Vietnam as well as tours in Korea and West Germany. Colonel Pappageorge has authored several articles which have appeared in professional military periodicals.

MR. KENNETH E. ROBERTS is a foreign affairs analyst with the Strategic Studies Institute. Prior to his present position, he was an analyst in the Office of the Chief, Research and Development, Department of the Army. He has a degree in international relations from The American University and a masters degree in international affairs from Florida State University. He is a member of the American Political Science Association.

MR. JOHN F. SCOTT has been a research analyst in the Strategic Studies Institute since 1963. He holds a B.S. degree in commerce and finance and a masters degree in social science. Mr. Scott has contributed to several Army studies on nuclear deterrence and strategy. He has been an instructor of adult remedial education and is the author of several articles on the application of social science to national security problems in the professional journals of the US Air Force as well as the US Army.

COLONEL MARTIN J. SLOMINSKI is an analyst of Soviet affairs. He has a masters degree in law and government from Columbia University's Russian Institute. He has had several assignments in Europe and at the Department of the Army level in intelligence and is a graduate of the Russian Foreign Specialist Training Program. Colonel Slominski is the author of professional papers which have appeared in military journals. He was a member of the Strategic Studies Institute from July 1970 to May 1974, and is now assigned to Iran.

MR. JAMES TRINNAMAN is a political scientist with the Strategic Studies Institute which he joined in 1973. Mr. Trinnaman holds degrees in political science and economics from Hobart College and the John Hopkins University. For nine years he was a research scientist in the American University's Center for Research in Social Systems. He has also worked as a senior staff scientist for Operations Research, Inc., and more recently as an operations research analyst with the US Army Logistics Evaluation Agency. He has published articles on psychological operations and military affairs.

DR. ANTHONY L. WERMUTH is a political scientist with the Strategic Studies Institute. He holds masters degrees from Columbia University (English) and George Washington University (international affairs) and a PhD from Boston University (political science). A West Point graduate, Dr. Wermuth's military assignments include brigade command; Assistant for Central Europe, (OASD,

ISA); and Military Assistant (Public Affairs) to the Chairman of the Joint Chiefs of Staff. He has taught at West Point and at the Army War College. Following retirement, he served for 7 years as Director, Social Science Studies, Center for Advanced Studies and Analyses, Westinghouse Electric Corporation. He has written many articles on military affairs in professional journals, and is a member of several professional associations.